the Visionary

the Visionary

entering the mystic
universe of joseph rael
beautiful painted arrow

WITH A FOREWORD BY JOSEPH RAEL

kurt wilt PHD

POINTER OAK

Pointer Oak / Tri S Foundation
Distributed by Millichap Books
www.millichapbooks.com

First edition, second printing 2016
Cover and interior design by Carl Brune
ISBN 978-0-9823274-0-1
Printed in the USA

LIBRARY OF CONGRESS CATALOGING-IN-PUBLICATION DATA

Wilt, K. V. (Kurt V.)

The visionary : entering the mystic universe of Joseph Rael Beautiful Painted Arrow / K.V. Wilt ; with a foreword by Joseph Rael. – 1st ed.

p. cm.

"A Tri S Foundation book."

Includes bibliographical references and index.

ISBN 978-0-9823274-0-1 (pbk. : alk. paper)

1. Rael, Joseph. 2. Rael, Joseph--Religion. 3. Rael, Joseph--Philosophy. 4. Tiwa Indians–Biography. 5. Shamans--New Mexico--Biography. 6. Visionaries–New Mexico–Biography. 7. Mystics–New Mexico–Biography. 8. Shamanism–New Mexico. 9. Mysticism–New Mexico. 10. Indian philosophy–New Mexico. I. Title.

E99.T52R38 2010

305.897'496--dc22

[B]

2010042841

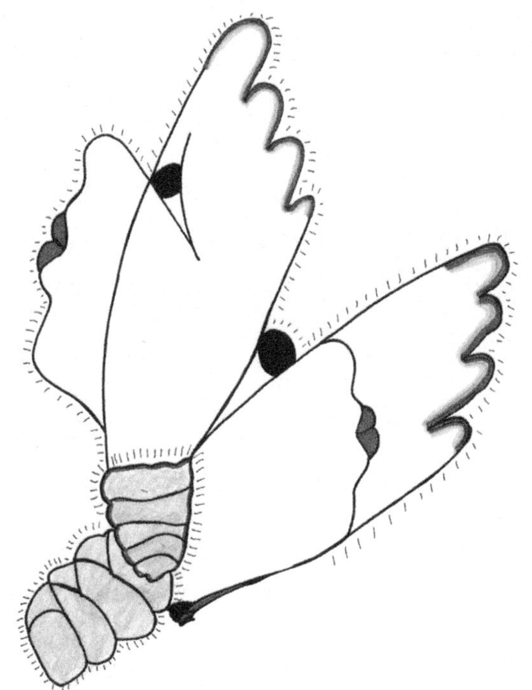

CONTENTS

part one theVisionary

part two Entering the Mystic Universe of Beautiful Painted Arrow

Row, row, row your boat gently
Down the stream.
Merrily, merrily, merrily, merrily
Life is but a Dream
"La vida no mas un sueño es."
(Life is but a Dream)

In 1947 at 12 years of age, at the seventh grade at Santa Fe Indian School, the "at" sound was unfolding a beginning of a lifelong dream, a dream made of pure clarity that would begin crystallizing into an unfolding spiritual journey of singing songs. At the age of 12, I became a first tenor in a boys choir under the direction of Ray D. Shinos. He had a masters degree in music and was our music teacher. Perhaps some of you remember him—those of you who attended Santa Fe Indian School in the 1940s and 1950s. Bernard Duran, Gilbert Mermeja, Jimmy Martinas and Alfred Nailer from Picuris Pueblo were in the all-boys choir. (The school also had a mixed choir where boys and girls sang together.) All of us who went to the Indian School in Santa Fe, New Mexico, City of the Holy Faith, as it was sometimes called, I believe, continued on to become mystics, to live inside a row boat traveling down life's stream. Some of us after a while became Santa Fe's Horse Head Mountain, from which waters came down and flowed past the boarding school.

Today I can still hear the beautiful voices of young men and young women in my meditations, voices which will continue to live forever in the House of Santa Fe, a beauty of divine presence.

—Joseph Beautiful Painted Arrow
Colorado, 2010

A Note about Tiwa from Joseph Rael

In my teaching and writing, I have often referred to the various sounds in Tiwa, the language spoken by the Indians in my father's village of Picuris Pueblo. The sounds in the word Tiwa are "Tii," which is the vibration of reflecting, or thinking; and "Wah," which is the vibration of universes.

Tiwa means "universes are reflecting, thinking" and therefore they have language.

Tiwa is not just one language, it is the vibration of all language. It is anything that has to do with sound. Every person who speaks any language, anywhere in the world is speaking Tiwa. If you are an English speaker (or German, or Italian, or French, or Spanish, or whatever language) you are very much a Tiwa.

In fact, every person speaking is the universe reflecting on the consciousness of the multiplicity of billions of billions of billions of universes.

In the same way, when I write or speak about Picuris Pueblo as the heart center, I am not marking out that particular locale in north central New Mexico in particular. Wherever I am, wherever you are, is the heart center of the universe, because we have language, and we are reflecting, thinking beings.

The sounds in the word Picuris are: *Pii*, which is the vibration of the center of the universe; *cu*, which is the vibration of "where it sits"; *iii*, which is "multiple states of awareness." Picuris is the vibration meaning "the center of the universe, where it sits in multiple states of awareness."

Language happened this way: first the Vast Self (Divine Presence) created Taa-Que Spirit of Tiwa, sometimes referred to as Plow Man (the vibration of universes reflecting), and then, out of that, the people were given language.

In 2000 I asked Joseph what I could do for him. He asked me
to write a book about his life, his teachings, and his unrevealed
visions. This is the result. I hope it honors him. I must thank
two people without whom this could not have grown: Denise,
who has inspired and partnered me, and Norman Marchand,
our Dharma friend, who has devoted years to preserving Joseph's
oral teachings and to photographing his paintings. I also wish
to acknowledge the contribution of my colleague and close
friend, Dr. B. L. Hobbs, who offered many insights on the text,
particularly regarding the Hero's Journey. Last, I thank Sally
Dennison and Millichap Books for publishing this and being
dedicated to Joseph and his work.

We dedicate this to our daughter, Yasmine, whom Joseph has
showered with love, and about whom Joseph said, "She is our
future and we are her roots." And finally, I offer this story as a
long-life prayer to Tsloot-ta-koi, who has blessed our family and
so many sentient beings. May he continue to do so for many
years and lifetimes.

Tutah,
KV WILT

THE LIFE OF JOSEPH RAEL
{A CHRONOLOGY}

pre-birth
- ~ Visited family as auric body/consciousness
- ~ Perceived in womb through mother's thoughts and feelings
- ~ Listened to vegetables, sensing energies of siblings

1935
- – Born in La Boca, Colorado, near Ute Reservation
- ~ Saw auras and rainbow bodies of family members

1935–41
- ~ Envisioned "little people," beings of the trees
- ~ Could not differentiate subtle and ordinary realms

1940
- ~ Lost in alternate reality on hill while shepherding

1941
- ~ Experienced out-of-body perception when head is injured
- – Departed from La Boca
- ~ Envisioned Elf Boy
- – Moved in with father's mother, at Picuris

1942
- ~ Envisioned kachinas in ship
- ~ Envisioned elderly lady with music houses, precursor of sound/peace chambers
- – Started Picuris Day School

1943
- – Began shamanistic training with Antonio Simbolo
- ~ Experienced visions in kiva, with sound, vibration, and color
- ~ Received back-to-back transmission from grandfather
- ~ Fed by spiritual presence during 100-year kiva ceremony, experienced center of medicine wheel
- ~ Experienced whirlwinds and Lord of Wind

1944
- ~ Underwent thunder caller clan training
- ~ Made blackboard approach in Picuris Day School
- ~ Slapped book, light engulfed him, and he learned contents

1945

~ Envisioned mother in coffin before she died

1947

~ Performed healing ceremony for woman

1947–52

~ Attended Santa Fe Indian School, concentrated on studies

~ Healed woman with cancer over distance

1948

~ Experienced eagle presence during thundercalling

– Antonio Simbola, *Pel-qui-weh,* went to Spirit

1954

– Started at Saint Joseph's College

1955

– First woman Joseph had healed returned to Picuris to die

1955

– Married Patricia Lucero with whom he had five children

1960–65

– Sun danced on Ute reservation

1961

~ Envisioned Earth Mother/Madonna after he almost died in gas explosion; Mother/Madonna (*Ki-ah-neh* in Tiwa) said, "You're going to be all right."

1963

~ Called by/envisioned medicine teacher, Grandfather

1968

– Entered University of New Mexico, developed capacity to read minds and books

1970s

~ Communicated with deceased relatives in Picuris and during sun dances with the Southern Utes

1975

~ Attended University of Wisconsin

1976

~ Read his professors' minds during MA exam

– Brokered peace treaty between Taos and Picuris

– Worked at Taos County Mental Health Council

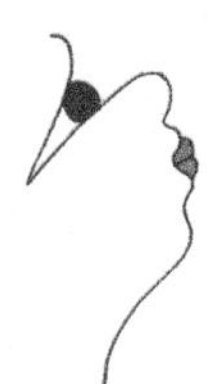

1977

- Worked at Office of Indian Affairs
- ~ Envisioned Hispanic ghosts on Picuris, sent them into Nah

1978

- Contributed to the Religious Freedom Act
- ~ Vision-traveled to find God in Hawaii
- ~ Envisioned life in bubbles underneath ocean

1979

- ~ Envisioned the end of time
- Worked for Indian Health Service

1980

- ~ Started the Long Dances
- ~ Lost in and escapes from the alternative reality of *Aah-suh-naa*
- Trained Picuris runners
- Given land by Southern Ute Tribal Council for life
- ~ Traveled with Jesus

1980s

- ~ Assisted by angels in Germany
- ~ Stopped rain for Robert Redford's making of *Milagro Beanfield War*
- ~ Stopped rain during ceremonial dances in Austria

1981

- ~ Envisioned map in Santa Fe office of IHS
- Started work at Picuris Health Center (Tu-tah Center)
- ~ Sent ghosts into the nah, subtle world, at Picuris Pueblo

1983

- ~ Taken to subtle world of Grandfathers, directed to build peace chamber, envisioned elder and infant, built first chamber in Bernalillo
- ~ Envisioned UFO on land near Hesperus
- ~ Gave man arrow so he could discover oil

1984

- ~ Envisioned mermen in California during purification ceremony
- ~ Saw shark on road

1986

- ~ Envisioned Drum Dance
- – Started Drum Dances
- ~ Encountered Lord of Wind while sun dancing

1987

- ~ Visited by 5 black-light beings (vowels/5 fingers of Taah-meh-ney) who asked him to take War Gods to lower worlds. Found and sent first War God to underworld
- ~ Heard dolphins speak through baby during ceremony for purifying ocean in Scotland for dolphins
- – Started Sun/Moon dances worldwide

1988

- ~ Envisioned 5-year old peace chamber child and elder angel in Bernalillo

1989

- ~ Envisioned the origin of Picuris while in Pennsylvania
- ~ Communicated with Ah-Keh, ancient prophet of Picuris people while leading sun-moon dance in Pennsylvania

1990

- ~ Envisioned ascent of peace chamber in redwood tree above Albuquerque
- ~ Found second War God in Scotland, sent it to lower world
- – Began to focus on visionary art

1991

- ~ Performed thunder calling ceremony in Colorado

1996

- – Diagnosed with, and recovered from pancreatic cancer

1998

- ~ Experienced trance-vision in Hesperus, in which he saw the alphabet, geometric shapes, numbers, mathematical formulas, and departed relatives, indicating future experiences.
- – Semi-retired to Southern Ute Reservation

2006

- ~ Envisioned Horn of Plenty while dancing in Australia

the Visionary

part one

INTRODUCTION

This is not a conventional biography. It could not be so. For
Joseph Earl Rael, Beautiful Painted Arrow, is a visionary, a
being blessed with extraordinary intuition, of not only personal
but also planetary import. Despite the fact that he has had all
the experiences of a contemporary American householder. In
this sense he is like the great yogis of Tibet, the *ngakpas*, the
white robed ones who integrate intense practice into so-called
ordinary family life, who live life as a spiritual practice. For the
Amerindian *ngakpas* with whom Joseph grew, everyday, life-
sustaining work is sacred and transformative. Invested with
presence, all so-called ordinary acts are holy plowing. Walking,
driving, talking, painting, writing, singing, scrubbing, officeing,
building, washing, planting, cutting, cooking, hunting,
fathering, and husbanding—all are essential, all are just as
important as questing for visions in kivas and lodges, as fasting
and dancing for days. They are all metaphors through which the
soul actualizes itself and Vast Self becomes present. Favoring
one necessary activity over another is a destructive act of the
ordinary mind. (How could eating be better than defecating?)

The reader will, however, notice that I have de-emphasized the
details of his householding, of his personal history. One reason
for this is Joseph's introverted, modest nature. He is a private
person; not a public figure. He has only shown himself because
he was directed to do so by Spirit. Even then, he usually resisted
Spirit's call until he became sick and/or the routine of his life
disintegrated. In talking about his resistance to the imperatives
of Spirit, he usually chuckles and invokes his stubbornness.

I have also de-emphasized details because we, as Joseph
repeatedly reminds listeners, do not exist; only Great Spirit, or

3

as Joseph prefers to say, Vast Self exists. And while Vast Self
is potential in most of us, It is realized in Joseph. Therefore,
the facts of Joseph's personal life are far less significant than
the ways in which Vast Self has expressed Itself through him.
Personal history (tidbits the drunken mind craves, imagining
it owns something) pales in comparison to what a real human
sees, feels, and senses—for the benefit of all sentient beings.
Joseph has shared what he wishes to share of his personal life in
his books. This book only adds what Joseph feels is relevant to
our growth.

Overall, this book aims at what Joseph has aimed at for most
of his life: understanding and transformation. It will, therefore,
be more truth than fact. While Joseph's mystical experiences
(which defy the ordinary senses and conventional logic) occurred
as described, they will necessarily be explained through
metaphor, an alternative, intuited model of reality. For instance,
Jesus performed many miracles, readily accepted by mystics, but
he explained alternate reality (the kingdom of heaven) through
parables and metaphors. So while your ordinary mind might find
little to chew here, I hope your subtle, imaginative mind will be
intrigued, challenged, even elated and inspired. I also hope that
you'll find Joseph's books, compact discs, web sites, and videos.
This way you'll also read about the events I note in the initial
timeline but neglect in the text. Better yet, I encourage you to try
to sit in his presence while he's still in his body (though he rarely
leaves his hermitage). "Energy, when it's transmitted that way
from body to body, is the essence of communication" (*House of
Shattering Light* 22).

While Part One of this story began at Joseph's hermitage
a decade ago, at his suggestion Part Two began while Joseph,
Marchand, Denise, and I were sitting in our kitchen before one
of his seminars, the final event of his stint as artist-in-residence
at Saint Leo University. We conceived the project as a meditation
manual so that his students, even people encountering his work
for the first time, might practice Joseph's visionary experiences
within themselves and their environment. It follows the trend of
Joseph's teaching, teaching that culminated in the publication

of *Sound* in 2009. *Sound: Native Teachings + Visionary Art,* about five years in the making, combines his most subtle teachings on light, sound, and energy with an extraordinary collection of his paintings and internet links to his chanting. Both parts of this book were updated to incorporate the new insights in *Sound.*

Another prefatory note: Joseph, who exists as one-third very subtle being, one third subtle, and one third perceptual/physical being, has never been exigent with dates concerning his personal history or with consistency—though he functions quite well in the time/space grid. Dates are the obsessions of the left brain, grid consciousness. Consequently, though I have assigned dates to some of the significant events in his life, they may be inaccurate, somewhat fluid. So what. And remember, communicating a vision, direct perception of the energetic dimension, via the ordinary mind is nearly impossible. Turning the eternal/infinite to the temporal/finite requires incredible funneling, lamentable framing. In order to better appreciate his mystical experience, you might do well to occasionally flip to the back of the book and engage in a practice.

Finally, Tiwa is an oral language. Over the decades in which Joseph and his publishers have been presenting his teachings, they have sought to convey Tiwa sounds and words into English in an authentic manner. In some cases English renderings have changed. English is, as you will see, much less poetic and rich than Tiwa. So, you will notice apparent inconsistencies.

At the end of this forward, before we consider Joseph's experiences and the way in which he's shared them, we emphasize, as Joseph has, that he does not teach the religions of his ancestors but his visions. In emphasizing this, we'll quote from *Sound:*

> I teach what has come to me from my visions. I spent fifty years becoming a visionary so that what I do in ceremony comes from Source and it works. I don't know how these ceremonies work or why they work, but they work. People who criticize me for sharing ceremonies with non-Indians don't understand that the ceremonies I am doing are not traditional or tribal. (80)

On the next page, re-iterating that everything he does comes from his visions, Joseph says that all our inspirations come "from that band of light-like energy that is full of the power of lifting" (81).

Part one, which follows, elaborates his visioning; part two communicates how we, too, can access, via inspiration, that "band of light-like energy."

Appreciating Vision

An important aspect of understanding Joseph involves understanding visioning. Visioning is just the most dramatic form of intuition, one that involves seeing subtle reality with or without the physical eyes. The most common form of visual intuition is seeing auras or the magnetic field, the radiance surrounding and pervading all beings. However, all the senses have intuitive capacity, or, said another way, intuition can function through all the senses. With heightened or subtle touch, we can sense or feel energies. With what is sometimes called audition, we can hear voices or vibrations from the subtle realm. Likewise, we can taste and smell phenomenon that are not apparent to the outer senses. Every outer sense has an inner/ subtle counterpart. Such experiences are well-documented by mystics around the world, in all spiritual traditions.

So, although I use the word "vision" because most people relate mystical intuition with seeing, Joseph experienced more comprehensive dimensions of reality via all inner senses. Furthermore, although many more people experience these intuitions than admit to them, most people function as individual selves rather than Vast Self like Joseph, and, therefore, have intuitions of individual, not universal, significance.

Though Joseph has crisscrossed most of the globe since we met, he is less known than the native visionaries Black Elk and Black Elk's nephew, Fools Crow, his spiritual brothers. Black Elk, the revered Sioux visionary who went to Spirit in 1950, has become an exemplar of native spirituality, indeed, an exemplar of wholesome and holy life in general. His visions, experiences and his recollections of his people's sacred ceremonies, told to Neihardt and Brown, have become Native American and spiritual classics, taught on many college campuses. Reading them, we are powerfully inspired by his revelations, communion with all beings, and spiritually rich way of life—then humbled by our ignorance and saddened by our pitifully meager lives.

Fool's Crow, perhaps the most extraordinary spiritual healer of the twentieth century, is best known through the testaments of Thomas Mails. Many non-Indians directly and indirectly benefited from his miraculous healings before he left his body in 1989. Both Black Elk and Fool's Crow experienced and lived from the primordial ground. Both served only the Great Spirit. Both loved all people—every entity is a person—and all races; both felt that the wisdom of this continent could help the planet and all sentient beings survive; and both emphasized the rigorous and uncompromising requirements for becoming an agent of spiritual power, a "hollow bone," as Fool's Crow said. All beings, seen and unseen, have benefited greatly because these native magi lived and because they recognized the pale-skinned scribes in whom they could confide.

Joseph is the next generation of native holy man. Unlike his Sioux predecessors, Beautiful Painted Arrow, pronounced *Tsloot-ta-koi* in Tiwa, has been transmitting his visions and the natural way to non-natives without intermediaries. Joseph's European shadings, his education by native elders and non-native teachers and university professors, and his insatiable inquisitiveness have not only fit him to teach Indians and non-Indians, but to do so worldwide. In fact, Joseph, who traveled abroad extensively for twenty-five years and whose students have built more than twenty sacred chambers outside the United States, has communed with many more people than the revered Lakota seer and Teton healer. And significantly, while the visions and healings of Black Elk and Fool's Crow can be appreciated by non-natives, Beautiful Painted Arrow's have unfolded for all beings.

Joseph became aware of his destiny to enact his visions among non-Indians in 1981. After earning an M.A. in Political

7

Science, *Tsloot-ta-koi*, whose name also means "Double Rainbow" and "Medicine Arrow," was working for the Indian Health Service in Santa Fe . One day, a vision of a map appeared on his office wall. The map, which showed a series of simultaneous scenarios, illuminated problems and infused him with ideas. Though he didn't know where to begin, he knew he was to teach non-Indians:

> The map directed me from the Age of Reason to the Age of the Heart. It was now time for the Indians to show the non-Indians how to think through the heart and not through the mind.
>
> So I started sharing the teachings that I had received, and over the years I have been all over the world leading workshops and ceremonies. I did not teach any specifics of the Picuris ceremonies. What I got at Picuris was a foundation.
>
> . . . I didn't have to translate this knowledge into supernatural power. It translated itself and became part of my repertoire, based on the vibration of the land. (*House of Shattering Light* 115)

So after forty-seven years of studying with teachers of the Indian, non-Indian, and spiritual worlds, being ever-directed by intuition and vision, Joseph focused on his spiritual work, which Joseph defines as "becoming involved in actions that promote awareness, compassion, carrying, purity, and higher mind." Though this vision of the map was personal because it involved his destiny, it was also impersonal because his destiny involves all sentient beings. He knows, as did Black Elk and Fool's Crow, that if the so-called advanced societies who destroyed and continue to destroy indigenous societies and nature don't receive and value what natives have, real life can not evolve— just progress and die. Not only that: Joseph, who was told his spiritual tribe would be composed of "rainbow people," has been given new ceremonies and revelations particularly relevant to the people of this time, the human tribe.

However, Joseph not only enacts and gives voice to his visions; he paints them, particularly since his semi-retirement to the Southern Ute Reservation of his mother. His home, the kiva below his evolving gallery, the dwellings of his students, as well as *Sound* showcase his extraordinary 'flat' art. These paintings and drawings, which Joseph calls "generators of light" (*Sound* 169), fulfill what Campbell considered the four-fold mystical, cosmological, psychological, and sociological functions of true, transformational art. They also link him to his Picuris ancestors, who painted on the walls of their kivas.

Though no one taught Joseph how to paint transformational art, he acknowledges studying with several masters of flat art, popular in the 1940s. At the Santa Fe Indian School, he was taught by Velino Herrara and had the opportunity to watch the process of Gerald Nailor, perhaps the most famous native artist today. He also acknowledges the influence of Ray Toledo, his art teacher at the Santa Fe Indian School. Ray taught Joseph how to mix colors and noticed an already present mystical gift. Though Ray soon forgot what he said, he told Joseph that he "had a direct pipeline to God and that when I drew, I was drawing images that were coming from the inner source, from the spiritual place" (*House of Shattering Light* 158–59).

As an artist, Rael is very much like William Blake, the European world's greatest visionary artist, who said that we, ignorant and flawed, aren't just possibly divine but *essentially* divine, and that we have not only mortal eyes but immortal eyes of Imagination which can perceive the ever-present subtle forms of eternity. Who was "a 'seer' in the literal sense of the word, for whom the realm of the spirit was every bit as tangible as the material world" (Vaughan, *William Blake* 1).

Blake, born in 1757 into a middle-class London family, was never formally educated but did attend drawing school at ten and began a seven-year apprenticeship to an engraver at fourteen.

During and after his apprenticeship, Blake became passionate about comparative mythology, Michelangelo, Raphael, and Gothic art, as well as Plotinus, Paracelsus, Boehme, Shakespeare, and the Bible.

His uniqueness, akin to Rael's, was attested to by his 1890 biographer, William Rossetti, who said Blake was "a man not forestalled by predecessors, nor to be classed with contemporaries, nor to be replaced by known or readily surmisable successors" (*William Blake* xiii).

Like Rael, Blake also perceived life in reverse, 'inside-out,' like the American nineteenth-century mystical poet Emily Dickinson, who wrote, "Much madness is divinest sense/To a discerning eye" (*Collected Poems* 22, lines 1–2). In order to better appreciate Blake's kinship with Rael, contemplate the following revolutionary statements selected from his great poem, "The Marriage of Heaven and Hell": "Man has no Body distinct from his Soul for that calld Body is a portion of Soul discerned by the five Senses, the chief inlets of Soul in this age"; "A fool sees not the same tree that a wise man sees"; "He whose face gives no light, shall never become a star"; "Eternity is in love with the productions of time"; "The most sublime act is to set another before you"; "The head Sublime, the heart Pathos, the genitals Beauty, the hands & feet Proportion"; " . . . All deities reside in the human breast"; "If the doors of perception were cleansed every thing would appear to man as it is: infinite" (*The Complete Poetry & Prose of William Blake* 34–40).

As these quotes suggest, Rael and Blake had precisely the same quest: to "cleanse" the "doors of perception," for themselves and others. Blake's "cleansed," immortal perception also allowed him to regularly converse with angels, prophets, his departed brother, and inspiring spirits; to see a funeral of fairies, a host of angels chanting as the sun rises, a "tree filled with angels, bright angelic wings bespangling every bough like the stars," and angelic figures walking among those making hay (Gilchrist, *Life of Blake* I, 7).

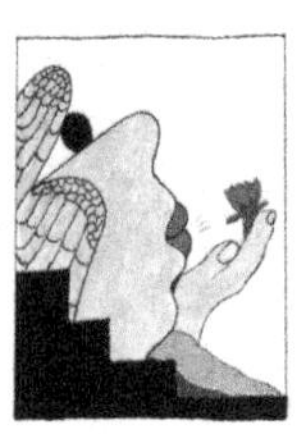

The correspondence between these two visionary artists is profound. The more one studies Blake's visionary poetry and designs, the more one can appreciate Painted Arrow's, and vice versa. For instance, for Blake, our collective and individual salvation depends upon Energy/Imagination, one of his four archetypal Zoas, rising up and resisting oppression by Reason, the tyrannical Zoa. In Joseph's work, this realization appears in our need to awaken to inspiration/intuition and free ourselves from "perceptual reality," as well as in the faces of innocence peering skyward, "drinking light" in his visionary paintings.

The Blake scholar and mystic Kathleen Raines echoes Rossetti in writing that Blake has had no successors in his striving to create a "new pictorial language." Though he draws on the indigenous and North American experience rather than the British, Rael might very well be Blake's successor. Therefore, what Raines forecast of Blake, may well apply to Rael: A "New Age" may yet discover in Rael "the forerunner of a new way of expressing the non-spatial interpenetration of spiritual worlds, and that spiritual collectivity of life of which he had so strong an intuition" (*William Blake* 124).

Joseph also evidences remarkable kinship with the great medieval visionary and mystic, Hildegard of Bingen, a Benedictine sister, who, like Joseph, was a writer, artist, musician, and healer. Though she "had felt . . . the gift of secret mysteries and wondrous visions" since early childhood, like Joseph, Hildegard's defining vision didn't occur until middle age, in the year of 1141, when she was nearly forty-three years old. After a heavenly voice spoke twice, directing her to speak and write, she wrote the following:

> . . . a burning light coming from heaven poured into my mind. Like a flame which does not burn but rather enkindles, it inflamed my heart and my breast, just as the sun warms something with its rays. And I was able to understand books suddenly, the psaltery clearly, the evangelists and the volumes of the Old and New Testament, but I did not have the interpretation of the words of their texts nor the division of their grammar. (Hozeski, *Hildegard's Scivias* 2)

Furthermore, the vision commanded Hildegard to say and write what she had experienced. When she procrastinated to do so, she would become ill. Joseph, as we will learn, has had the same reaction, losing insight and power, experiencing despair, when he does not enact visions. Hildegard's recorded and illustrated visions, approved by Bernard of Clairvaux and Pope Eugenius III and completed ten years later, comprise *Scivias*. Altogether, *Scivias* contains thirty-six pictures and descriptions of twenty-six visions, all detailing her encounters with Biblical figures such as Jesus, Mary, Abraham, Moses, Joshua, the Prophets, the Patriarchs, the Apostles, and a host of natural and celestial phenomena. After each vision a heavenly voice explained to Hildegard what she had seen. These explanations appear in the text, right after Hildegard's illustrations and descriptions.

"Probably the best known portion of this visionary work is its ending, which Hildegard set to music and which dramatically depicts the eternal battle between good and evil" (Fuhrkotter, in *Hildegard's Scivias* ix). Just before this, in vision twelve, Christ and a host of angels animate the four elements of earth, water, fire, and air, which cleanse the world. Then an angel blows a trumpet, summoning the bones of the dead, which take on flesh. The luminous among them ascend the second circle of heaven, to rest in the blissful lap of eternity. The once-anarchic elements have become harmonious. And "the sun, moon, and stars—just like embellished things—[shine] with a reddish gleam full of brightness and beauty" (*Scivias* 366). Hildegard recounted the vision's final scene in this way: "Thereupon, the sky got very bright, and I heard all the previously mentioned virtues sing in a wondrous manner to the various types of music. They persisted strongly in the way of truth as they sang the praises of the city of celestial joy" (375). She then recorded their songs to the various denizens of heaven.

Understanding herself to be in the line of the prophets, she recorded subsequent visions in two more works, *Book of Life's Merits* (1163) and *Book of the Divine Works* (1174). Like Blake, Hildegard was a householder. However, unlike Blake but like Rael, Hildegard, the mother superior, was not a reclusive visionary. She also founded convents, preached, healed, performed exorcisms, and exhorted the Church, clergy, and laity to spiritually awaken. Though she was Germany's first Christian mystic and a monumental figure of the Middle Ages, she like her male counterpart, Meister Eckhart, whose mystical meditations on nothingness and emptiness are strikingly similar to Joseph's, had been largely forgotten until recent years.

To deepen our appreciation of visioning, let us leap forward
about 750 years to consider two twentieth century visionaries,
one of whom the dualistic mind would consider a mystic, one
of whom it would consider a scientist. The first is a little-known
religious figure, a great Tibetan lama, one of many who intuited
the annihilation of Tibetan culture by the Chinese Communists:
Tulku Urgyen Rinpoche. Urgyen, born in eastern Tibet in
1920, was a reincarnate master, perhaps most revered for
communicating Dzogchen, the Great Perfection, the innermost,
non-dual nature of mind. Though he spent long periods in
retreat and meditated daily, he too was a householder, a father of
six, who founded five major monasteries in Nepal after fleeing
Communist Tibet.

In 1955, with the Communists threatening eastern Tibet, he
traveled from his ancestral home in Nangchen to Central Tibet
at the request of the Karmapa, the fifteenth spiritual leader
of the Karma Kagyu lineage. (Before dying, the Karmapas
generally write a letter indicating where they will reincarnate.)
Shortly after he had arrived at the Karmapa's monastery, he
and the Karmapa visited a shrine to divine the future of Tibet.
The Karmapa wrote his question on a slip of paper and placed
it under the mask of a Bodhisattva, a being who had achieved
Buddhahood, enlightenment. When they returned the next day
and unlocked the shrine they saw that blood-like liquid had
flowed from the mask, enough to fill three bowls. Subsequently,
the blood spilled onto the floor. The Karmapa told Urgyen, "The
Buddha's teachings in Tibet will probably disappear. What a
tragedy" (Tulku Urgyen Rinpoche, *Blazing Splendor* 293). (At
about the same time, another great tulku, Dudjom Rinpoche,
saw blood flowing for seven days from a statue of a Bodhisattva
near the capital of Lhasa.)

Shortly thereafter, Tulku Urgyen had a more explicit mystical
encounter. This occurred during a lucid dream in Moon Cave
where he was living. A "dakini of incredible beauty," a goddess or
female archangel, began to dance. Realizing she was a "wisdom

dakini," he asked her what would happen to Tibet. She replied, "The Chinese will come. . . . Thirty-six months from now the Buddha's teachings in Tibet will be stamped to the ground and the land left in darkness." He then asked if the Dalai Lama would go into exile, and she said, "There is no doubt. He will go to India" (295). To ascertain her reliability, he asked a last question about the Dalai Lama's whereabouts—which the *tulku* later confirmed. Fully aware he was in an altered state, Tulku Urgyen did not want to open his eyes, the *dakini* was so beautiful. Nevertheless, he opened them and could still see her a few feet away. Haunted by the vision's message, Tulku Urgyen and his family eventually escaped to Sikkim—even though the majority of Tibetans believed their country's spiritual power would protect them.

Finally, we have the example of Carl Jung, better known for his psychological discoveries and formulations, such as the Self, anima and animus, and collective unconscious, than for his extraordinary visions. In his autobiography, *Memories, Dreams, and Reflections*, Jung recounts a personal and transpersonal dream vision he had while three or four years old. Entering a "dark, rectangular, stone-lined hole in the ground," he found a "wonderfully rich golden throne," upon which sat a luminous lingam. "Only fifty years later . . . did it become clear to me how exceedingly unchildlike, how sophisticated and oversophisticated was the thought that had begun to break through into consciousness." It had "happened in order to bring the greatest possible amount of light into the darkness. It was an initiation into the realm of darkness," "the secrets of the earth" (12–13).

Though his entire life was marked by such visions, several others stand out. At age 38, when he was playing in order to recover the "small boy" within himself and repossess a "creative life," he had a series of profound visions, this time while he was awake. He "saw a monstrous flood covering all the northern and low-lying lands between the North Sea and the Alps." He "realized that a frightful catastrophe was in progress." Upon "mighty yellow waves," he "saw the floating rubble of civilization and the drowned bodies of uncounted thousands. Then the whole sea turned to blood. The vision lasted about an hour." Later, he realized the collective unconscious was showing Jung the coming world war. Yet "the idea of war did not occur to me at all" (175–76).

Two weeks later he envisioned a more vivid version in which "the blood was more emphasized. An inner voice spoke. 'Look at it well; it is wholly real and it will be so. You cannot doubt it.'" Over the next six months, he had a "thrice-repeated dream that in the middle of summer an Arctic cold wave descended and froze the land to ice." The land was "totally deserted by human beings. All living green things were killed by frost." About six weeks later, "on August 1 the world war broke out" (175–76).

I'll briefly recount one more of Jung's visions, this one because it involves the 'ascending' of Jung's subtle self, what Joseph would call his *nah*, and because it involves the transformation of Jung's consciousness and being. Also it parallels one of Joseph's later, more profound visions. In 1944 Jung suffered a heart attack and experienced visions when he "hung on the edge of death." While having these visions, his nurse told him it was as if he were "surrounded by a bright glow" (289). He found himself high up in space, looking down upon the Earth, India in particular.

He later figured out that he would have to have been a thousand miles above the Earth to have seen what he did. He turned and saw a house-size black stone, which turned out to be a sort of temple with a Hindu yogi sitting beside the entrance to an antechamber. As he climbed the steps he felt "everything was being sloughed away; everything I aimed at or wished for or thought, the whole phantasmagoria of earthly existence." In brief, Jung was experiencing spiritual death, the purification of the personal self (*solvae* according to the alchemist Basil Valentinus), the shifting of one's center of gravity to the impersonal and transpersonal dimensions. The "experience gave me a feeling of extreme poverty, but at the same time of great fullness." Soon his initial sense of "annihilation" gave way to the bliss of being free from the "box system" (290–91). This is just the experience that Joseph has wished to awaken in his students.

15

I've dwelled a lot on Jung, but Jung is a very important figure in the evolution of "Western" culture and consciousness, incorporating the wisdom of ancient and indigenous cultures. Ever guided by intuition, he strove to become more rooted so that he could branch farther. And repeatedly he warned against devaluing intuition and overvaluing reason. He said, "Rationalism and doctrinarism are the disease of our time" (300). Joseph, in fact, remembers meeting Jung, whom the Picuris called "The Man with the Pipe" when Jung visited the pueblos in his life-long attempt to reconcile the square (European mentality and practicality) with the circle (primitive intuition and emotion). In his autobiography, he even refers to these as the two parts of himself, recognized when he was a child.

Though Jung seems not to have written about his visit to Picuris, he did write about his visit to the much better known Taos. Speaking of his visit with a chief, Ochwiay Biano, Jung contrasts the shallowness of speaking with a European and the profundity of speaking with an Indian and "discovering new approaches to age-old knowledge." When the Indian remarked that whites were "cruel," "that they always want something," that Indians "think they are mad" and that whites "say that they think with their heads," Jung remarked, "Why of course. What do you think with?" To this Ochwiay replied, "We think here," "indicating his heart" (247–48). This is precisely what Joseph, perhaps thirty years later, was guided to teach non-Indians in the vision in his office.

The disease of reason about which Blake warned in the eighteenth century and Jung warned in the twentieth, is now an epidemic, accelerated by the so-called information explosion. And though recognition of our worldwide ecological crisis and of more wholesome perspectives offers hope, intuition, emotion, and instinct continue to atrophy. With this deification of the human biocomputer, computer, and information in general (along with the demeaning of the world's indigenous populations), we don't appreciate visions, guidance from the collective unconscious, save perhaps the periodic apparitions of the Virgin Mary.

Vine Deloria Jr., in his book recounting the extraordinary powers of medicine persons, bemoans the spiritual poverty of contemporary native people, a people whose existence in earlier times was predicated on intuition and vision:

> Even on the most traditional reservations, the erosion of the old way is so profound that many people are willing to cast aside ceremonies that stood them in good stead for thousands of years and live in increasing and meaningless secularity. The consumer society is indeed consuming everything in its path. It is fair to say that the overwhelming majority of Indian people today have little understanding or remembrance of the powers once possessed by the spiritual leaders of their communities. What we do today is often simply a "walk-through" of a once-potent ceremony that now has little visible effect on the participants. The exercise of spiritual powers still continues in some place but lacks the definitive intensity of the old days. (*The World We Used to Live In* xix)

This, of course, means that whites, nearly successful in erasing the 'red' people's physical presence and ceremonies, have nearly erased their spiritual presence. The attempt to eradicate Spirit was inevitable—because whites have only done to the survivors what they've done to themselves, all the while selling the illusion of progress. And imagining they've got 'it,' that they're the chosen ones.

From Joseph's perspective, materialism and this hegemony of mind over intuition, emotion, and instinct is further fueled by language. Many of us can understand how habitual phrasing fosters habitual consciousness, but Joseph refers not only to jargon and clichés, but to the language itself, in particular, to the language of English, the universal tongue. Europeans, the world's foremost colonizers, are what Joseph calls "noun people." European languages rely on nouns, static material entities. Things. The result is a sclerosed, skewed perception of life. Mental definition, image, and language ("perceptual reality") conspire to deaden living and give the illusion of what Buddhism calls "permanence." They also, by reducing living to a material

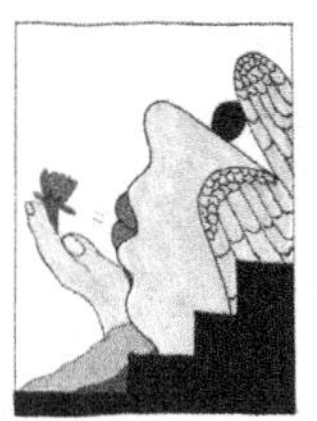

experience, promote the fear of death. Tiwa, Joseph 's second language, is verb-based, conveying happenings and metaphoric relationships rather than mere objects.

Joseph was aware of the limiting nature of English from the time he began to learn it; it is his fourth language—after Ute, Tiwa, and Spanish. As a result of what he realizes about English, Joseph manipulates the language to express "visioning," to bring about a shift in consciousness, or simply to accord with reality. He speaks poetry, plays with diction and syntax, breathing Spirit into the dead and deadening medium, trying to make English more like Tiwa, a language of essences, metaphors, and happenings. For this reason, left-brained, rational types, struggle to understand Joseph, even when they are attracted to him. Ironically, Western scientists, specifically theoretical physicists (with whom Joseph has dialogued), are creating a language and discovering a perspective similar to that of Joseph and his mystical forbearers—an imaginative language and perspective highly dependent upon metaphor, which defies the ordinary mind.

Finally, though Beautiful Painted Arrow usually refers to himself as a mystic, he has occasionally called himself a medicine person, a translation of a native term, as well as a shaman, a term "derived from the Vedic word 'sram'" (Halifax, *Shamanic Voices* 3). Though the words are often interchanged, one could rightly say that a medicine person is an Amerindian shaman. While I find both these terms limit Joseph's scope, they certainly convey aspects of Joseph's giving. Indeed, Joseph's acts are as miraculous as the medicine persons Deloria included in *The World We Used to Live In.* (Deloria passed to Spirit in 2005.) Furthermore, Joseph fulfills every one of the descriptors Halifax offers in *Shamanic Voices*, her survey of the world's shamans (which includes Amerindians such as Black Elk and Lame Deer):

> Shamans are healers, seers, and visionaries who have mastered death. They are in communication with the world of gods and spirits. Their bodies can be left behind while they fly to unearthly realms. They are poets and singers. They dance and create works of art. They are not only spiritual leaders but also judges and politicians, the repositories for

the knowledge of the culture's history, both sacred and secular. They are familiar with cosmic as well as physical geography; the ways of plants, animals, and the elements are
known to them. They are psychologists, entertainers, and
food finders. Above all, however, shamans are technicians of
the sacred and masters of ecstasy. (4)

Had Joseph become the theocratic leader of a pueblo, he
would be *cacique,* the role accorded to his step-grandfather and
primary guide, Antonio Simbola. He would, therefore, have
more properly fit the terms classifications of medicine man
and shaman. But as we shall see, destiny, universal design,
extended Joseph's scope, his spiritual influence, beyond both of
his parents' reservations. Joseph's tribe has become humanity. In
describing Joseph's life and spiritual quest, this book also aims
to convey that supernatural events are natural not supernatural.
This is so-called civilized people's greatest challenge, much more
challenging than outer space, because we have handicapped
ourselves and can no longer break through the barriers of light
like the young native runners.

In light of our many limitations, Joseph's experiences and
acts (as well as those of the other mystics I recounted), may
seem miraculous or fantastic. Or, if our belief system admits
vision, we may reject his visions as false or heretical. Though
unnatural, this is common, for as Joseph Campbell writes,
"Myth is somebody else's religion." Or because his visions
include prophets of established religions, we might associate
him with those. Joseph, whose realization includes all paths,
has not communicated some of his visions for just this reason.
He eschews all labels. Nevertheless, some who have ears to hear
and eyes to see, who are ripe for inclusive rather than exclusive
spirituality, who intuitively know that the body and creation
are the presence of the Creator, will embrace the natural way
he reveals. Above all, becoming natural (we only become when
natural) depends upon our manifesting several qualities that
mark Joseph's being and work: awareness, innocence, and
"teachability," qualities often invoked by Jesus, prophet, poet,
storyteller.

Finally, to more profoundly describe visioning, or, more precisely, to shift from content to process (from *what* to *how*), we'll include a portion from *Sound*. Though many, many mystics have had visions, both personal and impersonal, I don't know anyone who has conveyed the mechanism of vision with such poetry and precision:

> A vision is the soul drinking light. It starts with descending light, like falling rain. The descending light is feminine, the receptive. It is just light or undifferentiated energy. To someone perceiving the vision, it looks like a picture, or a phenomenon, but it is really just the action of the soul drinking light. The visionary transformation happens in the act of perception. The soul, or consciousness, or the Vast Self is drinking light that looks like awareness. It looks like receptivity; it has the quality of "as-above-so-below." It has the quality of "heaven is here now." What you want to achieve is here now, ready, given. Earth is fused with it; therefore, we can materialize it right now and make it real. (*Sound* 95)

Meeting Joseph

We met Joseph just before he devoted himself full-time to
promoting "awareness, compassion, carrying, purity, and
higher mind." We were introduced by a doctor who worked with
him in the Indian Health Service, and who considered herself
Joseph's student. Aside from his professional work introducing
preventative medicine to New Mexico's native reservations,
he had concentrated on creating a holistic health clinic; had
organized White Feather, a non-profit foundation for that
purpose; and had trained young ceremonial runners at Picuris,
his father's reservation. He had also dedicated himself to healing
native patients, particularly victims of alcoholism. In addition, he
had begun to guide and doctor several co-workers in the Indian
Health Service who had discovered his abilities.

In summer, we visited his Bernalillo home, where, three years
later, he would build the first peace chamber. He and his partner
had created an environment for holistic healing, a prototype of
the center he was trying to institute at Picuris. The first evening
we joined a healing sweat lodge for a young Indian suffering
from alcoholism. After the lodge, he discussed his work with
native alcoholics and those ill and dying in hospitals, away from
their tribes and medicine people. He told us how he perceived
their depleted and imbalanced energy fields, how his light body
tuned/traveled to the subtle realm and negotiated with their
"animals," their vital essences.

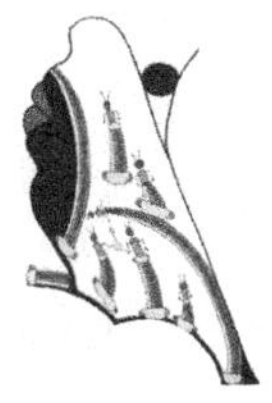

The next day he led us into the mountains around Picuris
where he was reactivating the ancient shrines and training
Picuris Pueblo runners to participate in the commemoration of
the 1680 Pueblo revolt against Spanish rule. Spaced periodically,
the shrines stretch in four directions from the center, or soul,
of the ancient village. They are like the subtle energy centers
along the human spine, the *nadis,* and meridians, except that
they extend from and return to the village center, the heart.
While the present pueblo of Picuris comprises twenty-five square
miles, Joseph explained that the shrines extended for thirty

miles, and the aura or sacred energy field of the pueblo extended for 200 miles in each direction. The shrines were set below the surface of the earth, like little kivas. Objects that had been collected or made were ritually arranged in the cylindrical holes. The shrines, which are not arbitrarily chosen, also signify the presence of the deities, the ancient angelic beings that protect and guide the pueblo.

Tending to the shrines was like planting a kernel of corn or an acorn. Planting, I would come to know, is one of the fundamental Pueblo metaphors. To grow into a real human, we must first be planted, and then continually nourished so we will develop roots, branches, leaves, and flowers/fruit. Sadly, non-Indians are rarely planted. Not only are we all visitors/conquerors to this continent, our technological culture, which despises Earth and views the body as tainted and the mind as holy, discourages the planting of spirit/light/energy deep in the kiva/shrine of the body, as well as the communion with Earth that might ensue.

Disconnected from what indigenous peoples call the Below or Grandmother, unplanted, fixated on the transcendent Above, we never grow spiritually and barely grow physically. All this cultural conditioning is aggravated by the pressure to move, to set out on our own, to conquer new territory. Consequently, our plant never grows, like the seeds of which Jesus spoke in the parable. Poorly rooted, not continually fed or tended, the sickly plant, seeking the sun, snaps, falls. Joseph's rootedness and paradoxical radiant buoyancy were palpable as he navigated the rocks and trails like a chipmunk, a deer, a bighorn sheep.

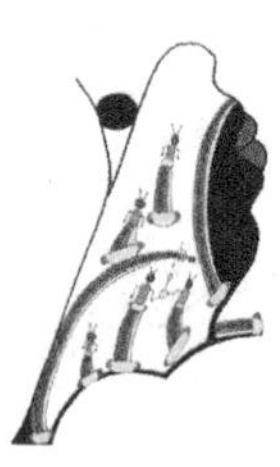

Feeding or recharging the series of shrines is linked to the Pueblo tradition of spiritual running, the tradition Joseph was attempting to re-institute among the young at Picuris. Four times a year, at the solstices and equinoxes, the Picuris would participate in a non-competitive relay, running from the pueblo's center/soul out about thirty miles in each of the four directions: eastward in spring, southward in summer, westward in fall, and northward in winter. On their way to and from the holy sites on the circumference, runners would pause at ancient shrines to give and receive energy. Eventually, as the holy runners pushed through second and third wind, they ran above ground, on light, like the wing-footed Hermes of Greek lore. Joseph told us as he had been told for some thirty-five years in the winters of storytelling time, by Antonio Simbola, storyteller, elder, and medicine man.

Joseph explained that the first runners from the center were always the young children. They always started because they were still strongly connected to the subtle light; they were still angels. The Picuris called these angelic runners, *pa-ne-ne*, "those who break through the barriers of light." Because they haven't yet mentally identified themselves with just their physical bodies, the clear white original light and the matrix of light, energy, and sound predominates in their beings. The barriers of light they break through for the older ones are the illusions that have caused the subtle light to crystallize into ordinary perception.

The young ones, recently arrived from the subtle realms, or heavens, refresh the light, keep it flowing to and from the material and non-material realms. They renew the spiritual connection for the entire tribe. All tribal/family members, adolescents, adults and elders, actualize a different direction and quality of light, light in various stages of embodiment. Furthermore, the people perform a collective, planetary and cosmic function. Joseph writes that the Picuris people "call themselves *tuu taah the nay* and then *pii tah*—where the center of life is, or where the kiva is the center. 'We are the people from the source—the center of the circle of light'" (*House of Shattering Light* 49).

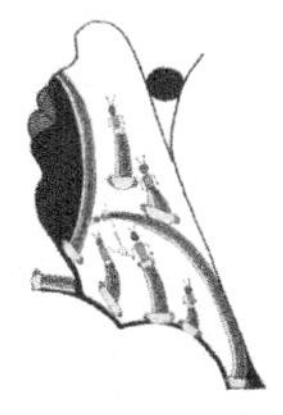

After feeding the shrines, we paused to eat on a peak. It was then that Joseph said he sensed the presence of our daughter, seven-months old in her mother's womb, and gave her (his god daughter) the very name he had just described, Pa-ne-ne. Looking over the distant highway and homes, he also explained how we, all of us, could orient and energize our homes as Picuris had been oriented and energized. Beginning at the Center, we could invoke the archangelic powers of the Above, Below, and the four directions, starting with East. We could then construct shrines outward in the four directions, at intervals, and periodically feed the shrines with sage, consciousness, and presence. He compiled some of these early teachings in his first publication, *Healing,* a booklet printed in 1981 under the aegis of White Feather, Inc.

Before we left Joseph to retreat in the Sangre de Cristo Mountains, we three also talked about our experiences as boy scouts, a subject we would often revisit in years to come. Joseph, in middle and high school years at BIA boarding school in Santa Fe, had briefly been a scout, an ironic feature of his initiation into the white world. While a scout, he had met and been impressed by one of American scouting's founders, its original Chief, Ernest Thompson Seaton. Seaton, who wrote several books on Amerindian mysticism and culture, had joined the scouting venture because of his deep involvement with native peoples and the natural life, but left scouting in 1915 because of its new military orientation.

In the 1940's, Ernest Thompson Seaton, who had by then re-established his Woodcraft League, invited Joseph and other native boys to perform traditional dances at The Castle, his center for native culture. Years later, after the Chief had left his body, the Chief's daughter sought out Joseph to heal a native boy she had adopted. In gratitude, she gave him a beautiful beaded pipe her father had made. Since our first conversation about scouting, Joseph has mentioned the possibility of infusing scouting with its original inspiration, the realization of nature and the natural. Once natural, we can become rooted, and once rooted, we can unfold, grow, in at least seven directions. To be more precise, we are Nature; Nature is manifest Spirit, the Vast Self we are, though it is not yet actualized in us.

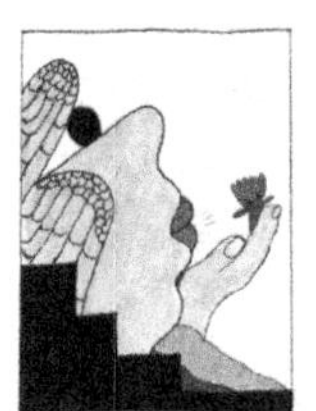

CHU-HA-MEN-TEN: IN JOSEPH'S KITCHEN

In his extraordinary *Hero with a Thousand Faces*, Joseph Campbell, a world pioneer of comparative mythology, explains the spiritual import of myth:

The trance susceptible shaman and the initiated antelope-priest are not unsophisticated in the wisdom of the world, nor unskilled in the principles of communication by analogy. The metaphors by which they live, and through which they operate have been brooded upon, searched, and discussed for centuries—even millenniums; they have served whole societies, furthermore, as the mainstays of thought and life. . . . For they actually touch and bring into play the vital energies of the whole human psyche. . . .

And so to grasp the full value of the mythical figures that have come down to us, we must understand that they are not only symptoms of the unconscious (as indeed are all human thoughts and acts) but also controlled and intended statements of certain spiritual principles, which have remained constant throughout the course of human history as the form and nervous structure of the human physique itself. Briefly formulated, the universal doctrine teaches that all the visible structures of the world—all things and all beings— are the effects of a ubiquitous power out of which they rise, which supports and fills them during the period of their manifestations, and back into which they must ultimately dissolve. (256–57)

The ubiquitous power that revealed Tiwa brought forth the first storytellers at *Chu-ha-men-ten*. Though commonly translated as 'long ago' or 'once upon a time' by scholars such as Harrington, according to Joseph the phrase literally means, "at the sand place." Though Joseph identifies the sand place as an area with sand dunes near the Rio Grande in south-central Colorado where he sometimes leads ceremonial dances, the place has metaphorical resonances. Picuris storytellers "use this expression to mean 'a long time ago' because every grain is an eternity and there are many of them" (*Sound* 39).

The shimmering, tingling sand place means the story is infinite, out of time, and yet, every time, always, now. It also invokes infinite place, the innumerable galaxies, universes, worlds. The unchanging story, the clothing of eternity as time, links the transpersonal and personal minds of the hearers. These two are linked by the intuitive, archetypal mind (which Jung might refer to as the quality of consciousness that accesses the archetypes of the collective unconscious). Upon hearing *chu-ha-men-ten*, the hearer puts the analytic, rational mind aside, to listen deeply and allow the vibration/story to penetrate deeper levels. The words of the elder (considered both grandmother and grandfather) break the barriers of light just like the *pa-ne-ne*, only in the opposite direction, from the uncreated light down and out: from very subtle, clear, white original light, to subtle light of awareness and the aura, to the gross, ordinary, biocomputer mind.

Repeat *chu-ha-men-ten* a few times. Listen. Focus on the sounds alone. Listen. Sense how you, your instrument, vibrates. Can you feel how *chu* sends breath/sound powerfully from the throat out through the lips? How the *ha* sends breath/sound downward into the chest? And how the *eh* in the last two syllables vibrates against the palate and is propelled against the top of the skull when you press the tongue against the palate to sound the final *n*'s? *Men-ten* rhymes, resounding like a gong inside the head, activating the sense organs and brain. Ringing radiance. Vibration is radiance.

In English, a foreign tongue on this continent named by conquerors after a conqueror, this is called synesthesia, one sort of stimulation's evoking another. Artists often experience this, seeing the shape and color of music, hearing a painting or movement, for instance. Some mystics experience this too, except they know that the vibration is the color, is the sensation. Phenomena are multi-dimensional and multi-sensational; most of us, however, function uni-dimensionally.

Our capacity to resonate and directly perceive that resonation prefigures our ability to understand Joseph and Tiwa mysticism. For mystics, understanding means synchronous vibration, the way two similarly tuned instruments in the same room vibrate when one is played.

In *Sound*, Beautiful Painted Arrow stresses this unchanging nature of the Tiwa stories, but he indicates they are not just expressions of universal doctrine necessary for Tiwa society, but important for the world:

All ceremony originally came from a vision somebody had

which gave instructions for exercising mystical power. These instructions were passed down from generation to generation unchanged, because if they were changed they would lose their power. The Tiwa creation stories were told over and over, from year to year, using exactly the same words. They still are. They are only to be told in the winter. They aren't just children's stories; they are really a source of mystical power. The storytellers repeat the stories not just because the new children coming up need to hear them. The very pronunciation of the words of the stories affects the psyche of the planetary resonance. It is affecting not only the Tiwa-speaking people, but all of the world, from New York to France to the polar regions. That's why it is very important to tell these stories in the same way every time. (23)

Joseph also records that "children's stories I had heard so often at Picuris Pueblo taught me how to think—to live as if I were perpetually in a state of omnipresence. I didn't have to translate this knowledge into supernatural power. It translated itself" (*House* 115). (While on one hand, original transmissions should not be changed, they must be and are added to by visionaries who are connected to the Source as it continually unfolds in time and space. This can be seen in the ceremonies of Fool's Crow, Black Elk, Wovoka [ghost dance], and Joseph.)

According to Joseph, all the Tiwa teachings, all the principal ideas exist in this frozen, subtle world of the "eternal now." When Tiwa tell these ancient stories, the winter ice melts. The melting water of ideas is luminous. "When this light, which is the water that drips off this frozen plane, falls like rain in tiny droplets onto the mind of all living things on the planet, it fuses ideas with the mind. It endows the mind with the life giving energy of chi" (*Being and Vibration* 169–70). *Chi*, one of the vibrational components of the Tiwa Great Spirit, is breath, energy, movement, and action.

These stories, told in the month following the solstice, are said to emerge from a place of ice, a place so distant it exists in the eternal now. Badger, the storyteller, is the totem animal of Picuris. Joseph, who expresses a particular kinship to the badger people, has a complete badger costume that he has worn on special storytelling occasions over the years. Imagine winter, just after the winter solstice, when the mind is clear, when the outer world of the senses darkens, when long nights evoke the unconscious, when the ordinary, conscious mind and body tend to hibernate. Envision the sloping white mountainsides and frozen rivers of northern New Mexico and southern Colorado.

In 2001 in the kitchen of his hermitage, Joseph had arranged two sets of ten vari-toned, three-quarter-inch stones in circles on the counter. He was about to tell us the Tiwa story that predates Pueblo emergence and corresponds to the Torah's explanation of 'The Fall'; the origin story told him by Antonio, perhaps in the same manner. Joseph began. He said that long, long ago, in the place of luminous consciousness, the Tiwa ancestors, the original people created by Spirit, were choosing the cosmos into which they would enter. They had ten worlds from which to choose. For the Tiwa, the cosmoses don't literally number ten; ten represents all the infinite potentialities. A vision showed Joseph that there are "worlds upon worlds, upon worlds, spiraling infinitely." The original people intended to enter the first world, a cosmos of "at-onement and infinite possibilities," in which Creator and creation are in perpetual harmony, unitive consciousness. (Joseph touched the top stone.)

But as the original people were about to enter this world of unity and infinite possibilities, Magpietail Boy thrust his long tail in their path, directing them to a second cosmos. (He thrust a pencil into the circle with one hand and picked up another stone, lower and to the side.) As a result, the ancestors and their Tiwa relatives have lived in this world of duality, perpetual opposition and effort. But the storytellers stressed that we shouldn't regret having left the first world, that all worlds, including this physical world, are endowed with great beauty.

In *Being and Vibration*, Joseph elaborates one of his visions of creation. He writes that before the first world was "only the dark infinite void," "no-form place" (175). From the dark, infinite void "there came the being of calling, of divine longing, and God called forth the light." Just as light came from the dark void, so does vibration come from silence: "Even before time was, silence was, and silence had the attributes of *keee* (placement)—*aah* (purity)—*teh* (stop). . . . Placement was the primary essence vibration that became the mother, giver of life, so that now life could create" (179). Elsewhere in *Being and Vibration*, Joseph calls the coming forth of light/sound from no-thingness, *taah-key*, the Big Bang (171).

The womb of Nothingness that metaphorically birthed/ breathed pure light is called *Ayin* by kabbalists and *Shunyata* by Buddhists. And the silent, no-form place corresponds to what sufis call *Zat*, silent life. The pure luminosity of creation before time that Joseph describes is what the kabbalists call *Ayin Sof Or*, Endless Light. The Tiwa ancestors, the ancient ones Joseph described in the kitchen, were subsequently exhaled into creation, toward the first world, as the light of knowing, Higher Mind. They are the original energy, light, and sound, means of Great Mystery's Self-knowing and the expression of Its Love. Together, kabbalists consider Ayin/Ayin Soph/Ayin Soph Or, Nothing/ All/Endless Light, to be divine pre-existence. Early in *Being and Vibration* Joseph merges all of these metaphors:

> We knew we were a people (a "vibration") who had come from the Infinite Void, from zero, from one's sense that we did not exist. We were made of appearing and disappearing light that came from the inhalation and exhalation of God's breath. We were from the very Heart of the center of the non-existence of infinity. (23)

Understanding this passage is essential to understanding Joseph's realization and teaching. His fundamental teaching, which I referred to earlier as emptiness and nothingness, is that "we don't exist." The people knew they were silence that became and becomes sound, that they were darkness that became and becomes light, that they appeared and disappeared, that they were and are non-existence that became and becomes existence. This is not a cliché, like saying that this is all *maya*, illusion. It is not nihilistic. It is a truth that can shock us out of the ignorance of duality, that we are things. It assaults ego and the fear of death. It can free us to re-enter the luminous first world, and the origin of All. The void from which every breath emerges and returns.

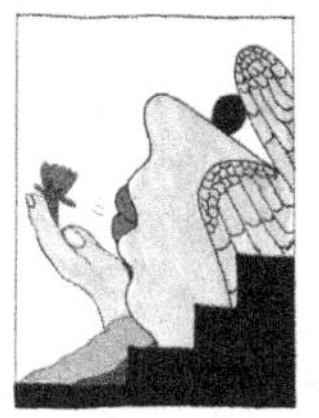

29

Mentioning the heart and the center, Joseph introduced *tu-tah*, which means center, kiva, mountain, and love. The people are *tu-tah*, the womb/kiva from which they emerged as vibration, the Center which is also above (mountain) and below (kiva). This paradox signals the uniqueness of Joseph's vision and Tiwa spirituality. It also invokes the medicine wheel, the matrix of sacred directioning that emerges from the subtle realm and transpires through the physical realm. Joseph's teachings on the medicine wheel are complex. For now, appreciating that Tiwa perceive reality as a circle is enough.

Continuing his explanation of the stones, Joseph said that once the ancient ones existed as pure breath, light, vibration, song (*chaah*), they chose which of the other worlds they wished to inhabit, where they would incarnate, or simply, in what condition they would exist. Though the Tiwa speak of ten possible worlds/stones, very much the way kabbalists refer to ten *sephirot* (ciphers or emanations), Joseph reiterated that the ten represent infinitude, like the crystals of sand in sand place.

Joseph also explained that the worlds, the 'universe' of ten stones, might represent the various angelic levels—the Neo-Platonic angels of creation, generation and salvation; the Zoroastrian Amahraspands and Yazatas, the archangels of the Jewish Hekaloth, such as the cherubim and seraphim, and ophanim. The stones also function microcosmically. (He pointed to the second circle again.) "Within me, this could be my liver, this my stomach, this my heart, my pancreas, my brain, my lungs, my kidneys." Then he explained that the Tiwa located the stones in the village that corresponded to the organ stones within and fed them with cornmeal to promote health. They are power points, similar to the shrines stretching along the mountain trails.

As mentioned, the Tiwa creation story/cosmogony and the arrangement of stones have many similarities to the Kabbalistic tree, the arrangement of the sephirot, which hang like fruit on either side of the tree's trunk or spine. Tiwa's original ancestors had wished to exist in the 'perfect' world of Unity and at-onement, a consciousness in which they would always experience the presence of the Creator (*tah-mey-ney*), in which they would be aware of themselves as the source, the endless, surrounding light and the dark infinite void. Some mystics call this consciousness the state of supreme identity. Kabbalists refer to this stone as Keter, the crown. In language similar to Joseph's, kabbalists say this first or highest world/state on the tree of life "contains all that was, is, and will be; it is the place of first emanation and return" (Halevi, *Kabbalah* 6).

The divine name or vibration of this sephirah is Ehyeh or Ehyeh Asher Ehyeh, meaning 'I am' and 'I am that I am.' These are the words by which The Being identified Itself to Moses on Sinai. The actual Hebrew words are significant and essential because Hebrew, like Tiwa, is an objective, revealed language wherein the vibration sounds the reality. Judaism is also more nature, body, and creation-oriented than Christianity, this continent's dominant religion. Each sephirah has numerous macrocosmic and microcosmic correspondences. Not only is each associated with a world, it connotes a world within a level, an archangel, a name of G-d, a divine quality, a human soul quality, a human function, an organ, a body part, a physical capacity, the 'evolution' by which revelation becomes appropriate action in the dualistic, sensual world where the Tiwa were misguided by Magpietail Boy, the trickster.

Mentioning Ehyeh, the 'I am' consciousness, is particularly significant because it corresponds directly to one of Joseph's visions, which we will contemplate later. It is also significant that while many mystics consider experiencing this transcendent unity to be the supreme spiritual realization, Tiwans do not. This is only one of the ten/infinite conditions/consciousnesses. Tiwans would relate the transcendence without creation more to the direction of Above, associated with the crown center. More to *tah-mey-ney* than *Wa-Ma-Chi*, the Vast Self. Vast Self, the most profound single idea of Joseph's teaching, is complete consciousness, incorporating all forms of perception, including the senses, all our relations, all stones. Independent of two-leggeds, Vast Self is present in/as Earth, as well as the galaxies. Only Vast Self heals our fragmented, delusional, destructive point of view.

The mischievous Magpietail Boy, a being whom other traditions would call a demi-god, titan, archangel, or deva, is, as Campbell says, not just a symbol or a symptom but the statement of a spiritual principle. For Tiwa speakers, all creatures and creations embody spiritual principles or archetypes, as Joseph sometimes calls them, because they are the temporary crystallizations of light and patterns of vibration, the manifestations of what we previously called meaningfulness. Emergence, vibration's taking form upon Earth, is another story. Magpietail Boy thrust his long, tapered, sword-like tail in their path, guiding them away from the Vast Self, into the world of duality and time. For this reason Magpietail Boy represents unpredictability, misdirection, and disruption, the cosmic shock that thwarts our intention, leads us from consciousness to unconsciousness, from action to reaction. In a word, Joseph says that Magpietail Boy is "unawareness," a condition that plagues us all.

Understanding Emergence

So, the first ones missed the world of infinite Oneness, of Oneness, and entered the finite world of duality. But Joseph nuanced their/our condition. The world to which they were diverted is our "primary world," the world of our "work." Though the finite, physical body, which Joseph refers to as crystallized light, is our root body, we participate in, and are composed of, all the other worlds, including the first world of oneness. "Our work is enriching our primary world with the essences of all the other worlds." (While describing this, Joseph smiled and gestured from the second stone, to the ten, to the first, to beyond, and back to the second.) "And," he smiled again, "by enriching this world with them, we enrich them." We pollinate all the worlds like bees. But here, upon Earth, we have our hive and make our honey. In this way, consciousness of Vast Self grows, and Vast Self, Itself, grows.

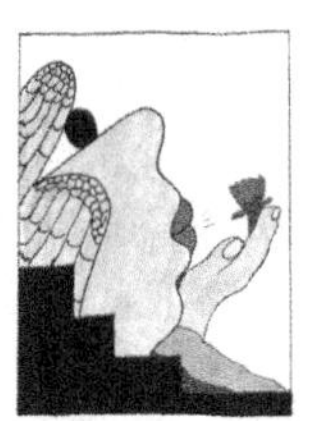

According to Joseph, by entering the world of duality, the ancient migrants ended in "perceptual reality." They forsook what Joseph calls Higher Mind, what contemporary psychologists call transpersonal consciousness, for personal consciousness. Tibetan mystics would say that they shifted from the Dharmakaya, the very subtle/mind, to the Nirmanakaya or gross level/mind. This very subtle level and transpersonal consciousness/mind to which we still have access (when we don't exist), is also known as Intelligence, the clear white light, primordial light/mind, consciousness without an object, and the Divine Mind. Revelation and true inspiration originate from this level/consciousness.

Perceptual reality/personal consciousness, what we have just termed gross level/mind, is the domain of dualistic, conceptual thought, generated by what we've called the biocomputer, as well as the senses. Having the personal consciousness as our primary world, we are susceptible to being intoxicated by the personal self, controlled by ordinary thought and emotion: self-image, egocentricity, memory, the known, computation, reason, self-love, desire, and aversion—in a word, what Buddhists refer to as ignorance. Joseph says being ignorant is being "unaware," being "caught in perceptual reality."

In other words, Magpietail Boy guides the ancient ones to his domain, his mental affliction, the personal mind. In all myths, place is also a state, a condition of consciousness. Subject to being unaware, to being caught in their personal selves and the notion of time, the people are in danger of forfeiting transpersonal consciousness. They struggle with mental illusion and afflictive emotions. However, to help them, they have awakened ones, ceremonies, prayers, the sacred structure of the pueblo, the stories, the vibration of the land, the cycles of nature, the archangels of the elements and directions, and the Tiwa language.

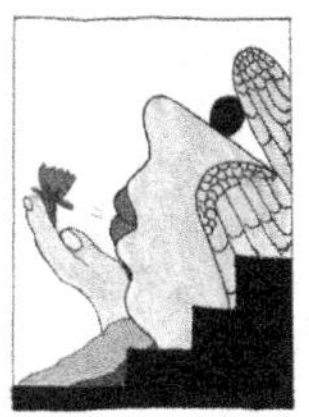

33

The implications of the Tiwa migration can be illumined by Hopi creation myth, and vice versa. The Hopi, perhaps one of the original Pueblo peoples who migrated southwest into Arizona, perhaps the Anasazi, refer to migration as spiritual, geographical, and anatomical. Frank Waters relates in *Book of the Hopi* that Taiowa, the Hopi equivalent of *Wa-Ma-Chi,* commanded Spider Woman to create humans in the first world. The first people were given wisdom; they understood themselves and were happy. But they forgot to respect Taiowa, to carry out the requisite rituals. They fell into unawareness, got caught in perceptual reality. Or, as Joseph often says, "They imagined they existed" (as mere personal selves). Waters relates that they started to use "the vibratory centers of their bodies solely for earthly purposes, forgetting that their primary purpose was to carry out the plan of Creation" (12).

As a result of the misuse of their vibratory centers (chakras), their becoming intoxicated with their personal selves, the top vibratory center in the top of the head through which they "communicated with the creator" sealed over (9). Division, discord, and duality entered the first world. Before destroying the first world, Taiowa directed the wise ones who still lived by the "laws of Creation" to gather at a certain place and be saved (13). Those who still existed in unity, whose transpersonal consciousness functioned, whose crown center (Keter) still pulsed and vibrated, followed a cloud and a star, gathered, and were led to ant hill, to be saved by the ant people below.

In mystical literature, the personal self is often referred to as the lower self. Ordinary thought identifies with the physical realm/stone, which is just a 'slowed down,' encapsulated version of the subtler worlds or levels of consciousness (of the soul, Blake would say). It is linear time, crystallized light. Rather than being aware, we identify with the physical realm as perceived through the ordinary senses and create an image of ourselves. The physical body corresponds to the kabbalistic stone of Malkuth, the kingdom; the identifying mind is Yesod, and desires and responses are Netzach and Hod respectively. Encapsulated in this limited self/consciousness, we are unaware of the presence of the sovereign, the crown, Keter.

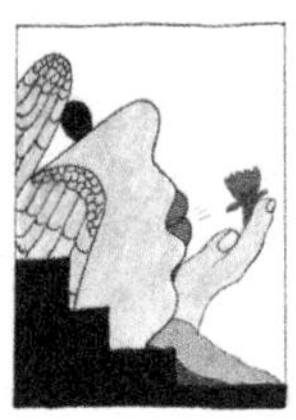

Because of Magpietail Boy's trick, we are not aware that Earth and our bodies are the Vast Self. In fact, governed by gross mind, we are rarely aware, period. Lacking awareness of the Creator in and as creation, we think creation is dead and meaningless. And we increasingly become more materialistic, addictive, and depressed. Such is the state of two-leggeds caught in personal consciousness. However, with what mystics call awakening, we can see how we contain infinite worlds. We have the possibility of Vast Self consciousness. We can appreciate how our primary world, Earth, contains infinite species, nations or cultures, or languages, similar to the many hoops Black Elk saw in his vision. Understanding these microcosms will help our understanding of the differences not only between natives and their conquerors, but also between the Utes and Pueblos, Joseph's peoples.

Between these two extremes of pure consciousness and form exists what we have referred to as the realm of meaningfulness and archetypes. Positioning this (though these realities exist in neither space nor time) between the transpersonal and personal levels/minds, we can refer to this as the impersonal level/ mind. What Tibetans call the Sambogyakaya or subtle level, or enjoyment body. Joseph refers to this as the realm of qualities and archetypes, principle ideas, of *nah*. Had the Tiwa found this world as their primary world, they still would have experienced duality, but of a much finer nature. For kabbalists this level comprises the stones from Tifereth (Beauty) to the aforementioned Keter: Geburah (Justice), Chesed (Mercy), Binah (Understanding), and Chokmah (Wisdom), as well as the hidden sefirot, Daath (Awareness).

Nah is the natural dimension of soul, perfect nature, our inherent, essential pattern of qualities and energies, the Self in Jungian parlance, the 'atman' in Sanskrit. The mental essence of the *nah* is awareness. *Nah* is also the realm of intuition, direct, non-analytic knowing. Becoming aware and intuitive, we become "the true human," "someone who is, moment by moment, totally merged with life" (*Being and Vibration* 67). Fully experiencing our *nah* gives us our first taste of spiritual freedom, freedom from illusion and reaction. We begin to watch and know ourselves. And we begin to receive direct intuitive guidance, independent of the known. Being aware eventually awakens us to our qualities or archetypal talents (Plato's Forms) that the Tiwa language and creation reveal. Mystics also call this impersonal dimension the causal, metaphoric, or abstract level.

When Joseph teaches that sensible (gross) phenomena are metaphors, he means what appears to be merely physical is the projection of qualities, the *nah*, the impersonal realm. When we spiritually awaken, we perceive the qualities transpiring through appearances (as well as G-d's luminous exhalations becoming archetypes—patterns of meaning, energy, light, and vibration). Death is merely the G-d's final inhalation. In death, what was crystallized light, becomes a pattern and hue of light, becomes light Itself, becomes the Void, "the very heart of the center of the non-existence of infinity."

For example, we see a tree with the sight sense. The gross mind identifies it as tree or cedar. The subtle mind, however, perceives a being growing toward sky, spreading to the horizons, like DaVinci's Universal Man, yet rooted in the earth, penetrating downward. For Tiwans, tree is wisdom. Joseph teaches that a tree is metaphor/energies of *le* (spreading), *lo* (descending), and *la* (ascending). Contemplating these great beings, we can become wise, moving trees. The subtle realm is also the level of impersonal feelings, the unselfish emotions (as we saw in the sephirot): ardor, joy, love, compassion, and generosity. When we feel these emotions, we are our subtle nature. They are the natural expressions of *nah*.

This dimension, which we often experience in dream, consists of patterns of light, sound, and energy. 'Timewise,' it is what we call eternity. Angels, luminous beings, as well as our own angelic natures exist at this level. Though the *nah* is sometimes called 'higher,' it interpenetrates this gross/physical world. When we see someone's or something's aura, their mantle of supersensible light (through our subtle senses), or when we hear the inner sound or sound of the spheres, we are perceiving this subtle world/energy.

Being aware, existing in and as *nah,* is essential because it bridges/permeates the transpersonal and personal selves and levels, thereby making possible the consciousness of Vast Self. In Tiwa stories this awareness and longing that shocks the ignorant Magpietail Boy, stuck in perceptual reality, is Yellow Corn Woman. It can also take place spontaneously, when beings are aware, as was the case with Joseph, Black Elk, Jakob Boehme, Plato, Saint John, and Moses. Or in profound states of meditation, as happens with myriad Tibetan lamas. Or, as Joseph teaches—during kiva, sweat lodge, and dance ceremonies. In these blessed, timeless states, the Tiwa ancients 'reach' the first world they intended, and more. The Medieval Christian mystic Meister Eckhardt says the soul enters (or realizes itself as) the Godhead, the divine in each of us. For the Neo-Platonist, the soul merges into Oversoul; for Hindu mystics, Atman becomes Brahman; for Tibetan Buddhists, awareness embraces essential luminosity, pure naked mind without centre or circumference, primordial ground, mother light.

The transpersonal Self is not only characterized by luminous 'conscious-without-an-object,' but by very subtle emotions: rapture, ecstasy, and ultimately the "peace passeth all understanding." The Vast Self, about which Joseph teaches is much more comprehensive than transpersonal. Vast Self involves immanence rather than transcendence. Or shall we say that Vast Self contains the transpersonal Self, is the embodiment of transpersonal Self. It is *Wa-Ma-Chi*, the medicine wheel, the seven directions, the ten worlds, in and as the body, the Earth, fully realized. What Joseph also calls Being, as well as Its infinite expressions as Beingness.

To appreciate Vast Self we must understand this inclusiveness, and overcome our conditioning of divine exclusiveness, the thought that heaven and Great Spirit are somewhere else, sometime. Vast-Self consciousness is not beyond. Vast Self is everywhere, everything, no-thing, always. And It is dynamic— plants produce seeds that produce plants—not static. At the end of *House*, Joseph explains it in a series of exquisite, interwoven metaphors:

> We ourselves are the Vast Self, that One Actor in the uni-
> verse, who creates continually in all moments. We are the
> Vast Self playing in creation as creatures, as individuals.
>
> In the experiences of my life, through loss and transfor-
> mation, ceremony, and story, I learned how to emerge con-
> tinually from the individual self that is Joseph Earl Head

> Rael into the Vast Self again. In the kiva, in the sweat lodge,
> in the sun dances and long dances, I have learned to die to
> myself in order to know the Self, dying from this House of
> Shattering Light into states of ecstasy, and then returning
> again, that the Vast Self might drink continually the light
> that It is creating. (199)

This is remarkable, a remarkable admonition from a humble being so spiritually gifted. Reminding us, both, that we must persevere/play, powered by ecstasy and that our perseverance is the Vast One persevering through and as us.

The Tiwa world and world-view is marked by hope and endless potentiality, not fear and loss. Though the Tiwa people's natural life has been threatened by invasion, materialism, consumerism, and repression, they maintain the means of 'dying' to our limited, material nature and awakening, being 'reborn' as subtle and very subtle natures. Spiritual nourishment, guidance, or grace, *who* in Tiwa. *Who* is embedded and built into every aspect of Tiwa life. Joe Sando, of Jemez Pueblo, who speaks Towa, a dialect similar to Tiwa, describes the pervasiveness of Pueblo spirituality in *The Pueblo Indians*:

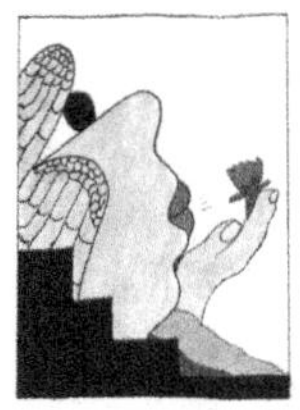

> The Pueblos have no word that translates as "religion." The
> knowledge of a spiritual life is part of the person twenty-four
> hours a day, every day of the year. . . . The tradition of re-
> ligious belief permeates every aspect of the people's life; it
> determines man's relation with the natural world and with
> his fellow man. Its basic concern is continuity of a harmoni-
> ous relationship with the world in which man lives. To main-
> tain such a relationship between the people and the spiritual
> world, various societies exist, with particular responsibilities
> for weather, fertility, curing, hunting, and pleasure or enter-
> tainment. . . . The calendar is so full that there is no time left
> for any new or innovative religious practice. . . . The religious
> rituals and ceremonials themselves maintained by the Pueb-
> los today, are the same they have practiced since their an-
> cestors lived in pit houses. The oratories, prayers and songs
> are the same. These observances are not spontaneous out-
> pourings, or outbursts of a trouble heart. They are carefully
> memorized prayerful requests for an orderly life, rain, good

crops, plentiful game, pleasant days, and protection from the violence and vicissitudes of nature. (22–3)

Having missed the mark through momentary unawareness, the Tiwa ancestors were given guiding powers and ceremonies as the means to unite the Center and circumference, Being and Beingness, the transpersonal, impersonal, and personal levels, both individually and collectively. In his paintings, Joseph utilizes ladders, into kivas and up and down the stories of pueblos, to represent this unifying function. They are reminiscent of, but more comprehensive than, Jacob's celestial ladder. Joseph characterizes the 'laddering' of ceremony in this way:

> Everything that exists is trying to unify itself with that whole. All ceremony exists to unify, to bring together, to bring into oneness—but within the oneness is the diversity of all that is. . . . There is a supernatural power that every human be-ing has, that cannot be cultivated by reading and writing. We must do something with our physical bodies and natural el-ements of the land, the fire, water, air, minerals, and wood. Native American ceremonies, some of which are very ancient, and many of the secret societies that Indians have, are based on this intention: to reconnect, over and over and over, to the land. . . .

> It is encoded in our physical make-up, by virtue of the fact that we have eyes and ears and mouths and noses and legs, that we are here to be catalysts and to connect the physical with the spiritual. . . .

> Ceremonies we do intentionally . . . focus our energies on certain acts and lift us powerfully into states of consciousness through which we are literally drinking light. We are drink-ing inspiration from all the heavens and connecting the above realms with the physical plane. This is what we come into physical form to do, and we are nurtured by doing it. . . .

> We may think we're sad because our physical needs aren't met or we need more success, but what we're really feeling is the natural hunger of the self for connection with the vast Self. And that can only come through ceremony. (*Ceremonies of the Living Spirit*, 2–3)

Before considering Magpietail Boy's redemption, we should

note that the ancient ones' missing unity and ending in multiplicity is not a 'fall,' as in the Judeo-Christian Genesis. Actually 'falling' has a very different connotation in Tiwa. Falling indicates loss of control, the presence of the unknown and unplanned that puts us in a state of childhood innocence and teachability. And Magpietail Boy is mischievous rather than malevolent. He's an immature prankster, not an evildoer. Tiwans do not have a word or concept of sin, which originally meant missing the mark. Joseph remarks that when Tiwans miss the mark, they shoot another arrow. Just as Tiwans have no concept of Satan or sin, they have no concept of guilt, hell, or heaven.

According to Joseph, after they (we) cultivate—clear, sow, nurture, reap, cook, ingest—the treasures of this second world (he picked up the second stone again), they will travel to and cultivate another world. (He picked up another stone.) Their parents and loved ones who left before, will meet them and take us to that next world, to the place they have prepared. And then the next world, and so on. (He pointed to the second circle of stones, showing that we would proceed to another universe after the first one.)

Ending his explanation of the myth, he said, "We need to communicate this model to the young so they know they are not limited, that we live eternally and have unlimited potential. We are all of this." He spread his hands. "We're here, but we're everywhere. We have a duty to cultivate this world and a duty to all the other universes." He smiled. Then he said, "I'm a shaman, an artist, a singer, a carpenter, a politician, an educator, a governor's aide, a parent. Maybe it is because I'm Gemini. Maybe I'm curious. Or maybe because I was presented with this model."

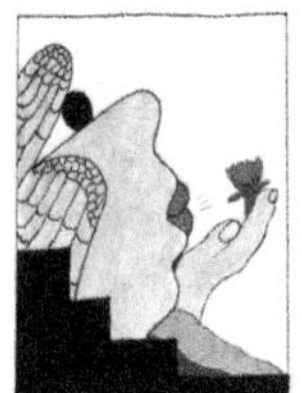

FOLLOWING YELLOW CORN WOMAN

Magpietail Boy doesn't always represent mischievousness and unawareness in Tiwa mythology. His story with Yellow Corn Woman conveys the hope of redemption from the Fall. Mystics and students of comparative mythology will note the significance of Magpietail Boy's having to go down to the kiva, to the Center, tu-tah, rather than up. Once the Tiwans/Tiwa inhabited this world and their 'world' within it, Magpietail Boy was transformed by the presence of his wife, Yellow Corn Woman, into a sacred clown, a holy trickster. Because of her, the elegant white and black bird can shock Tiwans in the other direction, from mystical sleep to awakening. The story of his transformation shows how we can emerge from perceptual reality and the illusion of the personal dimension. Though I'm summarizing the story, Joseph elaborates upon it in his book, *Beautiful Painted Arrow: Stories and Teachings from the Native American Tradition.*

Long, long, ago Magpietail Boy and Yellow Corn Woman lived with the people at Picuris Pueblo. Yellow Corn Woman belonged to the Society of Wizards, whom she visited every night. While she attended sacred ceremonies in their kiva, Magpietail Boy slept. Magpietail Boy finally started to awaken spiritually and noticed she disappeared at night. So, he pretended to sleep and followed her one night when she left dressed in ceremonial garb. His curiosity manifested spiritual longing and initiative.

According to Joseph, Corn Maiden (four Corn Maidens exist, one for each direction) is the Tiwa Field of Dreams, the exemplar of awareness. In *Being and Vibration*, he describes her as a young Indian woman standing "confidently in a corn field," aware "of the presence of the Great Mystery":

> The gentle breath of the Infinite blows a few loose strands of her silken long black, braided hair of the Infinite Void. Her graceful body is clothed in the muted tones of buckskin; of the cover wisdom it is made. A necklace is fastened around her neck, made of intricate bead-work and glistening silver; this is the place of the upper and middle worlds. On her feet are a pair of carefully hand-stitched moccasins, made of descending light, which are tied neatly with strips of rawhide, made of perpetual vigilance. In her hand she holds a planting stick, sharply pointed on one end. Her eyes turn downward and she examines the soil beneath, over which water now flows. She bends, ever so slightly, and with her stick probes the earth. (101)

The woman is the symbol of *co-weh*, the vibration that brings everything beautiful together in one place. It brings together the North, the South, the East, and the West, the up above, and the down below. The dress she wears is *oh-nee*, insight, the capacity to hear the sounds of innocence that come into constant review. The necklace is the metaphor of the connection between the earth and sky, of connecting thinking and feeling. She looks at water, the crystallized heart serum, that which comes from the sacred heart of the innermost place of enlightenment of God's greatness. Because the stick has a point, the moment she pokes it into the soil, she penetrates wisdom, which is ready to erupt and flood forth with awareness. "She stands on the awareness of the landscape of the infinite self and allows herself to be drunk through the feet of young woman" (101).

In Hinduism, the light Corn Maiden wields in her stick is *vajra*, the lightning bolt of illumination wielded by Indra, king of the Vedic gods. And in the Tantric Buddhism of Tibet, which retains much indigenous shamanism, Corn Maiden's stick is the *dorje*, the *vajra* scepter that meditators grasp in their right hands, reminding them of the supremacy of compassion. The presence that young women naturally drink through their heels, young men drink through the young woman within, the anima. In aggressive, over-heated, hyper-masculine materialistic America, the archetypal feminine is undervalued, even among women, rendering us largely unreceptive to the stick of Corn Woman (the pipe of White Buffalo Cow Woman, and, as Dr. B. Hobbs pointed out to me, the torch of Mademoiselle Liberty who stands at the mouth of New York City harbor). But then again, if Magpietail Boy appreciated her, we have hope, in spite of ourselves.

On this evening as she approached the kiva of the wizards, the moon shone on her moccasins, coloring them snow white. In the collective metaphor of the body, the moccasins represent the sensitivity that connects our feet, our earthly pole, with Earth. Even the goddess' feet are illuminated, permeated by the white light. By entering the kiva of the wizards, she marks the connection of "inner awareness and cosmic awareness" (*Beautiful Painted Arrow* 63). Wishing this healing, Magpietail Boy followed her inside and hid behind the roof poles. In this case his stealth indicates that "constant vigilance is necessary so that one is ready to experience only that which can come from the highest greatness" (63).

The Wizards created a rainbow (the subtle world) across the room and began ceremonies, showing that "only the physical body can catch the metaphors of awakened Awareness" (64). Unable to cross the rainbow, they searched inside and outside the kiva for an intruder. Finding no one they asked the Grass Owl, discrimination and perspicacity, to help. Grass Owl found no one outside, but searching inside, "the place of integrity," he saw the tail of the intruder among the poles (64). Notice that winged Boy is hiding above. He is ungrounded, unplanted, seduced by the Above.

The Wizards brought him down the ladder into the chamber, the "universal" (65). This indicates the vertical descent of Nothingness/All into which Magpietail is initiated. Joseph's understanding of the vertical and horizontal directions or paths of energy is profound. He calls this marriage of infinity/ transpersonal and time/personal the cross or grid. Bird Boy laid his head on his wife's lap; he surrendered. At that moment "Believing We Exist (ignorance/egoism) falls asleep and merges into Awakened Awareness falling" (65). "Believing we exist" is unaware and ignorant because the gross mind thinks we exist independently of the whole (which is also Nothing).

However, the next morning Magpietail Boy awakened in the horizontal ledge of a canyon wall. Joseph explains that put there by the Wizards, initiated into awareness, he must cultivate the capacity to act creatively and consciously in time, time being the horizontal ledge in which he is stuck. This is his first challenge after initiation, his vertical descent into the womb of Nothingness that is All. He is now the cross, the existential situation in which we all exist. Can we remain vertically connected to inspiration, can we evolve, act creatively, as we age horizontally? Or do we just react, perform habitually, perpetuating the past?

Elf Boy, who lived nearby, heard Magpietail Boy's cry for help

43

and stopped. Joseph explains that Elf Boy's arrival indicates that higher consciousness can only advance evolution by balancing and integrating "shadow and light, polarities, duality and reflection" (65). This conscious maneuvering is evident in the details of their interaction, which I only summarize here.

Eventually, Elf Boy conceded to help him, by challenging him to catch one of the spruce cones he dropped over the cliff edge. Magpietail Boy caught the last one. Then he dropped it to the ground as Elf Boy instructed. The cone grew into a spruce tree that ascended beside him; he descended. This indicates that the new initiate is responsible for creating the descending feminine and the ascending masculine. He was passive to these forces before; now he activates them. The spruce tree represents the connection between the above and below, Boy's growth to greatness. Remember I said that 'falling,' symbolized here by the spruce cone, has a positive connotation in Tiwa. Falling, the loss of control, permits 'teachability.' It is by falling that we surrender to and participate in the ever-descending, "passive" energies of the archetypal feminine, which creates "active," ascending matter, the archetypal masculine (67). This, a major principle of Tiwa metaphysics, will be dealt with later.

Elf Boy told Magpietail Boy, "You must place this worm by Yellow Corn Woman's bed . . . and not quarrel with her" (67). The boy did so, and the worm entered his wife's navel, ate her entrails, and killed her. The myth states that Magpietail Boy "lived happily ever after, alone" (60).

Though the story is cruel, it is the metaphoric telling of one human's, every human's, quest for wholeness and fullness of awareness. Joseph recalls that the storytellers told this story every winter. Listening to such metaphors in childhood plants seeds that are watered and sunned by experiences; experiences, in turn, trigger visionary insight, the opening of subtle and very subtle mind. Joseph's explanation of the story's metaphors shows how it illustrates what Campbell calls the hero's quest.

Magpietail Boy's outer journey (that is really an inward one), begins with his being called to adventure by the spiritually awakened presence of his wife. She heralds his potential and

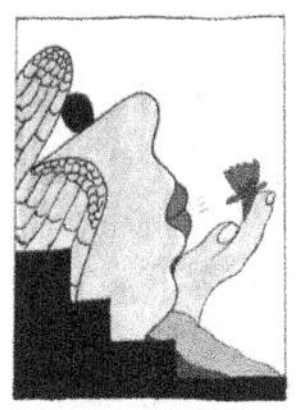

destiny. Once he submits to her and his longing, he crosses
the threshold from the known to the unknown, from Above,
to Below, to Center, when the wizards, his helpers, bring him
down the ladder of the kiva that is the "worldwide womb image
of the belly of the world" (Campbell, *The Hero with a Thousand
Faces* 90). When he lays his head on Yellow Corn Woman's lap,
he truly meets her, the goddess, for the first time. Then he is
initiated and sets out on the world of trials. He overcomes the
trial by enlisting the supernatural helper, of Elf Boy, who gives
him advice and a magical aid, the spruce cone. Magpietail Boy
catches the cone and follows directions, a principle prized by
Tiwa.

With Yellow Corn Woman's death, with her self-sacrifice of
compassion, "the triumphant hero-soul" experiences "mystical
marriage" with the "Queen Goddess of the World" and lives
happily (Campbell 109). With the fullness of Yellow Corn
Woman's awareness within him, Magpietail Boy can now
contribute to life. He effectively becomes, as Joseph explains,
an androgynous one, a wise elder. Redeemed, Magpie becomes
a *koshare*, trickster, magician, or holy clown: the embodier of
opposites, a Janus who can shock us into awareness rather than
out of it, who can lead us back to course rather than away from
it. No matter how much we are plagued by the young Magpie's
ignorance, the possibility of awakening exists. All we need
do is embrace and follow the Goddess Yellow Corn Woman,
awareness. Magpie's redemption, his hero's quest, is Joseph's
intricate telling of that universal mystical journey toward union,
inner alchemy and integration. The flavor of this journey,
however, with its culmination in relatedness with all of creation,
is purely Pueblo/Tiwa.

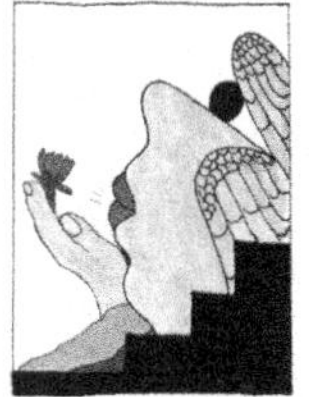

45

Magpie is a bit like Jack in the European fairy tale, *Jack and
the Bean Stalk*. Both men's quests are initiated by women—
except that young Jack does not actively seek awakening, having
been sent to sell the cow by his mother. Yet both receive magical/
spiritual help because they were teachable (though Magpie,
ever the boy, is more of a rascal). And both are transformed and
return as a boon for their people. However, the two are also

unalike. Jack ascends like the koshares then climbs down with symbolic treasures (actualizing Joseph's words, "We are drinking inspiration from all the heavens and connecting the above worlds with the physical plane"). Furthermore, Jack is the typical 'Western' hero, who conquers an ogre through cunning and stealth. By bringing down sky, he develops his animus, his yang. However, Magpietail Boy, a bird, knows transcendence well. He descends to Yellow Corn Woman, who was already rooted and illuminated. Magpietail Boy grows through his anima, his yin, his capacity to surrender. He mines the diamonds of the Earth, the Below, and is, therefore, healed.

He also teaches that we fulfill our work in this world by realizing our essential nothingness, the silence that exists between breaths, the flashing of Intelligence. The light of intelligence emerges from the silent nothingness (Ayin) with each exhalation, passes through (and creates) all three world/ levels, then returns into nothingness with every inhalation. We can experience Non-existence, our non-existence, after every inhalation. We can experience emptiness, nothingness in creation, at the end of every exhalation. This is a profound spiritual realization, very similar to Buddhist teachings on the void, but it is worth pondering because cultivating emptiness (of selfhood) allows us to be agents of miracle, full of the immanent presence of Great Spirit Mystery (in our kiva or spiritual womb). Emptiness allows us to give birth to the One, Vast Self. Listen to how Joseph poetically describes this exquisite mystery:

> . . . Every moment returns back to silence because its roots are there.
>
> Another way of describing silence is that we know its home is in the Infinite Void.
>
> Technically it is the no-form place or the place of nothingness. Consequently, the true measure of our success in life is how much of, or the degree of nothingness (emptiness) we can achieve.
>
> Do we really exist? The answer I can give, having viewed all the possibilities, is that, beyond all the levels of our highest goodness, we are nothingness, working diligently for more of the same nothingness, so that we may be full. The

true purpose of the practice of vibration is the self expression of the infinite in finiteness, because all of the One in the all is a sleeping, dreaming heart of Love. (*Being in Vibration* 180–84)

Among the indigenous of this continent, the Pueblo peoples are particularly conscious of what some mystics call divine immanence, the holy presence of the Creator in and as creation. They conduct their sacred rituals underground, in kivas, round wombs. "Going underground was a metaphor for entering the perfected self" (*Being and Vibration* 60). Like the Wizards, Yellow Corn Maiden, and Magpietail Boy, they descend into the perfected self on ladders. And each sacred chamber has an emergence hole, what Campbell calls the world navel, the center of the universe from which grace flows into this world. Through this *sibapu*, this fount of life, the first tribal humans rose from beneath the crystals of Sand Lake.

We, in all of the worlds within this world, need this medicine in order to evolve rather than progress and die. The next chapter will tell Joseph 's creation story, his coming to this world, the prelude to his quest. We will see that Joseph, who is very much a trickster, got a "little jump" on his journey.

Tibetans say that personal consciousnesses, while still beings of light in the subtle realm, can choose their parents based on an affinity of energy, light, and vibration. Tibetan Buddhist texts state that previously enlightened beings re-enter, reincarnate, to serve all sentient beings, that the parents that birth enlightened ones were often related to them in former incarnations. In fact, Tibetan Buddhism is so specific as to say that consciousnesses choosing rebirth are enamored with the light of a parent to be: males-to-be fall in love with their mothers (as pure light/energy); females-to be-fall in love with their fathers.

This explains Joseph's first vision, really his first seeing, his experience of being attracted to his family before he had a physical body. In La Boca, Colorado, in the winter of 1935 a "force was pulling" his subtle, angelic body "to these people, this house" (*House of Shattering Light* 20). He, his *nah*, composed of energy, awareness and subtle light, flew toward the house quickly like the wind, circled around, and entered, seeing his mother, father, brothers, and sisters. He flew through the walls and about the rooms, hearing his mother's voice.

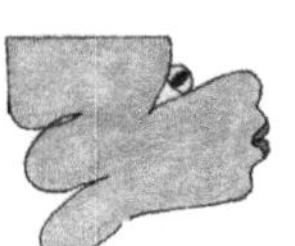

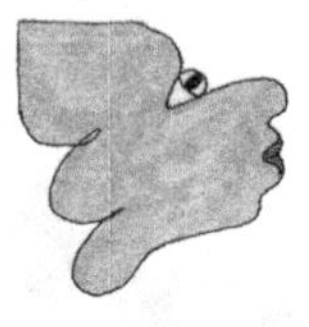

While in the womb, he thought his mother's thoughts rather than heard her voice. He experienced planting the garden and chasing away crows. He experienced life both directly and through his mother:

> Planting her garden was a pleasing experience for me in her womb because I could become the energies of the plants she loved so well. I knew the physical size of plants in the garden as well as what they were feeling. I had no concepts yet on which to base my perceptions. I was just listening randomly, experiencing the essences of things. Turnips were different from carrots in that they protested loudly for more growing room, and I think Mother heard them because she always planted them properly along the furrows. . . . I knew when my older sister and brother were near because they generated a vitality I could feel in my body when they entered the room. (21)

Joseph was in a pre-conceptual, purely perceptual state, "an ancient form of communication without words" (22). This is the state to which we moderns, over-conceptualized and gross-mind dominated, must awaken in order to become human.

Joseph was naturally practicing the mystical synesthesia described in the previous chapter. From the sound his mother made, he could see her moving. He was also 'thinking without thought, without a thinker,' a phenomenon talked about by the great twentieth century mystic Krishnamurti. He also learned how to think with his entire body by perceiving through his mother's body:

> Before I was born I was learning to hear sounds and glean meaning from them. I could see my mother's feet in the sound of her running—the vibrations of her feet on the ground.
>
> The sound my mother made when she ran was *Tol-liaah-who*, which in the Tiwa language I would later learn means 'Abundance of clarity that is aware.' . . . I was already learning to think words and images before they became ideas. I was learning to think with my whole body and not just my mind. . . . I had to rely on my mother's body to think. (22)

Joseph was being fed by and initiated into life by the sounds made by his mother. He remarks that this ability to be "alive inside our perceptions," to perceive vibration directly, without interference from the gross mind, "makes up all our insights – hindsights, mental telepathy, powers." Later in the same passage he reveals that her sounds fed a greater being as well: "Sound is how the physical world drinks other energies in its immediate vicinity in order to quench its thirst for existence" (23). Joseph says we are able to know our pre-birth because "reality is a circle" (22). Because time is both linear and circular, it spirals. Once he was "farther up the spiral," he was able to "look down and see where I started" (23). On June 2, 1935, perception through the womb ended. He emerged from the womb into a dream "made of gentle humming sounds" (23).

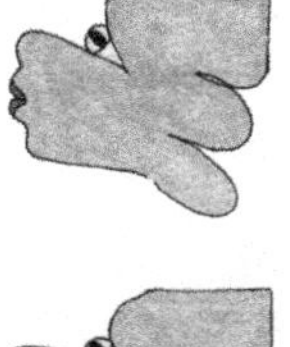

Joseph didn't remember these visions until he was about twelve, living in Picuris, New Mexico. The simple explanation was that he existed essentially as *nah*, as energy-light-consciousness *(pa-ne-ne)*. The gross mind, which remembers, had not fully developed. Consequently, "as a child I had a hard time knowing when I was in a visionary state and when I was in ordinary reality" (*House of Shattering Light* 23). In 2004 he described the twelve-year lag in remembering:

> I remembered those when I was about twelve, and I know why. I remembered them because I could think in abstract terms then. After twelve, I could think in abstract terms. Before that, I could think only in concrete terms, so I couldn't make sense of the worlds. Concreteness comes from the principle idea of planting whereas abstractness is born out of observation. I had twelve years to review what had been planted in my landscape, and so now I had the ability to observe them. Before that, I was the one and the same thing occurring. I was here and there, but I didn't know how to define. It was just one scenario. I was both the actioner and the actionee, and the vibrational perceptions had to become mental perceptions. They needed to be verified concretely for the psyche of my being. (Personal Communication)

Birthing to Two Traditions

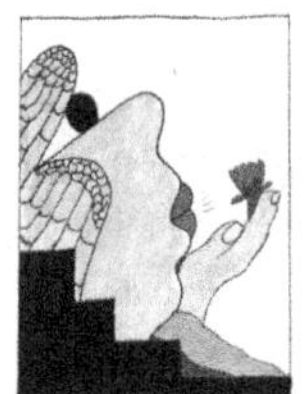

Joseph's mother, Beatrice Head of the Capote band of the Southern Utes, named him Earl for the physician who had delivered him. For almost sixty years, the Capotes, originally from the southwest San Luis Valley, on the eastern slopes of the southern San Juan Mountains and along New Mexico's Chama River, had survived on a sliver of reservation land in southwestern Colorado stretching from the La Plata to San Juan Rivers.

Smaller in stature than their eastern neighbors, the Arapaho, Cheyenne, and Sioux, the Utes "were a hardy, vigorous race characterized by high cheekbones, and deep copper-colored skin" (Pettit, *Utes: The Mountain People* 3). And though they were feared warriors and superb horsemen, they sought not immediate war but, at critical junctures, peaceful co-existence" with the Spanish, Mexican, and American invaders, even after repeated broken treaties (Decker, *The Utes Must Go* 12).

Their language belongs to the Shoshonean branch of the Uto-Aztecan linguistic family. Though they believe they have always inhabited the Rocky Mountains and the lands surrounding them, most scholars concur that they migrated into the area from Mexico in about 1000 AD.

Prior to acquiring the horse from the Spanish in the early 1600s, the Utes migrated by foot and pack dog in search of game and resources. With the horse they became a tepee culture, transporting their belongings, hide homes, and food long distances, even onto the buffalo-laden plains. However, within two hundred years of acquiring the horse, their traditional way of life was violated by settlers, miners, and Mormon colonizers.

By the end of the Civil War, the American invaders had penetrated the Colorado Rockies, the Ute heartland. And by 1880, the United States government had confined the far-ranging mountain people to two reservations: the Northern Utes, comprised of the Uintah, Grand River, Yampa, and Uncompagre in Northwestern Utah; and the Southern Utes, including the Muache, Capote, and Weminuche, in Southwestern Colorado. In 1895 Ignacio, chief of the Weminuche ('long time ago'), protested the government policy for the Southern Utes, left the Muache ('cedar bark people') and Capotes ('blanket people'), and established what became the Mountain Ute Reservation in the portion west and south of the La Plata.

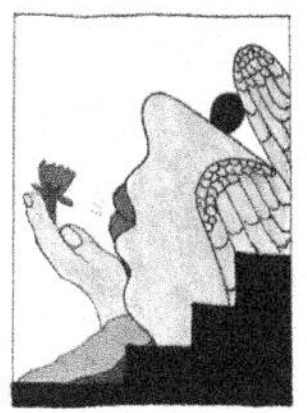

Beatrice was related to Capote chiefs on both her grandfather's and grandmother's sides. Her Grandmother's was the sister of the great Severo, who led the Capotes during the most intense oppression by the Americans, and who died at Ignacio in 1913. Beatrice also had French blood. She told Joseph about a French trapper who had befriended one of her male forbearers. The Frenchman promised to care for the Ute's wife if the Ute were to die. The Ute perished young, and the trapper and the Ute widow married, starting a family of their own.

The Head family traces its name to the time when one of its

young women was adopted by a Spanish governor named Cabeza
(Head). The young girl and her friend had contracted smallpox
due to the Spanish incursion. Not having a cure for the disease,
the Ute left her and a friend by a trail in southern Colorado,
near Conejos. The girls were found, cured, taken into the home
of Sr. Cabeza, brought up as Spanish young ladies, and later
repatriated to their tribe.

Joseph 's father, Alfred Rael, was a Tiwa Pueblo from Picuris,
New Mexico, east of the Rio Grande, between Taos and Española.
According to Pueblo oral tradition, the ancestors of the surviving
pueblos emerged from the underworld through the *sibapu*, the
emergence hole, north of New Mexico, at the aforementioned
Sand Lake. From there, the ancestors, led by their war chief,
migrated before many of them settled near the Four Corners.
Eventually, they occupied tens of thousands of square miles.
Today over 50,000 sites exist, primarily in New Mexico and
Arizona, with a few in Colorado and Utah. These Pueblo
ancestors are most often known as the Anasazi.

The Anasazi realized their constructions through the space
of nature. In canyons and on mesa tops, on cliff edges and in
caves, they built with the immediate substance of nature. The
refinement of Anasazi stonework was matched by their technical
command of astronomic alignments and repetitive orientations.
Pueblos more than thirty miles apart may deviate less than
one degree in the relationship of parts. Radiating from Chaco
Canyon, the Anasazi built more than 250 miles of precision-
engineered straight-lined roads that defy the terrain. With rare
style and profound understanding, they populated and celebrated
a land that now seems uninhabitable (Cook, *Anasazi Places* 3).

By the mid 1300s, driven by drought, disease, or warfare, they
had abandoned their complex civilization, migrated eastward,
merging with peoples already settled on the northern Rio
Grande.

Alfonso Ortiz, a Tewa anthropologist whom Joseph often
met at Picuris ceremonies, describes the Pueblo emergence in
a more detailed manner that prefigures the division of Pueblo
people into summer and winter groups, or moities. In the dark

earth beneath Sandy Place Lake in the north, "spirits, people, and animals lived together." Among them were the first mothers of the Pueblo, Blue Corn Woman near to Summer and White Corn Maiden Near to Ice, or winter. They asked a man, later to become Hunt Chief, to investigate the world above. He returned, accepted and blessed by animals, and appointed both a Summer Blue Corn Chief and a Winter White Corn Chief who will each guide the people above for part of the year, inspired by their respective mothers. Assisted by medicine men, sacred clowns, war chiefs, and a women's society, each chief guided half the people south along the Rio Grande, Summer people on the west, Winter people on the east. After they had each stopped twelve times, the two groups merged at the legendary Pueblo of Posi, perhaps the ruin now known as Po-shu-ouinge. From Posi the various bands migrated south and southwest, forming subsequent villages (Oritz, *The Tiwa World* 13–16).

When the Conquistadors and priests arrived in the Southwest in 1539, forty-seven pueblos existed in central and western New Mexico and northwestern Arizona. Today, after five centuries of conquest, subjugation, disease, and materialistic influence, only nineteen pueblos survive, most along the Rio Grande and its tributaries. Though the nineteen share a traditional religion, life-style, philosophy, economy, and participation in the All Indian Pueblo Council, each maintains its own political integrity.

Joe Sando, a historian and educator from Jemez Pueblo, describes Pueblo leadership in this way:

> The titular head of the traditional Pueblo is the cacique, together with his staff, the cacique being the theocratic leader, 'from the time of the emergence from the underworld,' as the people say. A few pueblos no longer have a cacique, nor do they have religious societies. Responsible to the cacique and his staff are the war chief and his assistants. They are the functioning arm of the leadership that enforces the rules, the regulations, and the ordinances of the theocratic system. (Sando 8)

Sando goes on to explain that each pueblo also has a governor, a position established by the Spanish to control the Pueblos and

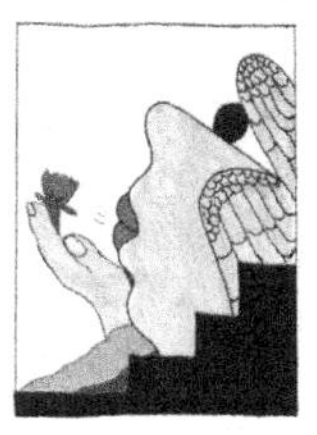

53

undermine their traditions. The Pueblos eventually undermined the Spanish by converting the role from dominator to protector. The governors, first selected from among the tribes by the conquerors but later elected by the members themselves, shrewdly maintained their independence and supported the caciques. Presently, the governors are responsible to the caciques, where they exist, and oversee all tribal interaction with the modern world.

The Pueblo peoples have three distinct language families: the Keresan, Tanoan, and Zunian. The Tanoan language, itself, has three dialects, Tewa, Tiwa, and Towa. The Tiwa dialect, the language of Alfred Rael, and later his family, is spoken at Picuris, Taos, Sandia, and Isleta. In addition to their tribal language, most Pueblos speak English, and many of the older generation speak Spanish, as well.

Joseph traces the Rael surname to a lieutenant serving under an invading conquistador with the surname Vargas, probably General Don Diego de Vargas, who re-established Spanish domination twelve years after the Pueblo revolt of 1680. Both de Vargas and Rael married Pueblo women. Joseph feels the name to have portended his destiny:

> . . . The Rael name comes from the original word 'Israel.' The Raels were Jews who were running away from persecution in Spain. They were called *los conversos*, meaning those who converted to Catholicism in order not to be killed as Jews. The name Rael on the family coat of arms means 'bearers of light.'
>
> Maybe in fact I was destined to play the role I am playing in the world today because it is the unfolding of that particular mystery of the 'bearer of light.' (*House of Shattering Light* 29)

Israel, the name of the Jews revealed during the age of Jacob, literally means those who struggle with El, the Hebrew solar god, a reference to Jacob's struggling with the angel, who was his heavenly counterpart. Also, Rael is close to Raphael, the archangel associated with the Sephirah Tifereth, meaning beauty and compassion. In Hebrew Raphael means, 'healed by El.' We will see in the pages to come how Joseph is 'healed by' El and 'heals by' El, *Wa-Ma-Chi* in Tiwa.

Elaborating on the description of his father's people, in *House of Shattering Light,* he wrote, "Picuris people don't call themselves Picuris. They call themselves *tuu taah teh nay* and then *pii-tah*—where the center of life is, or where the kiva is the center. 'We are the people from the source—the center of the circle of light'" (48). Echoing his vision of the creation story, Joseph evokes the kiva consciousness and the cultivation of nothingness as the paradoxical function and purpose of the people:

> So if they are the people who are at the core of existence, then they necessarily must also be the expansion of that. They're calling themselves "the No-form creating the form." . . . That's why they call themselves *tuu taah the nay*, which suggests that they don't exist, but also suggests that they do exist in states of non-existence. Non-existence is what gives validity to existence. Non-existence is black, and existence is white. . . . The magpie is black and he is also white. (48–49)

One doesn't solve the mystery of non-existence or one's existing in/as states of non-existence, which Joseph continually describes. One must experience the mystery. Joseph, like the great Tibetan masters who draw upon an extraordinary mystical legacy, has devoted his life to this supreme realization. One can say that non-existence is not physical death but a psycho-spiritual state. One begins to taste nothingness, the void, as one detaches from egocentricity—which is tight, aggressive, ambitious, dense and fist-like—and embraces 'selflessness,' which is hollow, empty, receptive, relaxed, and aware, like the cupped palm.

The cupped palm is, of course, the kiva, the spiritual symbol of the Pueblo people. Complementing the kiva, the oracle of empty space, is the mountain, symbol of the Utes. Together, in Joseph, they are the spinning, dancing, interpenetrating yin/yang symbol. The kiva represents the southern, dark receptivity of yin. The mountain represents the northern, bright upward, outward, dynamic yang. The kiva and mountain also express the yoni (female) and ligham (male) of Hindu culture. Though the two features express life's inner and outer complementary/

contradictory forces, Joseph says that the mountain peoples and the pueblo peoples come from the same center. "Mountain" in Tiwa means center. Kiva in Tiwa can also be a metaphor for center.

After sixty-seven years of conflict and conciliation, Joseph came to this realization about his being a kiva/mountain man with European spicing:

> There are certain challenges that are put to half-breeds, people who are of one tribe and also of another. I think they are put there purposely by the universal Intelligence as a way of cultivating people who will be able to take those two cultures and catapult them both to a higher level. Evolution comes from struggle, from two entities colliding. Out of that struggle comes something better. (*House of Shattering Light* 38)

Eastern mysticism, ancient alchemy, and Carl Jung have made us aware that each of us is a metaphorical mixed breed, a human with an anima and animus, archetypal female and male. That our happiness and health depend upon our integrating, spiritually wedding Magpietail Boy and Yellow Corn Maiden, what alchemy calls our inner White Queen (relatedness, receptivity, intuition, feeling) and Red King (autonomy, action, instinct, mentality). In alchemy the wedding takes place in the inner athanor, or amphora, entered through the abdomen; in Tiwa mysticism, as we have seen, it occurs in the kiva, our sacred black emptiness.

Acknowledging and reconciling this inner polarity heals us, as well as our relationships. We no longer project our own inner dysfunction, but harmony and resolution. Moreover, Joseph teaches that mixing forces expands and elevates consciousness, not only individually but globally. He realizes, like Krishnamurti, that we are each the world, a teaching he enacted as an elder, with the building of the peace chambers on every continent. Mixing forces causes consciousness to expand and elevate in the society, as well as in the mixed, who contain opposing forces.

In *House of Shattering Light,* Joseph describes accustoming himself to life as an infant, in a body, governed by duality and time, perceiving directly rather than through his mother. The people and things he originally met as vibration he now met as unfocused images in a realm of bright light. His parents and siblings seemed like luminous "giants." Joseph recalls his awareness as a "glowing light superimposed over my infant body." Functioning primarily as *nah,* more subtle body than physical body, he perceived the auras, subtle light, not only of his family, but of animals and plants: "Living in this place of light was like living in rainbows of ever-changing, colored energies" (23). Gradually, as he perceived the physical individuality of his environment, he perceived his own. And gradually he experienced love, the glue that eternally connects us.

Because of his heightened awareness, his expanded sensitivities, Joseph was already experiencing Departure, the first stage of Joseph Campbell's Hero's Journey. Yet, while most of us only experience onset of Departure, "the call to adventure," when we are forced or choose to leave the safety and security of our familiar environs, Joseph was experiencing the transition from subtle light and his mother's womb, tempered by the force of love. And while most of us experience Departure by plunging from the limited conscious mind (perceptual mind) into the unconscious, Joseph was experiencing the journey in reverse. Coping with duality was always his biggest challenge.

In the womb, he had experienced them through awareness and the mind. "Mind energy is cold, impersonal. Heart energy is warm." Because of this warmth, this eternal connection, native elders invite the ancient relatives. When they invite them, they are really saying, "We bring in the heart" (24). Though Joseph came to rely more and more on his mind, heart, and ordinary senses, as we all do, he retained his subtle capacities. We will learn, however, that he turned to the kiva, sweat lodge, long dance, and sun dance, to maintain and deepen his spiritual perception.

In his autobiography Joseph relates the hardship of life in La Boca. The town six and a half miles south of Ignacio, the environment proved inhospitable. The family, Joseph in particular, experienced enchantment, mystery, accident, and death, the full range of human tragic-comedy. In the summer Joseph and his siblings would do a tree-spirit watching ceremony:

> "We'd go up around big trees, lie down . . . and just watch. Pretty soon, we'd see the lights of the trees, almost like they were Christmas trees, and then we'd see the beings in the trees. They would manifest into some kind of humanoid appearance or something else" (*House of Shattering Light* 36).

Clearly, Joseph's consciousness was toggling back and forth as he entered perceptual reality.

When he was five, becoming accustomed to his body and perceptual reality, Joseph envisioned another dimension of the subtle world, another face of alternate reality. A face that challenged his determination to incarnate. If he hadn't experienced his "call to adventure" before, he certainly experienced it then. Sun was setting. His mother had sent him to retrieve a wayward sheep (a symbol used in the Gospels, as well as by Blake). Suddenly, he couldn't see his mother. Fear arose, and he sought safety by squatting amidst the tall sage. He heard his mother's voice calling his name. A white cloud of mist pervaded the landscape. Then a warmth reminiscent of his mother's womb coursed through his body. Feeling secure, he stood.

"When I looked in the direction of her voice and concentrated, a light came from my eyes and made a hole in the cloud-like mist, so that I could see my mother on the other side" (16). The eyes both perceive light and emit light. His glance, a phenomenon cultivated by Eastern mystics, pierced the veil that separates this world from what we call heaven. The little boy, ever on the edge between the gross and subtle levels, slipped out and back into the world of crystallized forms. In conversation sixty-four years after the experience, he described the experience this way:

That's when I looked, and remember that light comes through my eyes, I didn't realize it at the time that apparently when I see something, or anybody sees something, there's a light going out of their eyes toward the object that they're observing. There was a large mist, a white cloud area, so I couldn't see where my mother's voice was coming from. All I heard was the sound of the direction my mother was. When I looked that way and I concentrated, apparently a light came from my eyes and made a hole in the mist, like a cloud, and I could see her on the other side. So I just went through that hole. What is mist? Mist, as far as I know it, is movement that is infused with awareness that, as it crystallizes, it stops in mid-air just before it disappears into breathable clarity. (Personal communication)

Joseph's description of the mist is poetic, derived from Tiwa, his understanding of vibration, and his visionary intuition. From the perspective of the ordinary mind, the description is metaphoric, symbolic. But from the Tiwa and Platonic perspectives, meaning, principal ideas, precede physical form. Mountain, mist, hole, boy, sheep, eyes, mother—all are simultaneously forms and principal ideas. And Joseph, as consciousness, (in a way similar to Jung's discussion of numinous dreams) was all these 'things'/principal ideas. As we shall see, Joseph's teaching cultivates a stereoscopic consciousness that links the dimensions of form and principal ideas, what we have heretofore called gross and subtle perception. In this experience, it seems as if the subtle realm were trying to reclaim him, to prevent him from individuating.

During the same year, Joseph had a serious accident on the back of one of the family's horses. He had gone out across the river with his father, Alfred, to cut hay on the acreage given to his mother, Beatrice. Alfred had hitched two horses in front of an alfalfa mower. Alfred and Joseph each rode a horse; Joseph rode Sandy, a horse his father had just broken. After they finished mowing, his father dismounted, unhitched the horses, took the reins in hand, and walked them to the gate. When he released the reins to open the gate, they bolted with Joseph atop Sandy. Joseph bounced back and forth; one of the metal spikes on the collar penetrated his skull. While the doctors operated on his pierced, crushed skull, Joseph's subtle, light body floated above his physical body, near the ceiling. From there, in that auric body, he, pain- and fear-free, watched the doctor operate. Joseph was impressed by the young doctor's confidence. Joseph recovered but still has a dime-size hole in his skull.

A more tragic accident befell his older sisters, Corleen and Gloria. Across the dirt road from their home ran a railroad track. Joseph loved to kneel beside the track, put his ear to the cold steel rail, and listen to the subtle vibration of oncoming trains. Listening to the vibration attuned him to what he calls the inaudible vibration, what other mystics call the abstract or inner sound. Doing so awakened the *nah,* carried him into the subtle, impersonal level. One day when he was six, he decided to show Corleen and Gloria how to do it.

All three lay their ears against the rail to hear the oncoming train. But they were so entranced with the sound, so tuned to the subtle realm and untuned to the gross realm, that they stayed there, neither noticing nor moving from the train. Joseph was thrown from the train. His sisters were killed. Something about La Boca seemed to enhance the presence of subtler, supersensible realms and the children's ability to enter them. In this case, his two older sisters went to the subtle *nah* reality and prepared the way for their family. Before long their mother would join them. But before this, the family would leave La Boca, sell Beatrice's allotted land, and move to Alfred's former home, Picuris Pueblo, in Northern New Mexico.

Arriving at Picuris: Meeting the Little People

In 1941 half of the Rael family set off for Picuris. It would be another of many experiences of Departure. Yet, the young hero was also beginning the stage of Initiation, wherein he is introduced to the energies of psycho-physical-spiritual transformation. Manuel, Joseph's half brother, had entered the armed forces to fight in World War II. Mabel, his older half-sister,

was boarding at Albuquerque Indian School and would continue
to live on the Ute reservation. Beatrice and Benito, Joseph's
youngest brother, would stay in La Boca until Alfred, Joseph, and
Tayo and Fernando, Joseph's older brothers, were settled.

Enroute to Picuris, Joseph had one of his many encounters
with the little people, beings considered less subtle than angels,
variously called nature spirits and elementals, who inhabit
another of the worlds that interpenetrate this world. They
heralded the transformative experiences of Initiation that lay
before him. He would soon learn that the beings he encountered,
Elf Boy and Old Man Beaver, are well-known characters of Tiwa
stories. Elf Boy, a key figure in the Magpietail Boy and Yellow
Corn Woman story, would again feature in Joseph's life some
thirty years later. Like William Blake, Joseph has maintained his
capacity to communicate with nature spirits, fairies, angels, and
the departed throughout his life.

The four Raels and Nathan Bird, in whose truck they were
driving, got stuck crossing a stream between Vadito and Picuris.
While the men pondered a solution, the boys played on the
hillside. Joseph paused to gaze at the stream and saw a luminous
small being sitting across the bank, a boy about three feet tall
with oversized eyes. The two youngsters engaged in telepathic
conversation, exchanging light through their eyes. Joseph says he
was "listening with his eyes and seeing with his ears" (*House of
Shattering Light* 34).

Elf Boy told Joseph that his family would be okay. Elf Boy's
family was coming to lift the truck and take it to the other side.
In the meantime, he invited Joseph to play, to walk on the water's
surface. Joseph tried but slipped in up to his waist. As he was
slipping, Joseph sensed the presence of another, older nature
spirit, Old Man Beaver. Just then, his father called the boys.
When the elders started the truck, it miraculously floated to
the other side. In Joseph Campbell's formulation of the Hero's
Quest, Elf Boy and Old Man Beaver functioned as threshold
guardians, but also as helpers when they transported the family
chariot over the "threshold of adventure" into a new realm, in
this case the stage of Initiation—a stage of intense preparation

and purification that lasted almost forty years.

In *The Hero With A Thousand Faces*, which has inspired innumerable scholars, artists, and inquisitive persons since 1949, Campbell described the passage to Initiation in this way:

> The mythological hero, setting forth from his commonday hut or castle, is lured, carried away, or else voluntarily proceeds, to the threshold of adventure. There he encounters a shadow presence that guards the passage. The hero may defeat or conciliate this power and go alive into the kingdom of the dark (brother-battle, dragon-battle; offering, charm), or be slain by the opponent and descend in death (dismemberment, crucifixion). Beyond the threshold, then, the hero journeys through a world of unfamiliar forces, some of which severely threaten him (tests), some of which give him magical aid (helpers). (245–46)

Joseph's innocence and spiritual power were the "charm" which allowed him to communicate with Elf Boy and Old Man Beaver and pass into a new realm. In years to come, Joseph often returned to the riverbank to meet his friend. Though he didn't reappear, Joseph often sensed his glance.

Picuris, the smallest of the nineteen pueblos, was named by Don Juan Onate, who called the people *Pikuria*, those who paint. Though they numbered about 3,000 in the mid-thirteenth century when they inhabited a much larger pueblo in the Pot Creek area, they now number about 334. The present pueblo, which Tiwans have inhabited for 750 years, is located sixty miles north of Santa Fe and twenty-four miles southeast of Taos, near the town of Penasco, where Joseph finished high school. In Picuris, the Rael men lived with Alfred's mother for about a year. Grandmother's house, though embellished, still stands, on the right of the road, after one crosses the bridge into the pueblo.

In *Being and Vibration* Joseph describes Grandmother Rael's joyful, loving presence and her carrying the descending light of the heavenly planes. In addition, she was his first guide, his first initiator into the Tiwa mysteries. She taught the Rael boys that even the simplest, mostly quotidian tasks, like sweeping the floor, was sacred: "She would sweep the floor with a hand-brush of straws harvested from the fields. These brushes were holy because the herb the straw was taken from was sacred. Thus sweeping the floor and cleaning the house were really a ceremony of beautification, opening the gateways to the upper heavens, to awareness" (31).

She also taught them to cultivate the precious energy of awareness by exhorting them to "pay attention" to the helpful voices of their ancestors. Were the children to remain unreceptive to the guidance of those already gone to the subtle realms, they might easily "get lost in the metaphors of life" (32). The Tiwa rely on the guidance of those in the subtle world, which, as we said, penetrates the primary world of crystallized light. Having learned his grandmother's message, Joseph has been guided by light beings, ancestors and non-ancestors alike, for more than seventy years. Getting lost in the metaphors means not realizing that what appear as solid things are epiphanies, the incarnation of qualities, the embodiment of pure meaningfulness, revelations of the Vast Self. If the young ones are not aware, their gross minds will know only dead things, not metaphors, not epiphanies. They will, as Joseph says, succumb to illusion.

His grandmother illustrated metaphorical reality by explaining the significance of the dirt floor on which they ate:

> "The floor is important," my grandmother would say. "It represents the floor of life where everything comes from. It holds everything. Everything that comes, comes from the floor, or the foundation of life. It feeds us, it clothes us, it houses us." She would make reference to the fact that our

houses were made of adobe, from earth, and so we were being supported by the soil of the earth, which symbolized the vastness of the inner self. The earth was the flower garden and we were her little flowers. (33)

They sat cross-legged on the dirt floor, eating upon cloth mats, with gourd dippers. They participated in sacred ceremony three times daily. The house was a temple; the floor and the objects upon it were an altar. Grandmother sang about the bowls and food. She showed them that eating is reverential. She taught them that everything in life is eating: Life is eating all that lives, and all that lives eats life. And while our physical body eats matter, our *nah*, our soul, drinks light. When we humans make effort, strengthening our *nah*, the Vast Self, eats.

As they ate from the clay bowls and gourds, she told them that the gourds, from which Tiwa made rattles, were their bodies. That they, the food they carry, and their bodies are made of music. They ate for the purpose of tuning the instrument to make beautiful sounds; not just beautiful sounds, their personal songs. Saying this, she was telling them to sing their unique song, the song that no one else can sing, the song without which the universe, the Vast Self, is incomplete. She also taught them to listen, not only to the voices of ancestors but to the voice of the Great Spirit:

> To become a true human, one must become conscious of listening and hearing the voice of the Great Mystery speaking through everything, through the sound of a tree, or the bird flying overhead, or the wind in the room, or someone breathing, or someone talking, or a moment of silence. The activity of sound is what made the people. It is, therefore, simply through listening, and using that listening, and paying attention, that one finds the guidance of the Great Mystery along the path of life. (*Being and Vibration* 34)

As a boy, Joseph saw that the generation after Grandmother, those who had been to boarding school, were already forgetting and forsaking this holy knowledge and practice. The invading mind said, still says, daily, natural life is unholy; only otherness, the artificial, the abstract, is worthy of worship.

Joseph vividly recalls his grandmother's two-room house:

> The outer walls were slightly rounded and made from adobe,
> a mixture of mud, straw, and micaceous clay. When the sun
> shone, the tiny pinpoints of gold, which were everywhere in
> the micaceous clay, would reflect its rays, giving the whole a
> glistening golden quality.
>
> Inside, the walls were painted with red clay from the
> ground upwards for about three feet and were whitewashed
> the rest of the way up to the ceiling. Overhead, the ceiling
> was constructed from pine poles which had been stripped of
> their bark. (*Being and Vibration* 30–31)

Telling him and his brother that her house was "modeled after the first house," Grandmother introduced the perception of the "House of Shattering Light," the title of Joseph's autobiography. The dwelling of the house, as a shell/structure as well as a container, what Eastern mystics call an *akasha* or capacity, is a metaphor for this condition of existence, life with Earth as the primary world. Literally made of glittering earth, the houses of Picuris reflect the physical body, which is crystallized light, and the subtle auric body that interpenetrates it. Every thing (the entities that appear to be mere objects) will dissolve, dismantle, shatter, as Grandmother said.

In fact, solidity and permanence is illusory; every apparent thing is shattering, right now. We simultaneously non-exist and exist and are every subtle state in between. In this sense, the house is the slice of white light, the white stripe of the koshares. Joseph also likens the house to a moment in which we exist that allows us to change before we and the moment slip back into the black of non-existence. Understanding the metaphor of the house of shattering light allows us to understand time, creativity, choice, responsibility, and possibility, all in the context of inherent (egocentric) non-existence.

Perceptual reality, the gross mind, what Blake called "our mind-forged manacles," prevents us from perceiving the many-layered, transitoriness of creation. The gross mind is, in fact, too slow to perceive the successive instants or slices of light. Just as it perceives a film to be continuous rather than a collection of still images. The gross mind only notices the drama of death, when light/breath/*chi* no longer penetrates form, the subtle body detaches from the gross body, and eternity disengages from time. Of course, death doesn't exist for the Tiwa, just life in another condition. Joseph sees the gift as well as the limitation of our living in and as the House of Shattering Light, this second-choice world. The 'slowed-down' nature of the mind and the senses allows us to make meaning of each moment—if we can awaken.

The adobes were a perfect multi-level metaphor in the spiritual school of the pueblo. They were made of earth/Earth, yet they glistened with subtle, interpenetrating light. And they were impermanent; they dissolved from the moment they were made. They necessitated continual care, just like our bodies. Moderns, however, attend the materialistic school. They identify with what dissolves and, therefore, fear dissolution. They build illusions, create metaphors of permanence and false security, erect granite headstones.

The shape, as well as the composition of the adobe homes is symbolic, and ironic. Being square, they represent the archetypal masculine. Yet they are the domain of women, who are in charge of the home. The anima, the moon, is within the masculine. Kivas, on the other hand, where men go for spiritual training, represent the feminine. The animus, the sun, the masculine, is within the feminine. These symbols of alchemical reconciliation are the equivalent of the Taoist yin/yang circle, in which yin is a black circle within the white arabesque and vice versa. Even as a body of seven, Joseph perceived the "round structure of my femininity was expanding the potential in my masculinity because alchemically I was growing into my opposite, that I might learn balance of male and female" (20).

Being *nah* as well as body, they could be aware of each shattering instant, each "ringing-bell slice of light. . . . However, the ringing slice of light passes quickly and we are then involved in the next slice of light and the next moment. There again, we see it mentally, emotionally, physically, and spiritually" (35). Remember, Joseph teaches the pulsing of the appearing

and disappearing Vast Self. On the exhalation, the *nah* can experience the slice of creating: form and time, which are really just epiphanies of light and vibration. And on the inhalation, the *nah* can experience the uncreated: the infinite void and silence. At the young ages of seven and four, the Rael boys were being taught stereoscopic consciousness by their first Tiwa sage: to be aware of the subtle and gross worlds, eternity and time, simultaneously. By cultivating *nah*, by listening and paying attention at the mental, emotional, physical, and spiritual levels, the boys would be "living inside the perceptual reality" (36).

But it is much more descriptive if we can understand it. And it is a cornerstone of Joseph's teachings. When we *live* perceptual reality, we think, feel, and sense/act reactively, unaware of our state. We are, as we said earlier, 'asleep.' We are on automatic pilot. This unconscious state would equal living outside perceptual reality. When we live inside perceptual reality, we are aware of these internal manifestations, at the impulse stage, even before we express them. This is so because awareness energy is so much quicker than mental, emotional, and physical impulses. And, from its still center point (on the medicine wheel) it can perceive the 'still small voice' of intuition and inspiration, the spiritual level. The phrase itself, "living inside perceptual reality," centers us within our own internal tempests, as well as the tempests stirring around us. Until the internal and external disappear and one exists in the 'what is' of choiceless awareness, the non-dualistic consciousness (Dzogchen) taught by Tulku Urgyen.

"Living inside" also distinguishes Tiwa mysticism from the transcendent mysticisms prevalent in both East and West. Joseph does not simply teach the cultivation of 'higher' consciousness, an awareness, which, at its zenith, detaches us from life and responsibility. Instead of cultivating this 'beyond the beyond' perspective, he cultivates 'within the within': living inside perceptual reality as the first step toward freedom and non-duality. Living inside/perceiving through reinforces the Tiwa fact that the physical body/Earth is our primary world. This is a more challenging awareness and mode of living, but it is necessary to fulfill our primary spiritual work, work that can only be accomplished here and now.

Living within also adds new meaning to the spiritual cliché of being centered. When we are within the within, living inside perceptual reality, we are the Center. One of the many renderings of the Kabbalistic Tree of Life, discussed with regard to Tiwa cosmology, shows the tree as the concentric rings of a literal tree, with Kether, the crown, as the center, and Malkuth, the kingdom, as the outer ring. Furthermore, when we live so far inside perceptual reality, the inside becomes outside, and we become the Center and Circumference, the Vast Self. This essential understanding relates to two other features of Joseph's teaching: kiva-consciousness, which we have already mentioned, and the medicine wheel, upon which we'll elaborate later.

Appreciating Picuris: Spiritual Place

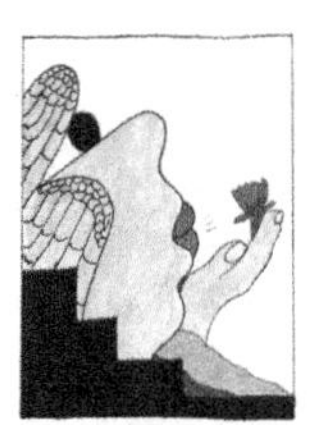

Grandmother's adobe house of shattering light was also a metaphor for the pueblo in which it stood. As Joseph walked, breathed over the land of his grandmother, he realized that Picuris "was a living being with a psyche of individuals made up into a group." He describes the discovery of the Picuris group soul in the first chapter of *Being and Vibration*, his introduction to Tiwa sound mysticism. Through listening and paying attention, he learned the "village was not just a physical place, it was a mental, and emotional, and a spiritual place as well" (19).

He was beginning to learn what he many years later outlined for me in the Sangre de Cristo Mountains. The center or soul of the pueblo, representing the original emergence hole, is the empty plaza, flanked on the northwest corner by the Mission of San Lorenzo. "The elders had been very careful to find a place of power and had made it the heart of the village. The power is something that you can feel; it can also be seen by some. The elders and medicine people built their homes close to this center and then the people built their homes around them (*Beautiful Painted Arrow* 55). The heart center of the village becomes a pole erected once a year before the August 10 corn dances. The pole, about twenty-five feet high, is cut from a tree on the mountain, erected in the southwest corner of the square, and climbed by the sacred clowns at the culmination of the festival, after a day of sacred ceremonies, feasting, running, and dancing.

After hilarious play, one of the koshares succeeds in climbing the pole (like Jack, various prophets, and Greek heroes); he unties a sheep, bread, and a watermelon; and he brings them down, assuring the people continual material and spiritual sustenance. In *Ceremonies of the Living Spirit*, Joseph describes how, watching the clowns ascend and descend, he understood that new inspiration was being brought to Earth from the Very Subtle and Subtle planes. The people (people also means vibration in Tiwa) feed on this new inspiration, and the consciousness of the people/pueblo is "pushed upward." They were, in fact, recreating "how perceptual reality comes into being" (35).

Though it only exists physically during this festival, once a year, the sacred pole represents the spiritual axis that penetrates the center connecting the Above and Below. The pole, a tree shorn of its branches, becomes the Kabbalistic Tree of Life, once again envisioned in its vertical form, with the crown at the top and the kingdom sunk deep in the earth. It also represents the human spine, up and down, along which energies circulate, along which Up and Down circulate.

Campbell calls the point at which the pole penetrates, in fact, the entire town center, "the world navel" (40). It seems surprising that Campbell's language sometimes resembles Joseph's. Perhaps it is not so surprising if we consider that it was his study of Amerindian life that inspired him to study comparative mythology. Through this sacred opening, embodied by the spiritual hero herself/himself, "grace, food substance, energy: these pour into the living world" (40):

69

> The torrent pours from an invisible source, the point of entry being the center of the symbolic circle of the universe . . . around which the world may be said to revolve. . . . The tree of life, i.e., the universe itself, grows from this point. It is rooted in the supporting darkness; the golden sun bird

perches on its peak; a spring, the inexhaustible well, bubbles at its foot. . . . Thus the World Navel is the symbol of the continuous creation: the mystery of the maintenance of the world through that continuous miracle of vivification which wells within all things. The dome of heaven rests on the quarters of the earth, sometimes supported by four caryatidal kings, dwarfs, giants, elephants, or turtles. Hence, the traditional importance of the mathematical problem of the quadrature of the circle: it contains the secret of the transformation of heavenly into earthly forms.

From deep within Grandmother Earth (the yoni, the sacred womb), the pole (the lingam) rises to pierce Grandfather Sky, "the dome of heaven." (Of course, the pole was first put into the hole.) Together, the Center, Down, and Up form the native trinity. The two extremes, created by the Source, the hollow Center (the heart) continually re-merge with it and emerge from it.

Another example of alchemical marriage. The *koshares*, the black and white magpie clowns, are infused with the spiritual longing and intent of Yellow Corn Woman. Colored and clad in the colors of sacred Mother Earth and Father Sky, they gravitate to the navel/pole, circle it, play beneath it like children, all the while surrounded by the tribe, some of whom they pull inside their inner circle. They are the blinking black and white lights, the uncreated and created, male and female, yin and yang: all opposites. As the embodiments of regenerated Magpietail Boy, in whom opposites were resolved, they can climb the pole and bring down the spiritual treasures tied to the pole's tip. Like Jack they can ascend the vine and gift the people with the symbolic revivifying treasures, what Campbell calls "grace, food substance, energy." And by climbing the pole, the koshares counterbalance the people's ongoing descent into the kivas.

From this hub/heart extend the breath of the four cardinal directions, considered by natives to be great beings, guardians; what Campbell calls "caryatidal kings," meaning column-kings; what followers of the Abrahamic and Zoroastrian religions call archangels, specifically the archangels of the throne. "The

houses formed a village medicine wheel. Animals, fields, and places of work snuggled close to the mountain, west of the village. The place of burial was to the north, as was the Sacred Chamber that I experienced when I was nine. The meeting-place for the tribal elders was set off, east of the living centers, in the mind's direction" (*Beautiful Painted Arrow: A Medicine Story* 55–56).

Just as sacred energies flow up and down the pole (even when it is not physically present), sacred fundamental energies of life flow back and forth from the directions to the navel, through the gates guarded by archangels. The relationship between the directions and the people was reciprocal. The Picuris fed the directions through conscious work and ceremonies. Different directions dominated life according to the seasons: east in spring, south in summer, west in autumn and north in winter. The people honored and reinforced the flow of sacred energies by running from the pueblo center to each of the directions on the equinoxes and solstices. And the aura or energy field of Picuris, its subtle body, extended far beyond the pueblo's physical boundary, far beyond their running feet. In truth, the pueblo extended as far as their consciousness, as their prayers for the planet and the cosmos.

Joseph saw that the pueblo had several geographic levels. Behind the empty, hollow, luminous town center, the pueblo rises, and rises once again as one ascends into the surrounding mountains. In traversing these levels, Joseph was experiencing and knitting the three worlds/the three levels. "The village was architecturally designed so that the physical people lived alongside the supernatural beings who would manifest themselves through the sacred ceremonies" (21). In addition, buried in the ground every twenty feet or so were shrines, consecrated points which carried special blessings. The children were taught they were "pressure point activators." When the children, the *pa-ne-ne*, caressed the hidden shrines with their feet, they charged themselves with energy and archetypes. They communicated with the spiritual beings that composed the pueblo's atmosphere. Because they lived as energy, youngsters

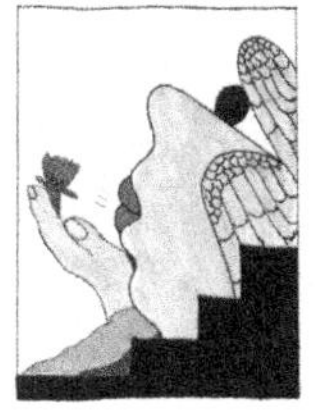

"began to understand that everything in each designated location was the resonating vibration of the play of principal ideas" (*Being and Vibration* 21). The holy shrines enhanced the psyches of individuals and bonded the community in love. The shrines, the Tiwa magi taught, also sent energy in all directions, far beyond the pueblo. Again we find the Tiwa caring for other beings and peoples, even those who would destroy them.

Also, Joseph was learning that walking has great spiritual significance for the Picuris. When walking, he was/is "Time and Purity, Beauty, and Awareness of God's Light." When walking, therefore, we are time and awareness; we fuse the gross and subtle levels, manifesting purity and beauty. Walking, *taah-chi-who* in Tiwa, is also related to plowing, also sounded as *taah*. So, though the moccasin, shoe, or foot touches the surface, the energy descending through the sole plows, penetrates and turns over the earth, exposes that which had been dark and hidden to light. By walking then, we prepare the soil for the seeds of newness and feed Earth. This is conveyed by *chi*, which means energy, awareness, and movement. 'Planting' our feet and moving, we charge the Earth and seed our becoming. Finally, in doing this, *who* happens. *Who* conveys the mysterious presence of the Vast Self, the Great Spirit. An individual and collective blessing.

To some it seems remarkable that a so-called primitive people who rarely left present-day New Mexico should have such an 'expanded' consciousness and concern. But the subtle Self, the *nah*, is not limited by time and space, and the Vast Self includes all. So cultivating awareness and compassion, not only permitted but necessitated the Tiwa's global, even extra-terrestrial concern. In comparative spirituality, we find this altruistic concern among Buddhists who pray for all sentient beings. In their own perfect way, the Tiwa practice the Four-Immeasurables Prayer, the generation and dedication of compassionate wisdom (bodhicitta), sending blessings of love, compassion, joy, and enlightenment to the four horizons, then throughout the universe.

Picuris Pueblo spirituality is carried by the Tiwa language, as
we have already indicated, a language based on verbs and rich in
metaphor. Joseph says that Tiwa is the vibration of Northern New
Mexico, the revelation of the Vast Self, the Great Spirit. Though
Alfred spoke Tiwa, Joseph didn't know it when he arrived at
Picuris. From the start, he understood that Tiwa carried a
vibrational aliveness, the vibrations of Mother Nature, the land
(*naa-meh-nay*), which is the embodiment of the Vast Self:

> The Tiwa language is like an energy that resonates in that
> geography. I was eating from that resonance, sleeping it, so I
> needed to speak it. Tiwa was the vibration of that geography,
> which extended for twenty or thirty miles.
>
> Everything that exists on the surface of the land is really
> an extension of the land. Ceremonies are about these exten-
> sions of land, or how land expresses itself in its highest natu-
> ral form. And land is the symbol of the vast Self that is in a
> state of purification. Land is flowing with waters that purify,
> with rivers, with rain, with snow, with the ocean like a big
> lung, constantly freshening the air. (*Ceremonies of the Living
> Spirit* 6–7)

This accounts for the extraordinary power of Tiwa language
and Tiwa mysticism. The language, which is the vibration of
nature, which is itself the Vast Self, makes the Vast Self ever
present. In fact, to emphasize this, Joseph recently said, "Tiwa
is not a language; it is a collection of sounds," meaning that the
sound of Tiwa, an oral language, *is* the meaning. The sound is
what is happening; the words themselves are creating. For noun
people words represent reality, at best. For the Tiwa, every act is
ceremonial, and all so-called things are sacred participants. The
practical function of so-called things exists as metaphor. For
instance, what English speakers call 'hands,' Tiwans call *ma-nay-
nay*, meaning creating, manifesting. And Joseph translates 'cup'
(*tii*), which is really 'cupping,' as "the power of crystallization
that is influencing the awareness that is holding something in."

Because the Tiwa, Pueblo, and natives in general, did not originally distinguish between spiritual and secular, nature is always Nature. Physical happenings not only express the Presence of Spirit; they metaphor pure meaning; they actualize the subtle realm of Platonic forms, make it perceptible through the senses. This is why Joseph's teaching is a medicine for people reared on spirit/matter, soul/body duality, who routinely destroy what they consider things. Who destroy Vast Self, Spirit's immanent presence. His medicine connects the transcendent, very subtle world of Spirit (Being) to its subtle existence as patterns or energy, light, and vibration, to its manifestation as Earth and universe, as physical expressions of Beingness. Being as meaning/archetype as Beingness.

Joseph's reference to "life's unfolding from the inner recesses of the land" also relates to the kiva, the underground sacred chambers of the Pueblo and their kin, the Anasazi. The Pueblo peoples emerged from the earth, from the hole that symbolically sits on the floor of every kiva. So it is natural that they descend to perform ceremonies (like the wizards) and meditate in Mother Earth's womb in order to most directly merge with Vast Self. This is the best way to dispel duality and cultivate the inner kiva, the sacred space within us.

Tiwa was/is very different from the three representational languages he already knew—Ute, Spanish, and English. While his first three languages were mental, these new sounds were intuitive, and every sound and word was a metaphor expressing an aspect of the Great Mystery, *Wa-Ma-Chi*:

> With a mental perception, the human psyche [via the senses] first apprehends and then quickly assigns placement, or definition. With vibrational perception, or intuition, definition is not necessary, because vibration unfolds the essence of the thing perceived. The perception comes with a resonance. It comes complete, like a flower, or a song. Instantly, we perceive it in its fullness; we drink its light and it becomes a part of us. (*House of Shattering Light* 39)

Intuitive perception and mental perception occur on different levels the subtle/*nah* and the gross/personal levels. The *nah* level is not only the level of direct perception, or as Joseph wrote, of vibrational/intuitive perception, but is the level of subtle light and energy, meaningfulness, archetypes, inspiration, and, ultimately, creative imagination. As *nah* we actualize our subtle nature in all its aspects as well as the perceptual means to experience the subtle, unsensed, archetypal nature of creation. Joseph's experiences and resultant teachings bear an uncanny concordance with the ancient Persians, the Mazdeans and Zoroastrian magi. And knowing a little of their visionary teachings will further illuminate his. Mazdeans call the supreme, original being Ohrmazd; Zoroastrians call It Ahura Mazda, the Lord of Light and Wisdom.

In Zoroastrianism, Ahura Mazda is surrounded by six "supreme Archangels" or Amahraspands, who constitute the 'highest' dimension of the *nah*. Together, the seven correspond to the seven directions. Just below the Amahraspands are the Fravati, "who are at one and the same time the heavenly archetypes of beings and their respective tutelary angels." Every earthly being has a "heavenly archetype or Angel, whose earthly counterpart he is." This heavenly condition or heavenly I is said to be the "menok" nature while the personal, physical nature is the "getik" state. "The distinction is . . . a matter of the relationship between the invisible and the visible, the subtle and the dense, the heavenly and the earthly, provided it is clearly understood that the *getik* state . . . in itself by no means implies a degradation of being" (Corbin, *Spiritual Body and Celestial Earth* 7-10). The *menok* state, the heavenly archetype, applies to all natural beings, not just human beings. The ancient Persians placed particular importance on one's realization of the angel of the Earth, Zamyat. This understanding of creation's (even the elements of earth, water, fire, and air) having a heavenly and terrestrial nature relates not only to Joseph's experiences, but to William Blake's.

Perhaps more relevant to appreciating Joseph is Corbin's description of the faculty of consciousness necessary to perceive heavenly, archetypal nature of people and things. To perceive the Angel of the Earth, "the Earth irradiated and transfigured

by *Xvarnah,*" "the Light of Glory" (29). Many who are limited
to the mental domain believe true visionaries to be fantasizing
and hallucinating. This illuminating, revealing faculty is active
imagination, what Jung called creative imagination:

> We must ask ourselves whether the invisible action of forces
> that have their purely physical expression in natural process-
> es may not bring into play psychic energies that have been
> neglected or paralyzed by our habits, and directly touch an
> Imagination which, far from being arbitrary invention, cor-
> responds to that Imagination which the alchemists called
> *Imaginatio vera* and which is the *astrum in homine.*
>
> The active Imagination thus induced will not produce
> some arbitrary, even lyrical, construction standing between
> us and "reality," but will, on the contrary, function directly
> as a faculty and organ of knowledge just as *real* as—if not
> more real than—the sense organs. However, it will perceive
> in the manner proper to it: The organ is not a sensory faculty
> but an *archetype-Image* that it possessed from the beginning;
> it is not something derived from any other perception. And
> the property of this Image will be precisely that of effecting
> the transmutation of sensory data, their resolution into the
> purity of the subtle world, in order to restore them as sym-
> bols to be deciphered, the "key" being imprinted in the soul
> itself. (*Spiritual Body and Celestial Earth* 11)

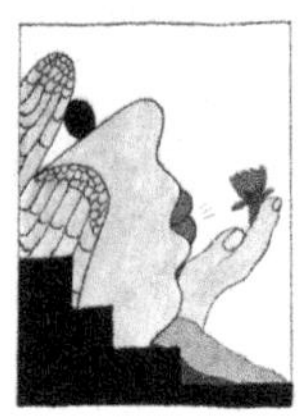

This passage, written by one of the great scholars of
comparative mysticism, in part elaborates what we have already
said concerning levels of consciousness. But, more importantly,
it clarifies the crux of mystical experience and vision, the essence
of Joseph's life. Furthermore, it explains how active Imagination
reveals the archetypal world to which Tiwa awakened Joseph:
Active Imagination "possessed" *the archetype-Images* "from the
beginning." (Blake equated Jesus with Imagination.) Living is
Self-Revelation. Joseph's insight, however, with its emphasis
on the "transmuting" quality of active imagination and the
revelation of archetypes as symbols, is uncannily analogous to
Mazdean/Zoroastrian vision.

Furthermore, in Tiwa, Joseph learned the relationship not
only between these abstract/heavenly and concrete/terrestial

worlds, but of these two to the Very Subtle world of primordial purity and Non-existence. Silence (non-existence) becomes vibration, becomes living 'things.' The fluidness or continuity of these states, conditions, or perceptions accounts for the inherent no-thingness of things:

> My first instructions at Picuris were that all material or non-material forms are alive and, secondly, that all of life's for the sole purpose of revelation—that everything we do or see teaches us what the No-thing looks like. This is important because essentially, we do not exist; therefore, we are born to learn the meaning of non-existence. Non-existence wants us to know Its meaning, so we come to participate in states of concreteness which are perceptual. Our life here is a dialogue between abstractness and concreteness. (*House of Shattering Light* 39)

RECEIVING A TIWA NAME AND VISIONS

In the months before Alfred, Joseph, Tayo, and Fernando were joined by Beatrice and Benito, Joseph not only learned Tiwa; he also received the Tiwa name *Tsloot-ta-koi*. He received his name from the spiritual leader of the pueblo, Antonio Simbolo, *Pel-Qui-Weh*. *Pel-Qui-Weh* (meaning "Annual Race" or "365 Days Covering the Four Seasons") would soon become his guide and later, his grandfather. Tsloot-ta-koi can be roughly translated into English as Beautiful Painted Arrow. Alfred had introduced his son as Earl. To Antonio, Earl's being sounded like an arrow, a medicine arrow.

The Picuris have a tradition that certain archetypal names must always exist in the pueblo, that people must carry the names in order that the sounds will vibrate whenever the people are addressed. Tsloot-ta-koi is one of those essential vibrations. An elder who had carried this vibration had just left his primary body. So, Earl, needing a Tiwa name and resonating with the Beautiful Painted Arrow vibration, was given Tsloot-ta-koi. From the beginning Joseph Earl loved it because in it he could "hear the sound of an arrow being released from the bow, flying through the air, hitting its target and, as its feathered end vibrates, painting the air around it with beautiful colors" (*House of Shattering Light* 37–38).

Joseph explains that the Picuris keep a magic painted arrow in the quiver, never using it for hunting or warfare. Westerners might say it is kept for an emergency. Joseph tells the story of a hunter who had become lost, having wandered into the mountains to slay a deer. The hunter shot his painted arrow back to his encampment, a distance of some miles, where it was retrieved by the medicine man. The medicine man created a rainbow (much as Magpietail Boy does with his tail in some stories) that stretched back from the camp to the hunter. The hunter stepped on it with the deer and was transported back to camp.

The arrow, in general, represents the power of intention and one-pointedness, powered by the exhalation of the breath. In Greek mythology, the arrow is personified by Hermes, herald and messenger of the gods, who flew by virtue of the wings attached to his sandals and hat. Endowed with swiftness, shrewdness and sagacity, he was also empowered to take the souls of the departed to the next world. Because of his unique capacity to traverse the worlds, he was considered the hierophant, the patron of the spiritual mysteries. In Egyptian mythology he is known as Thoth, or the 'Thrice-Great Hermes,' the bringer of wisdom to humanity. Joseph, a sacred runner and dancer, often describes himself as running above ground or flying. This, his visionary capacity, as well as his crossing the perceptual barriers of the worlds and communicating with subtle and once-physical beings, liken him to the ancient herald.

The young visionary's appreciation of Tiwa vibration and energy was heightened by his being a half-breed. At six he developed the consciousness of the outsider, the mystical witness. A consciousness that would be later intensified by years of white education. However, the outsider savored the new world, even as he struggled to compensate for his late start. Joseph believes that those who like himself are "split" have a special destiny. Often spurned by the cultures of their parents, they can internalize and integrate the opposing cultures, elevating both. From internal struggle comes evolution, the reconciliation of opposites. In his own life, he credits this confrontation of languages, of thinking and intuiting, of enabling him to perceive both ways simultaneously. Half-joking, he also attributes his koshare-like dual-perception to the hole in his head, received when he was a child at La Boca.

"The child with the hole in his head" had many dream-visions in his grandmother's house, for which he was teased when he shared them at breakfast, in the manner of Australian aborigines. One heralded the worldwide work he would carry out some forty years later. In this dream-vision, a wise old woman stood before him. In front of her were seven tiny oval-shaped chambers that seemed to be chanting with human voices. As he watched the singing ovals, the grandmother cried with joy. Perhaps as a result of the family's jesting, he forgot the vision for almost fifty-nine years. By the time he remembered the wise old mother and her metaphorical offspring, he had already consecrated more than eighty chanting chambers around the world. This vision, consigned to his unconscious, was both personal and impersonal, like his later vision of the map. The chanting chambers were, in fact, referenced in one of the many scenarios he was to see in his Santa Fe office in 1981.

Though he had many visions in the house of his first spiritual guide, he had another one, this time in waking consciousness, that would be elaborated in a future vision. This one involved meeting the Blue Stone people. According to Joseph, this pair of boulders is the most remarkable of Picuris' many shrines. Referred to as the blue stone, it is really two stones. Though they once sat exposed outside his grandmother's house, they now lie elsewhere on the pueblo, buried for protection. As a child, Joseph watched in awe as *Pikuria* came to honor and 'feed' the blue stone with corn meal. He also saw many subtle radiant beings feed the blue stone. This vision involved beings from other solar systems, kachinas:

> I saw a transparent ship come down from the heavens and
> land next to my grandmother's woodpile. In the ship were

two kachinas. They were very tall and they were wearing black and white robes. They got out of the ship and moved from the west end of the house to where they stopped, and the next thing I saw, the Blue Stone people were there and the kachinas started feeding the blue stones. I just took it for granted that maybe they were using cornmeal to feed the stones. (*Sound 85*)

The follow-up vision to this would occur half a century later.

KIVA-ING WITH ANTONIO

Joseph's first meeting with Antonio Simbola, his primary supernatural guide, had occurred when Joseph was still living with Grandmother Rael. When Antonio had heard Joseph as Tsloot-ta-koi. Because he received his name as a child rather than a newborn and by a medicine person rather than a midwife, his naming (and his brothers' naming) was unusual for a Pueblo child. But as we have already seen, so much about Joseph is atypical.

Traditionally, Pueblo receive several names, at different times. In *The Tewa World*, Alfonso Ortiz, whom we have already quoted, describes the various naming-giving ceremonies among the Tewa, close relatives of the Tiwa. His disclosures reveal how naming is closely related to the creation stories, how all aspects of Pueblo living are related. The first name is bestowed by the "naming mother" four mornings after birth. On the fourth morning after birth, the naming mother and her assistant (who are also the child's midwives), present the new-born to the rising sun. Then beseeching the presence of Blue Corn Woman and White Corn Maiden, who are believed to give the child her soul, naming/cord-cutting mother names the child. Though Joseph did not experience this extraordinary ritual as a newborn, he often presented himself to the being of the rising sun, *To-le-ne*.

The second naming ritual is the "water-giving" ceremony, carried out in the child's first year. This baptismal initiation, into either the Summer or Winter people, is held once a year,

depending on the moiety (seasonal group) the child is joining. Children always join the moiety of their father. This name, chosen by the parents and conferred by the chief of the moiety is only used for ritual purposes within the moiety. Before conferring the second name, the moiety chief says a short prayer and offers the child a drink of sacred water from an abalone shell. These rituals are exquisite and highly symbolic. One should read Ortiz to appreciate their details (*The Tewa World* 30–37).

As a whole, Pueblo society and rituals parallel the original two-ness of creation. (Even in Joseph's vision of the arising of Picuris, two kachinas were involved.) Unity (Center) and the duality (Above and Below) which proceeded from It and returns to It, are mirrored throughout Tiwa life. At emergence Earth and Sky, Above and Below, already existed. And before that, Silence and Sound, Nothing and Everything, Darkness and Light, Wet and Dry. The original White and Blue Corn women of the underworld, Demeter figures, established the Pueblo's essentially feminine, Earth-based, matriarchal orientation. Blue Corn Woman represents summer, warmth, right-sidedness, and yang (though in a goddess way). White Corn Maiden represents winter, coldness, left-sidedness, and yin. One must be careful in systematizing the Pueblo because the people themselves valued intuition over rules, as Joseph learned when he arrived. For instance, the Winter people, aligned with White Corn Maiden, were the hunters, not a typical yin/receptive activity, unless one considers a goddess such as Artemis.

As I said, Joseph knew Alfonso Ortiz and was impressed by the anthropologist's curiosity. Alfonso, says Joseph, was particularly interested in the role and essence of the koshares, and would often visit Picuris during festivals to observe koshare activities. Though Ortiz revealed many of his tribe's ceremonies, he may have missed, as an academic, the essence of the inner teachings. When Joseph's father, Alfred, had presented his son to the cacique, Alfred had asked something like, "Can you do something with this loco son of mine who has a hole in his head. He keeps telling our fortunes and the future at the breakfast table." Antonio, Pel-Qui-Weh, had said something like, "Sure. I know what's wrong with him. Leave him with me." Antonio, recognizing the boy's gift, told Joseph to tell only him what he saw in his dreams and visions.

Antonio, whose particular medicine involved working with the four elements of earth, water, fire, and air, trained Joseph rigorously. This involved preparing him to break all boundaries and limitations, not just to participate in the rituals of his clan. Austerities came easily to Joseph. He could run long distances, experiencing second, third, and fourth 'wind' (during which energy floods the physical body from subtler worlds, the subtle and very subtle selves.) He could fast from physical food. And, most importantly, he could fast from the perceptual reality, the habitual thoughts of the gross mind.

Joseph has never broken the vow that clan members make not to divulge activities of the clan. (And Joseph was brought into the ceremonies of many clans because most of the young men had left for World War II.) But he has characterized Antonio's tutelage in his first and second books, *Beautiful Painted Arrow: A Medicine Story* and *Being and Vibration*, as well as *House of Shattering Light*. In *Beautiful Painted Arrow: A Medicine Story*, we learn that Antonio, called Te, was synonymous with the mountain, the earth (The Below) reaching to become sky (The Above). Beyond this, the mountain, home of Te, was harmony and integration of the finite worlds, of body-mind-emotions-intuition, of the medicine wheel and the six directions. It was, therefore, a whole, holy place. Presence of the Vast Self.

When *Beautiful Painted Arrow: A Medicine Story* opens, Joseph, Chewaa, is hurriedly returning to the mountain, the holy life, from the illusory, secular life of perceptive reality. Soon however, transported by drum and song, he becomes a child again. With Te. Te taught him the old ways, wherein they had "ceremonies for everything," wherein "life was wondrously reverent" (5). Wherein they would honor the rising sun through the east door, with chants, Te would smudge the cabin with sage, and Chewaa would run up the mountain with yucca leaf on his leg, in order to bring Te a certain plant or root. This is Joseph's first published account of his running with the eagle, singing his song, feeling the eagle's wings lift him from the earth.

Joseph also describes the first healing ceremony in which he assisted Te. The ceremony, to heal a "spirit wanderer," one who was alternatively vacant from her body or possessed, lasted seven days. On the morning of the seventh day, Te told her family members that:

> three lost Spanish souls had been earth-bound, had entered the woman, and had made her actions and mind as they had seen it. "We are going to bring the healing water to her now. . . . I have sent the serpents after the lost ones and the serpents will bring the beings to me." He then directed the lost ones to go into light. The thunder beings had spoken for the woman and her broken soul at that time and the light, fused with purity, had won. She would now be well. (18)

Laying the foundation for Joseph's future healings, Te told him,

> Medicine, Chewaa, is the way one brings a person back into the center of the medicine wheel. If they have too much emotion, the wheel is out of balance. If the mind is too strong, or if the desire for things becomes too great—even desiring too much spirit—will take the wheel out of balance. We are all made up of the elements, and to be alive and well we must keep them balanced.
>
> Work hard during the day. Eat the right foods. Enjoy your time on earth. Purify yourself often. And when you are older and have found a mate, make love at night. Simple. It is all very simple. (24)

Joseph's first major contribution to healing another occurred in 1947. "A man and a woman came in a horse-drawn wagon to get a healing from [Antonio]" (*House* 63). After the afternoon preliminaries, during which the visitors introduced themselves, offered food, and described her ailment, they all slept. When they gathered the next morning for breakfast, Antonio asked Joseph to recount his dream. Startled that his grandfather knew he had had a healing dream, Joseph commenced, and Antonio replied that, in reality, the lady had come to be healed by Joseph. So, Antonio orchestrated a procedure whereby Joseph could heal and the lady would think it had been Antonio: "At some point when I'm doing the healing for her, I want you to come in. You'll bring some water in as if you're bringing it for me, and I'll ask you to apply it as if you're doing it under my supervision" (64).

The woman had had back problems for many years and was nearly paralyzed. Looking at her back, Joseph could see where the blood was flowing and not flowing. Afraid to be there, doing that, Joseph nevertheless applied water up and down her spine four times, as well as over to the spot where he could see the blockage. "She started trembling and jerking up and down. Grandfather was holding her down, and I was standing there afraid and not knowing what was going on. I thought maybe she was dying or maybe I did something wrong (65)."

> All of a sudden I saw light coming from her as if she was translucent. Right after she stopped shaking, she was in some kind of shock. She went from purple light to an almost translucent state. She opened her eyes and I could see they were full of amazement and surprise but, at the same time, of joy. She got up and she was well, healed on the spot.

Joseph asked Antonio if people were always healed in that manner. Antonio said that Joseph had a special healing gift. After that event, people came to Joseph to be healed and Joseph was guided to do so. Antonio thought that illness is not just the result of a cause, an accident, or because we don't eat or care for ourselves properly. For him, illness often occurs for a larger purpose, often impersonal. In the case of the lady, Joseph's first patient, she returned to Picuris when Joseph was eighteen, in 1953. She wanted to die at Picuris, the place where she had been healed.

> The people had a big feast for her. . . . The elders did a ceremony for three days because they said the particular illness that she was carrying was for some reality on the other side of the cosmos. They did that ceremony for her because she was connected to those people on the other side." (66)

Joseph's most profound early experiences occurred in kivas. In *Beautiful Painted Arrow: A Medicine Story* and *House*

84

of Shattering Light Joseph describes several long-term vision quests. In his first book he spends six weeks in a hole, a sacred chamber, when he is nine; in *House of Shattering Light*, when eight, he stays many days in his grandfather's kiva, performing a ceremony "done once every hundred years" (54). In both cases a holy woman or women bring him food, described in *House* as corn stew. In *Beautiful Painted Arrow* sounds (called subtle or inner sound in Asian mysticism) play a major role, notably a roaring waterfall, growing roots, and music. He also "smelled the perfume of other worlds. Then lights emerged from the dark silence. "Soft white light began to grow from the walls and touched me with a mist of magic feathers that moved in the song of silence. . . The light became so bright that I had to shield my eyes" (30). That is when a golden entity, an angel, communicated to him without words. "Other light beings gathered around." Soon the first angel was smoking a sacred pipe with sacred substances, and others were drumming and chanting.

Then he saw the medicine wheel map. Then he was initiated into the clan of the Thunder Callers by the fire of Father Sky. After this, yellow lights and a new set of beings entered to teach him. Then "red lights and small words came to teach me of the earth and the living understanding of all that is here" (33). Water came, trees sang, they all shared their "oneness in time," and he "knew how to honor all of beingness—the Plant, the Animal, the Mineral—and I became them all" (33). Finally, a blue-lighted being arrived, and he felt profound peace. They "traveled far and looked into sacred places of the earth travelers" before they were rejoined by yellow and red.

In *House of Shattering Light*, Joseph was fed by Spirit beings, lights, and vibrations, who "fed me physically" (55). He feels he was "part of a discourse with all the other powers of the four directions that make up the center of knowledge, the center of wisdom, the center of the circle. He was the center of the medicine wheel, surrounded by the directions of beings, lights, and vibrations. He heard extraordinary choruses of a kind he has never heard in perceptual reality, sometimes called the music or harmony of the spheres. Periodically, the sounds would reveal themselves as light, the choruses would become prisms that would dance about the kiva as angels. Joseph was "continually in a state of awe" (56). In both accounts Joseph does not want to leave when his grandfather comes to bring him back to consensus reality. In the chamber he was empowered, in awe, and peaceful.

Joseph continued to be trained by Pel-qui-weh and to experience non-consensus reality (spiritual magic) with Pel-Qui-Weh until the elder left his body in 1946 or 1947. Joseph has chronicled a few of these events in his books and related others in conversation. One involved his grandfather healing the boy's dislocated knee with ashes. Another miracle involved his grandfather's inviting him to say the rosary at Hispanic masses to which the medicine man had been invited. Painfully kneeling, he saw angels, created by the energy of prayer, flying around the church. Still another early miracle involved Pel-Qui-Weh's telling Joseph and other children to concentrate upon the kiva wall. Their collective concentration and Pel-Qui-Weh's power allowed the teacher to walk through the kiva wall. Though the season was winter, the medicine man walked into a summer meadow long enough to search for a healing herb before returning into the dark kiva.

Though the elder regularly transported Joseph and his contemporaries to the subtle/eternal world of energy, light, color, and vibration, in *Being and Vibration* we learn that Pel-Qui-Weh's greatest legacy to Joseph came though direction transmission. On this occasion, during summer, they slept in the kiva. Antonio built a fire, sang and prayed, then asked Joseph to lie beside him—back to back. This is because cold chi energy "goes out through the backs of our bodies. These are the tracks that we leave behind, physically as well as philosophically. . . . We leave behind our trail of moments for those who come behind us to resonate to" (44). A transference took place, initiated by brilliant flashing lights that emerged from his body.

> They were the different powers in ideas that were currently living in the village. They lived within us and in our relation-ships with other planets and stars. . . . There was a powerful

sense of wholeness or holiness in those lights because they were made of a sleeping dark night time that was planting lights on its dark fields. (45)

Joseph believes "that experience translated the sound vibration of the Tiwa language," which created in him "an awe of life" and the desire to investigate all languages (45).

Through that experience I came to understand that the earth has always been talking to us, but many of us have lost our sensitivities to sound and to vibration, so we do not hear her. Through sound she is telling us exactly what is going to happen next, but we haven't been able to hear her because we have lost our sensitivity to work as worship. We have forgotten how to listen to what our efforts have been saying. (46)

This is profound. We have moved from the center of the medicine wheel, far to the east, the direction of mind. The physical laziness engendered by modern life has had consequences far graver than obesity and laziness. We do not cultivate a respectful, loving relationship to Earth or our bodies. Instinct (intuition and emotion) atrophies, as does intuition; not only because we reject intuition as effeminate and soft, but because we don't make the effort necessary to break through the barriers that have come to separate gross/perceptual reality from subtle reality. Intuition is that bridge between subtle and gross, soul and body/mind, unconscious and conscious. When we do not move in beautiful, intuitive ways, the existing, all-living G-d, *Wa-Ma-Chi*, is not present within us.

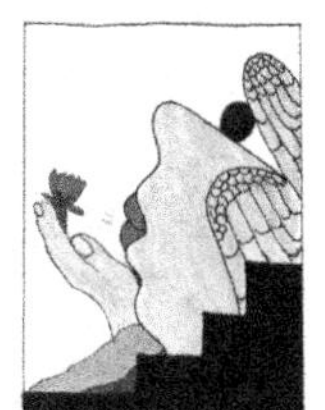

When Beatrice and Benito arrived, the family remained with Joseph's grandmother for about six months. Then the family moved to a small ranch owned by the Picuris, about three miles from the Pueblo, near the town of Shamisal. The Picuris called this land *Tol-Ke*, "Grace/Greatness Where Sun Meets Heavens." The Spanish called it Arroyita Del Agua, the Little Arroyo of Water. Here, the Raels flourished, raising horses, sheep, and chickens, and cultivating crops. Joseph relates the correspondence between the Picuris people and the Land, the Vast Self, in *Sound*:

> As we plowed and planted the land each spring, we were revitalizing and empowering ourselves. As we tended the crops, we were developing our own individual strengths. And as we harvested and prepared and ate the food, we were completing the cycle, taking into ourselves the energy we had poured into the growing and hunting and gathering of our food.
>
> . . . .
>
> The food that we harvested and that we ate was spiritual food for the sustenance of the Infinite Self. It encoded the essence of spiritual law. We were children of the soil and the soul was made up of all things remembered, all the plants and animals and people who had lived and eaten and planted there before us were part of the humus that produced the food we ate, and all our history and tradition was there in its vibrations.
>
> . . . .
>
> I learned by observing the rhythms of the land, paying attention to the early spring times and the birth of tiny new grass blades pointing through the fresh soul of the furrows just plowed. Every spring I grew in knowledge of the Divine Woman as I followed my father behind the horse-drawn plow. We plowed and we planted. In the dropping of the corn kernels we created the resonance of woman. So it was

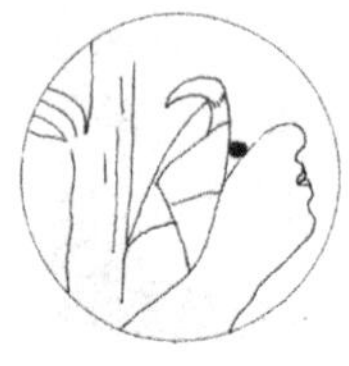

in each season; I learned by being part of something beyond myself, part of the rhythmic beauty of the ever-changing land. (5–7)

For the Picuris, and Pueblo in general, "As above, so below," attributed to the Thrice-Great Hermes, the mythical bringer of wisdom, is better stated, "As without, so within." This is not to say most Picuris experienced what Joseph did—we know from the Hopi story that worlds ended because fewer and fewer Hopi did. Only that their exquisite, difficult Way supported it and reminded them. Joseph was living dynamic Unity, ongoing revelation through which love, wisdom, and beauty accrued. Through which the Vast Self grew. Eden, however, was soon shattered.

Beatrice was ailing. She walked with difficulty. Her neck swelled. Doctors advised a goiter operation. Before she was taken to the hospital, Joseph experienced his next significant vision; he saw his beloved mother in a coffin. Because of this, he was afraid to say goodbye when the ambulance took her to Taos clinic two days later. An omission he has regretted for the rest of his life. He describes this tragedy and his long-term suffering in *House of Shattering Light*:

> . . . As she was getting into the ambulance, she called to me. My older brothers were at the door of the vehicle saying goodbye, but I hung back in silence. I was afraid that if I said goodbye to her she would really go, and that if she went, she would really die. I knew death was connected with her illness, because I had already seen her in the coffin. Because of this, I did not say goodbye.
>
> From the ambulance, she said, "My son doesn't love me any more, and he won't tell me goodbye," and she left. In that moment I knew that my mother was gone forever, and I was never going to see her in exactly the same way I had seen her. It was as if my whole world ended. (45)

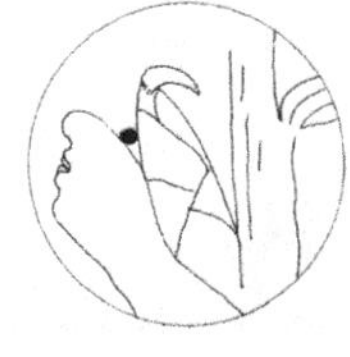

He saw her next as she had been in the vision. He had not gotten to express his love. He grieved doubly for many years, carrying the emotion in his lungs, making him susceptible to colds and allergies. Many years later a South American shaman released his pain in an ayahuasca ceremony. His mother's passing to the next world had many outward repercussions as well. The most dramatic was Albert's having to place the children with various Picuris relatives and foster families. He could not care for the ranch and the children alone.

Joseph was received by Lucia and Agapito Martinez, who had recently lost their adopted son, Filbert, in World War II. Joseph came to love them very deeply, considering them a second set of parents. Lucia was Jicarilla Apache, of the Sandoval family of Dulce, New Mexico. Agapito was Picuris, so they were a mixed-breed couple just like his own parents. As their only son, Joseph handled the horses, tended in the gardens, and worked with the entire village tilling, planting, and harvesting crops and performing ceremonies. Joseph, like all Picuris children, had many guides in all of these endeavors. Joseph has remarked that Lucia, whose name means "light," "the brightest star," gave him the capacity to become enlightened.

Also, her Apache relatives took Joseph into the sweat lodge purification, not native to the Pueblo peoples. Agapito, whose Tiwa name (Chu-quay-nay-nay) means "Where Eagles Perch," awakened in Joseph the power to pass through the gates of the four directions, where the cardinal powers 'variously called the four eagles, Grandfathers, or Chiefs' abide. Though Joseph came under the spiritual influence of Lucia and Agapito, and continued to be taught by his grandmother, as well as other elders, the passing on of his mother affected a deeper tutelage with his primary spiritual guide, Antonio. These two events drew Joseph more deeply into the Initiation stage of his quest.

90

INITIATION INTO THE GRID

While for most of us meeting a being like Joseph is an initiation, for Joseph confronting the strange white world was the major initiation of his life. As we have seen, Joseph was a natural mystic and visionary, who corrected his teachers at times, because the spiritual energy descending through him was eternal yet fresh, immediate and for time and space: a solution to the current problem. Though he made tremendous effort; effort came easy to him. He was a spiritual phenom, a prodigy.

In order for him to eventually fulfill his destiny of communicating primordial reality, wholesomeness, wholeness, and holiness to the white world, he had to know it. To experience the pain of its incompleteness and lopsidedness. Eventually, were he to emerge from the ignorance of the flat world, of mere perceptual reality, he could integrate the worlds—use his understanding of grid mentality to heal those ready to emerge from it. Though he struggled to think with his head as whites (and people made white), he would compensate by relying on his intuitive powers.

His immersion began in earnest when he was sent to a BIA Indian school in Albuquerque (though the representatives of the church had tried to indoctrinate him). These five or six years from 1947 to 1952 are skimmed in *Beautiful Painted Arrow: A Medicine Story* and *House of Shattering Light*. Though Joseph was always highly aware and intuitive, he accepted his sometimes harsh introduction to white life with innocence and gratitude. And when he returned to his family and extended Picuris family, he reverted to a more natural mode of living, continuing to receive subtle guidance from his beloved Pel-Qui-Weh. This contrast between environments, values, and approaches was eased when the federal government determined he should complete the last two years of high school at Penasco High, just off the Picuris reservation. Overall, his "school experiences took me into the white, Western world with its scientific mode of perception. Now and then, however, a mystical experience something like those of my early childhood would break into my everyday world" (*House* 88). To learn more details about his metaphoric departure from the natural/primordial and reverse initiation, please read his other books.

According to Joseph, his biggest shock in his early life, other than the death of his mother and guide, was his being told that he had to leave Picuris after graduating from Penasco High in 1954. This was because native tribes are matrilineal and that he, as an adult, officially belonged to his mother's tribe. And Joseph's older brother Fernando had returned there when he had come of age. Though Joseph had sometimes visited the Ute Reservation in the twelve or thirteen years since his departure and some of his mother's relatives still lived there, it was not a warm, nurturing environment. This was mostly because Joseph was an outsider, a half-breed. Being so, he experienced discrimination—as he had in the white world. It was also because the Utes had suffered more degradation than the Picuris, and more recently. Fewer of the Utes survived the late nineteenth-century wars of extermination that followed silver and gold fever. And those that survived were forced out of their beloved mountains, now called the Colorado Rockies, onto two small strips of land in Southern Colorado.

In addition, the cultural wars against the Ute had been more successful. For the most part, until World War II, the Pueblo assimilated Catholicism into their spiritual life and practice and continued some of their ceremonies despite being forbidden to do so. The Utes were not as fortunate. Their spiritual practice had been curtailed. More than the Pueblo, the Ute of the mid-twentieth century were more dependent on the irresponsible and malicious federal government; displaced, they were no longer able to live in the old manner. More importantly, they had been convinced of their worthlessness. They despaired. They hated themselves. When an imperialist power, an authority, or even a parent convinces us of our worthlessness, to hate ourselves, they have defeated us. Of course, the white government(s) had learned centuries before that they could manipulate natives, who had never brewed liquor, with firewater. Joseph would not be immune to this form of murder and suicide.

Joseph describes his journey from Picuris to Ignacio in *Beautiful Painted Arrow: A Medicine Story*. The book also describes Joseph's encounter with two beneficent elders who remembered his mother and her spiritual proclivities. Within a year of arriving in Ignacio, Joseph married Patricia Lucero. Patricia had been engaged to Joseph's older brother, Fernando, who had joined the military. Joseph, who had seen and been attracted to Patricia on previous visits, happily married her and adopted Fernando and Patricia's child. Through family contacts, Joseph found work in construction, landscaping, and plumbing. Though his and Patricia's first child died shortly after birth, she gave birth to five more children. Aside from providing for his growing family, Joseph helped other relatives through various financial crises. He was also, however, becoming an alcoholic, falling into the pattern of many Western males, who are challenged in their capacity to "hold their liquor." Who self-medicate to mask the pervasive insanity/disease wrought by materialism, capitalism, repression, prejudice, rootlessness, and overall imbalance.

He only records his alcoholism in his first book, in the chapter entitled, Walking on the Shadow Path. There he wrote that "drinking had helped me to turn away from the challenge that my quest had given me, and my feelings of loneliness had grown into a painful monster" (107). Feeling despair at being trapped, I drank more and more to rid myself of the painful gnawing that was growing from a soul demanding to be set free" (107). He had been thrust (Departure) from a condition of relative enlightenment and bliss into the darkness of ordinary consciousness to confront his and his society's demons. He had become one of Blake's innocent children dying under the effects of Experience. He was, as Campbell would say, experiencing the Belly of the Whale, the crisis of Initiation. Appropriately and poetically, Joseph was working as a caretaker in a cemetery.

Joseph was trying to forget Spirit, but Spirit would not permit this. In 1961, he experienced one of his best-known visions. Constructing a home in Bayfield, he was caught in a gas explosion. He was thrown some fifty feet and landed with his legs bent backwards beneath him. The Virgin Mary appeared to him saying that he would be healed (and heal others) despite having horrific injuries. Though he writes about the vision in *House,* in an almost off-handed manner, he does not reveal that before the Virgin of Guadalupe appeared, arrayed in turquoise, another woman appeared, Earth Mother. Brown, squat, round, this female archangel and embodiment of the Earth presence,

The Below, watched over him—before changing form into Mary.

Not totally giving in to his demons, Joseph (Chewaa) took spiritual direction, participated in the Sun Dance for four consecutive years—experiencing terrifying visions in three of them—and endured an operation to remove cancer. Yet his alcoholism persisted. Until, one day when coming out of a bar, he was confronted by one of Te's/Antonio's former apprentices who had since become "a most powerful medicine woman" (118). She functioned in the archetype of what Campbell calls the "herald," a being who summons one to spiritual heroism. She said that "Te's spirit-rising-time was near and he had sent forth a call for me to come. 'You must go now, she said.'" (118). The call of his spiritual teacher, whom Jung refers to as the Wise Old Man or masculine initiator, who awakens, in Joseph's case, re-awakens, the Self, the soul. The *nah*.

Joseph's journey back to the mountain, the pinnacle of consciousness, the Center of the medicine wheel, is chronicled in the beginning of *Beautiful Painted Arrow: A Medicine Story*. Pel-Qui-Weh was physically dead; his spirit had risen some seventeen years before. Nevertheless, he had the capacity to contact Joseph, to whom he had transmitted his spiritual legacy, just as he had done in the years immediately after his departure, while Joseph had been in school. If Joseph did not make the journey with his physical body, he made it as his *nah*. Or he journeyed interiorly to the presence, the energy of his teacher within himself. However it occurred, and it may have occurred in all three ways, Joseph was transformed, shocked from his despair and spiritual paralysis. He had defeated the inner demons, emerged from the shadow.

94

The mountain is the site where so many prophets and mystics have encountered the Divine, the Oversoul, the Godhead, the Great Spirit, the Dharmakaya, Intelligence, the Goddess of the World, the Father—supreme consciousness in a guise for every consciousness. It is also a place, a state of consciousness in which some have stayed, preferring isolation to society. In the venerable Hindu and Buddhist traditions such beings are called *arhats*. In addition, Buddhists contrast *arhats* with bodhisattvas, those who sacrifice the solitude of nirvana and develop *bodhicitta,* the wisdom/compassion that benefits all sentient beings.

Campbell calls this acme of Initiation, the pinnacle of mountain consciousness (Keter), Apotheosis (*The Hero with a Thousand Faces* 149–52). And Campbell uses the Bodhisattva ("whose being is the essence of enlightenment") Avalokitesvara as the "pattern of the divine state to which the human hero attains who has gone beyond the last terrors of ignorance." More importantly, Avalokiteshvara is "The Lord Looking Down in Pity," the one who descends the mountain out of love of those who suffer. Coming down from his mountain, being invested with new life, Joseph took up the reins of Initiation.

Convinced of his destiny to help others, Joseph became involved in the healing of the Ute people. (His mother had been a healer). This is the stage Campbell calls Return, the coming back to ordinary life and consciousness to share with other suffering beings. He worked on community action programs. He developed federal grants to offer educational and vocational opportunities, advocated for urban housing, and represented the poor. As a result of his astute and indefatigable advocacy of his people, as well as those of other tribes, he was chosen to represent the Ute people in state and federal commissions and negotiations. Joseph was so competent and trustworthy that he was engaged by other tribes, eventually representing both the Pueblo and Apache tribes. It soon became clear that he needed more white education in order to more effectively advocate for all native peoples. While he was doing this, a parallel quest inspired him: to meet all the mystics, all the illuminated souls, in and out of perceptual reality.

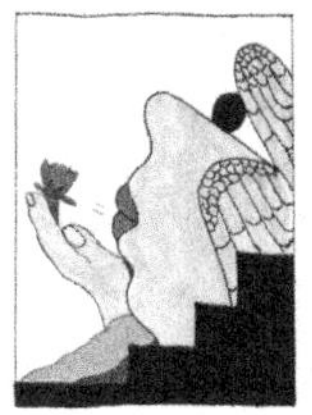

So, with the support of his two tribes, as well as the various government agencies with whom he had been working, Joseph attended the University of New Mexico in 1968. In six years, all the while working for the tribes and the state government and supporting his family who had come with him, Joseph graduated. Joseph's marriage with Patricia ended. Joseph remarried, completed a Master's degree at the University of Wisconsin, married for the third and last time, and began approximately five years of governmental service that ended when he had the vision of the map in 1981. One little-known event in Joseph's life involves his encounter with a distant relative from San Idelfonso Pueblo. When Joseph had been en route to Albuquerque to begin his B.A., he had met this medicine man related to his father. This elder asked Joseph where he was going. Joseph said he was going to college. The sage said, "Why don't you sit here and study with me." Joseph graciously declined. However, eight years later when Joseph had earned his M.A., he remembered, sought out the sage, and sat beside him (Personal Communication 2002).

Visioning in Kauii

In 1978, before he dedicated himself to teaching the rainbow tribe full-time, Joseph vacationed in Hawaii, ever vigilant to meet this world's living mystics. On the island of Kauii he found an underground bunker built during World War II. Being reminded of kivas of his youth, he spent four days in the kiva, without food, water, and thought. He made a vision quest. The intent of his quest was to "look for G-d."

After a couple days, Joseph found himself (his *nah*) traveling very fast through a tube of light on a kind of sled. He realized he was passing through the infinite ten worlds:

> I passed a lot of universes along the way. At the threshold of the first subtle world, galaxy, or universe, I was stopped by two guards who looked at me funny—I was dressed like a tourist—asked me what I wanted. I told them that I was looking for God. They looked at each other and laughed, and finally they told me to go ahead because the next guards would surely stop me. When I got to the next gate, I slowed down. There were two guys there again. They asked me who I was and what I wanted. I said I was looking for God and they said, "Just go ahead and let him through anyway because they won't let him through at the main gate any-way." When I got to the main gate, nobody was there, so I

went right through because I was looking for God. The next thing I knew, I felt a loud pop and I came back through my crown, into my body. And my reaction was, "Ah gee, this is no fun." I had all these expectations of some giant mother/father being of the awesome beauty and power of sunsets and mountains. There is just us. (Personal Communication, June 2001)

This realization is common among mystics who experience the full range of beingness. (Blake: "Men forgot that all deities reside in the human breast.") It corresponds to what some call Christ consciousness ("The Father and I are one"). Though Joseph points out that his experiences are not bound by religion. The Sanskrit phrase that denotes this realization is *Aum* (primordial vibration) *hamsa, so ham Aum*: "It is I; I am It." And Moses (whom Joseph met in his subtle journeys through the worlds) conveyed this supreme identity in a similar way. When he communed with El, the Great Mystery atop Sinai (pinnacle of consciousness), he asked Beingness how It should be called, how the people could refer to It. Beingness identified Itself as Ehyeh ("I am") and Ehyeh Asher Ehyeh ("I am that I am"). The existence of one primordial consciousness accords with Joseph's teaching (echoed in all his workshops and mystery schools) that "We don't exist." Only the Vast Self, immanent in and as all, exists.

Before ending his retreat, Joseph had another vision. Like his better-known vision of the mermen, it involved ocean. Joseph saw a vast balloon emerge from the ocean. Suddenly, the scene shifted, and Joseph saw the same balloon or a similar balloon at the bottom of the ocean. Instantly, he understood that this is how we would exist in the future, in cities constructed within bubbles, at the bottom of the ocean. He saw people among the skyscrapers, transporting themselves through the air with powered backpacks (Personal Communication, June 2001).

97

Throughout his life, Joseph, like William Blake, has communicated with those who had once existed in the body. Sometimes they have been what we would call ghosts, lost souls, who have not entered the luminous part of the subtle world that we call heaven and wander what is sometimes called the astral or lower astral plane (related to Yesod, Netzach, Hod). Sometimes these unevolved beings possess other beings, such as the woman brought by her family to be healed by Te, who cast them out. Often times they have been luminous beings, such as Joseph before he had incarnated into perceptual reality. And often times they have been illuminated beings, bodhisattvas who remain available to guide humans. All these beings would be considered subtle. As we have seen, after Antonio, Pel-qui-weh, had left his body, he continued to teach Joseph. *House* indicates that elders and teachers who had died were often present when Joseph was "doing a ceremony and . . . couldn't remember something" (42). Sometimes he would recognize them and ask them for help. Most times he would have to use his intuition. Obviously, the subtle realm is broad and contains many realms or worlds within itself.

In *House* Joseph recounts his meeting with the ghosts at Picuris where he was building a holistic health center, in 1981. Joseph had transported some Vista volunteers out to the pueblo for an adobe-making workshop. During the workshop, he heard two Hispanic males laughing at one of the volunteers. Joseph "noticed that my brain was vibrating at a higher frequency than normal, that it felt ticklish." The men who were laughing at the girl "kept fading in and out of my vision, so I realized that they must be ghosts. I closed my eyes and asked inwardly, 'Who are these two souls' and I heard one of the voices saying, 'At last, someone has seen us' (112).

Joseph realized "they probably didn't know they were dead, or if they did, they didn't know how to get out of here." So Joseph attempted to reconnect with their dilemma, and "the only thing

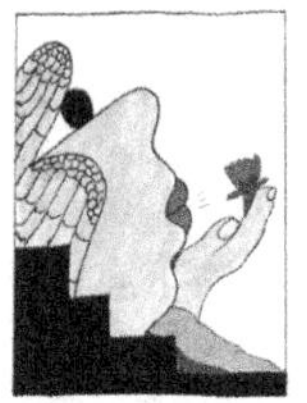

I got was the image of a car turning over about three miles from [Picuris], from where the road curved toward Penasco. Two Hispanic boys were in it, and it was a blue car." Consequently, Joseph drove over to the area he had seen in inner vision, found a few houses, and asked the inhabitants if two boys had died there in the late forties. "They said, 'Yeah there were two young boys. They were driving too fast and they turned over and they got killed." Realizing that their spirits were confused, he drove back to Picuris. "I took a match and said to them, 'When this match is lit the curtain will open and the energy will come and take you.' I lit the match, and when I did, I could almost hear the wind, as they went through into the spirit world" (113).

Joseph experienced another sort of communion with the dead when he was working at the Santa Fe Indian Hospital, in the early eighties. A medical anthropologist from New Jersey came to the hospital to carry out Ph.D. studies. "She wanted to show in some way that Indians were actually drawing from the spiritual realm." Ironically, she thought that Joseph, who been active in art, was lying about his spiritual influences and inspiration. "She got upset with me because she thought I was either making it up or just trying to agree with her" (*House* 159).

> As we spoke, my body started getting hotter and hotter and hotter, and I knew I was in trouble because when that happens, the power of the supernatural comes through. . . . It's a presence that has a hard time staying in my body, as if it's vibrating at fifty megacycles to my twenty-five, vibrating in every single cell in my body. This presence came into me during the interview with that lady. My face began changing, and I became a woman, a grandmother. I could see my face because I also became another being right there where she was standing. The anthropologist stared at me; her eyes kept getting bigger. I spoke to her, or rather the presence did, and it turned out it was her aunt who had died about five years ago. The presence said something like, "You don't believe anything, do you? You don't even believe your auntie over here." (159-160)

Joseph experienced everything as his body became less charged, and his regular vibration returned. Joseph's friend, a Vista worker who had been working with the visitor and experienced the entire exchange and change, said to the researcher, "You went to all the Indian reservations and you talked to all the Indian artists. The last person you came to see had what you were looking for all the time" (160). In this case Joseph acted as a medium to affect a healing between the woman and her aunt, as well as the woman's interior conflict between her mental and emotional natures.

Another experience, also related in *House*, occurred before this when Joseph was in Bernalillo with Ruth. He and Ruth had gone to visit the body of Carmelita, his father's sister, in the Hood Mortuary in Durango. "While I was there, I took an eagle feather and laid it across her hands. The instant I did this, one of the candles near her coffin popped and caught the rug in front of the coffin on fire" (162). Putting out the fire, Joseph recognized that Carmelita was enjoying herself. When he went to the church for the funeral mass the following day, he saw Carmelita and her son, Faustin Tucson, hovering above. Carmelita told him telepathically, "We're all right. We're fine. We're leaving now" (163).

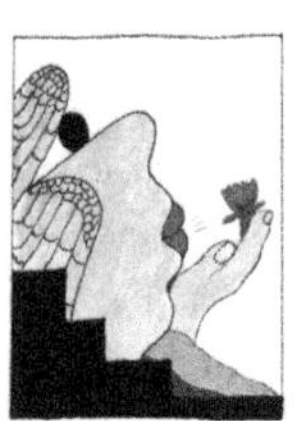

Some time afterward, he attended the rosary for his foster mother, Lucia. Uncomfortable "because I had resisted saying goodbye to my mother when she died" and fidgeting in the pews, he "saw white light coming from the heads of all of these people." Looking up in front of himself, he saw Lucia and Agapito, holding hands. After communicating telepathically that they were well, they floated over the heads of the people. Joseph closed his eyes and saw them traveling south until they came to a mountain where the "Picuris teachings say that Picuris people go after they die." When they got to the mountain, "the side of the mountain opened up, and I could see some of the people from Picuris who had died years before. . . . All these people met my foster parents. They went through the tunnel to the Other Side, and it closed and I saw just the mountain there" (164).

As mentioned, Joseph often met dead friends and relatives

when he sun danced. Sun dancing on the Ute Reservation in 1983, he met a childhood friend who had died in 1979. Having danced for two days without food or water, Joseph was resting in his sleeping bag. Suddenly he felt a presence on his left. He looked over and saw George Durand. Forgetting that George had died, Joseph asked him why he was there. George said, "Well, I'm here. I'm just keeping you company because I know you are going through a hard time." Joseph replied that he was struggling without food or water. Then George said he was taking Joseph somewhere to have some food. Joseph relates that he "left my physical body and in my etheric body I went with him," across the dance ground into another dimension (165).

There "on a long table were all kinds of fruits, watermelons, and an abundance of food." Joseph asked why George had done this, and George replied, "Well, because when you sit down to eat, you always feed us symbolically in your prayers. You have never forgotten to pray for the dead." Joseph ate, and then he returned to his body lying inside the dance circle. "For the next day or so, my body functioned as if I had eaten a big meal" (165).

He saw George again, during another sun dance. This time George and other Picuris people were "standing in a field with hoes. . . . But they were not planting corn or peas or beans as they used to do. . . . They were seeding new eternities, planting other realities." Among the people of his pueblo was his mother. This is the first time he talked to her, communicated with her since envisioning her in the coffin. She was young. She recognized him. He only recalls telling her how much he missed her. In the same sun dance, but in a later scene, Joseph saw his father with Carmelita, his sister. "They were going from one building to the next. They were basically ignoring me because they were onto something. They were aware of his presence there, but they didn't stop to talk to me because they were involved in a different reality," one parallel to this one (166). Perhaps all of his deceased friends and relatives were cultivating the same stone in the cosmological map.

A few pages later, he also tells of communicating with Lorencita Simbola, his sister-in-law. After she died, Joseph put a candle in the sound chamber and was outside hanging clothes, when he felt her presence. He could clearly hear her thoughts saying, "I was a diabetic because that was the way I was purifying myself. That was what I needed. Now I am free, and I don't have to come back here to do this over again. I'm free." When she told him that, "there was gold light everywhere." Referring to the golden light that lasted a few more minutes, she said, "That's what it's like here. It's really beautiful, and I don't hurt any more" (170).

These encounters don't include Joseph's many communications with the departed in dream time. (Joseph said recently that at a certain point he asked not to receive visions during dreams—because he tended to forget them. He also said that he may have developed the ability to travel to the other side in order to say goodbye to his mother.) In this chapter, Joseph also sums up his understanding of inter-dimensional communication and simultaneous realities, referring indirectly to his story of the ten/infinite stones:

> Apparently, when we die, we are no longer physically here, but we are here; we're just not in the same form. In fact, we're not perceivable as we perceive the material plane, but other than that, apparently, we are still here.
>
> I think maybe you and I are already there in those other realms as well. We exist simultaneously in this physical, perceptual realm and in other realities. Right now we are in these physical forms which bring together several realms. One realm is just the fingernail archetype. One is just the skin archetype or reality. Here we have a combination. We have the fingernails, skin, hands, a heart. All those are separate realities. Here in this reality they are all put together.
>
> It's not that those other realities are less complete than this one, it's just that they're each doing their own thing. They're holding themselves. They're totally complete in themselves. Over here, we get to wear the whole suit. In other words, if I am an eye and I am in that other reality, I know all the other parts, but I am just experiencing that one part.
>
> I am held in the pattern of being an eye, but in some place, there is still a form of me—my emotional body, my

spiritual body, my energistic body—that is simultaneously here but also in a finer vibrational form connected to, I hope, the other beings who have a finer vibration. (168–69)

Joseph continues to explain that we, the various aspects of the body, do not exist—do not exist as we think we exist. Though we perceive ourselves as limited in time/space, "[we] have a finer vibrational form than that of this reality." We are limited, limited to the last stone, by our limited perceptions. "So, since we don't exist, we appear and disappear, not only in this realm but in all the other realms" (169). We are the strobe light of G-d's breath, emerging from and returning to the infinite darkness, passing through the infinite worlds on Its journey.

Visioning in Bernalillo: Meeting Jesus

In 1979 Joseph was still working for the Office of Indian Affairs in Santa Fe and living in Bernalillo, the site of many healings and visions. One day, while in the office, Joseph was visited by a German man, whose name Joseph doesn't remember—if he was told. The man, a member of a German secret society (perhaps Rosicrucianism or Anthroposophy) delivered a message. He said that his society had prophesized that an Amerindian named Joseph would significantly contribute to world peace. Joseph had seen images of his future work on several occasions, but he had yet to receive explicit directions to link the images. The visit was an omen, for, several years later, Joseph found himself in Germany. Uneasy about traveling on the trains, he was assisted by angels, disguised as middle-aged men who loaded and unloaded his baggage at various stations. The angels rendered supernatural aid, then disappeared.

During the winter Joseph had one of his most profound visions encounters and travels, one that he has not recorded elsewhere. While Joseph was meditating, Jesus appeared and asked Joseph to travel with him to the underworld. Joseph said, "I don't like to go to the underworld; there are too many demons there." Apparently, Joseph did not have a choice. He found himself gliding through worlds of light, as he had done in Kauii. But this time he was traveling to dimensions of less light rather than more. They "stopped in a dim place where demons were rolled up in balls having orgies. Where there was a lot of fecal matter and a stench."

He heard a voice say, "Bow to my messenger." And two little demons bowed to Jesus who stood beside Joseph. "Jesus said all of these people are stuck." Joseph saw "animals who looked like cows but had a heavy coat like a rhinoceros." Jesus then directed Joseph to pick up a stick in the path. "Take this stick and tap these beings there (pointing to the back of their necks) because there are souls stuck in there, and you have to free them."

When Joseph tapped one, light rose up from its neck and out the top of his head. Jesus told Joseph to "keep doing this." He turned around, but Jesus had left him standing there, holding the stick in the underworld, and Joseph had a vision within a vision:

> In a timeless instant I saw all the details of the sun-moon dance, long dance, and drum dance. In the sun-moon dance we dance back and forth to the pole, which is the stick; in the drum dance we dance back and forth to a feather; and in the long dance, we dance from dusk to dawn without stopping—if possible. I've never told this in my books because I don't want people to associate this vision with a religion. This is not a Christian vision. This is not what I'm about. I come from the light. All my visions are principle ideas, metaphors. They show the Divine Presence is unfolding in all these activities. In the sun-moon dance the dancers hit the pole in the center. The pole is the stick that releases souls. But it's really the stick that hits the dancers. When I go to another reality, someone always takes me. (Personal Communication, June 2001)

Meeting Jesus and receiving the stick and the dances was yet another instance of the hero's receiving the Ultimate Boon.

Toward the end of his tenure with the Indian Health Service in Santa Fe , Joseph had less dramatic, more impersonal glimpses of the future. In some ways similar to Hildegard's Twelfth Vision of the Third Part of *Scivias*, one involved the end of time. Joseph describes it in this way:

> At the end of the world, there's going to be a building, a round building, and everything's getting dark—it's not completely dark. The clouds are low.
>
> This chamber is out there in a flat landscape, like a prairie. And there's a house there. And people are dropping their implements, like their hoes and picks, and everything—symbolic of the fact that they're going to stop everything they're doing, all work, all activity. And they get into this line. And there's going to be lightning and thunder. It's more like lightning and rolling thunder, with lots of roaring going on and the people are getting in line and going toward that light. When they walk into the light, they disappear, and they do not return. And that's the end of time. I don't know when it will happen. It may take two or three billion years, or trillions of years. (Personal Communication, June 2001)

Impersonally, the vision portrays the end of Earthly time, as well as the end of a single life when we stop working, and our internal energies orient themselves to the primordial light, which we become. Or it can portray a single moment—when thoughts stop and surrender to the clear, very subtle light of pure consciousness. At that moment time stops as we leave perceptual reality. From that transformative instant, that resurrection, we become primordial light, whether we continue to live a physical life or not.

This vision also contains many symbols of what Jung, and spiritual alchemists, refer to as the reconciliation of opposites: Earth and sky, male and female, left and right sides of the brain and body, conscious and unconscious minds. Sky descends upon the Earth. Light emerges from the Darkness. The flat plain contains a round chamber (female/natives) and a square building (male/moderns). True resurrection of energy/light/consciousness only happens when inner duality has been overcome, when the inner woman and man, representing all duality, experience tantric marriage. This is the stage Tiwa refer to as *key-aah-ta-meh-nay*, Mother-Fatherness, which theoretically occurs at fifty-five. When/if we become Mother-Father, when the microcosm (the elements within) is in harmony we can finally come to peace with the macrocosm (the elements without).

The second significant vision, more personal, occurred in his Santa Fe office. This is the aforementioned vision of the map, described in *House*. The map showed "ten or fifteen different scenarios playing out simultaneously. I absorbed the meaning of all of them in depth through one flash of light, replete with information." The map was alive with "problems in this Indian and non-Indian world" (107). The scenarios and ideas of the map flowed into him until he "became the map." Images were triggered, images of what he would be doing in the next ten or fifteen years. Then, however, he had another problem, he had to simplify and decode the impressions into perceptual reality. Once he did that, the next stage of Return, of sharing with humanity, could unfold.

Sun Dancing to Long Dancing

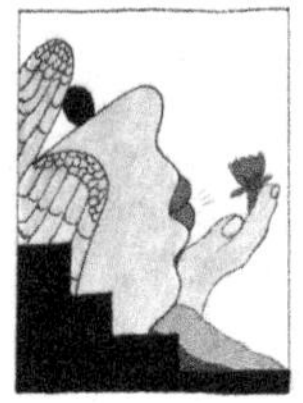

We've seen that many of Joseph's visions occurred while he ceremonially danced. He danced as a boy in Picuris, and he sun danced as an adult, with the Southern Utes as well the Lakota. While dance, like all the arts, has a sacred origin in European culture, in a time before sacred and secular were divorced, Westerners usually regard it as art or diversion (though this dualistic notion has begun to change—evidenced by the inclusion of dance by some mainstream Christian churches). In Amerindian cultures, however, dancing is not only integral; it is essential to individual and tribal growth. And the ceremonies were not circumscribed by tribal consciousness. Amerindians often danced for all sentient beings. Joseph relates that the

Pueblo sometimes danced for the planet and its powers, the archangelic, even for the solar system and galaxy. "Every dance, every ceremony, is both for you and for the cosmos" (*Sound* 59). The multi-dimensional effects of human dance will be more tangible later, when we have discussed his most recent vision.

In *Sound* he describes one of his many sun dance visions (across from his painting "Dance Chief calling the Sun-Moon People from the Spirit World to come and Dance"), a vision that revealed the creation of the medicine wheel and cornerstoned the dances he was to create for Indians and non-Indians alike:

> While sun dancing I had a vision of how God created all that is. I saw a light appear and then it radiated out in an instant, at the speed of light. The sun dance pole, made from a tree, was that point of light, that center from which the circle of light flashed out. When it flashed out, it connected with the mental, emotional, spiritual and physical parts of my being. We humans have four parts. We are emotional, we are mental, we are physical and we are spiritual. And those are the same parts that make up the medicine wheel.
>
> The flash went out from the One and then it came back into the One and disappeared. In that time, that instant, I knew a lot of information. All that information came as that point of light flashed outward. I saw that as a circle of light. There was no circle until the light went outward from that center point. As it expanded it created the circle. And then the periphery disappeared and the light came back in.
>
> When the light went out, it was being pushed out by space. And when it was coming back, time was pulling it back to the center. In another split of a split of a split of a second it would go back out again in the same process.
>
> That is how life is occurring.
>
> We dance in order to expand the potential for something to happen. It works because the word for dance is *pu-leh,* and that vibration contains the powers we need. (55)

Understanding dance to be the perfect enactment of *Wa-Ma-Chi,* (breath-matter-movement) of the cosmic interplay of Brahma (creating), Vishnu (sustaining), and Shiva (destroying), and of the paradox of our being simultaneously formed and formless, he longed for an authentic yet new way to share it. In 1980, after the vision of Jesus and the stick, Joseph started the first of the three dances he led regularly for almost twenty years, the Long Dance. In the long dance, dancers dance in a circle throughout the night. For half of the night they dance clockwise (sun-wise), and then they dance counterclockwise (moon-wise) for the rest of the night. These movements, male and female respectively, create the medicine wheel. According to Joseph, once the dormant male energy is awakened by the descending feminine energy, it becomes mental energy and moves clockwise, to the south, west, and north. Upon reaching the north, it spirals upward and lifts. Simultaneously, some of the energy, feminine energy, moves counter-clockwise, and is also lifted. Together, "the spiraling energies form a double helix that lifts. Now the All-that-is can express a higher purpose, a fuller awareness," "a higher consciousness" (*Sound* 103). The long dance, then, also quickens our medicine wheel.

"The long dance is performed at night because the night light is symbolically the 'blackness' or black matter, and the long dancer is the symbol of the 'blowing' (moving) aspect of blowing darkness." As they dance, they blow "in the dark blackness of the nighttime light. . . . Matter is black light that has been changed into white light so it can be seen as lighted stars or as materialized forms on this planet" (*Sound* 112). So, dancing throughout the night until the dawn, dancers awaken the black light of their own nothingness, as well as the white light of their thingness, which the white light becomes during exhalation.

In 1986, six years after starting the long dance, Joseph created the drum dance in response to an undated earlier vision he describes in *Being and Vibration*. "Men and women dancers were moving rhythmically back and forth on an open field from inside a giant drum that was being played. The dancers were moving forward and backward" from the present, to the future, to memory, the past. The drum was fashioned from a hollow log. And "the people who were playing the drum said that when doing a drum dance, the dancers would bring forth greatness

because the wood is greatness." Bouncing back and forth like
the sound waves inside the drum, the dancers could feed the
entire planet with fine vibration. After fasting and dancing for
three days, "a golden plate forms over the heads of the dancers
and another plate" forms beneath their feet. Intermittently,
golden light spirals upward from the lower plate, "connecting
Earth energy with sky energy," "where it becomes a ring of light
that spreads around the Earth" (165–67). This risen light then
descends as part of the rain, which nourishes life and enters the
food chain.

A year later Joseph initiated the sun-moon dances. Of the
three dances, the sun-moon dance is most like the sun dance.
Participants fast and dance for parts of four days. As in the sun
dance, they dance in a corral, under an arbor, dancing to and
from the center pole, the stick, the tree of life. The corral is the
medicine wheel, the picture of the universe, the seven Powers,
(the six Powers, plus the Center) from the perspective of this
stone. With the middle of the pole being the Center, the top of
the pole being Grandfather Sky, the bottom of the pole (under
the surface) being Grandmother Earth, and East, South, West,
and North being the remaining four (Directions, or caryatidal
kings, as Campbell would say). Each of the dancers moves from a
given spot on the perimeter, symbolic of our each starting life in
a certain Direction, under the primary influence of a Power, also
our primary part or function.

Fighting the influence of time, which would keep us in
duality, in our personal selves, the dancers move to the Center,
the One, Kether, Unity, the first stone they missed. As they drive
their bodies back and forth, blowing bone whistles, symbolically
never turning their backs to the Center, they become the
original, always first, flash of radiance Joseph experienced in
his sun dance vision. The flash that pulses from the empty
Uncreated Void, creates the Directions and the circumference
and then bounces back, returns, healing the multiplicity it
just created. At a certain point, not willfully determined, the
dancers, pulled inward, hit the pole, often falling, sometimes
experiencing visions. Hitting and falling represent surrender

109

of the personal, egocentric will to the Overwill, the Vast Self. Enacting another aspect of the Lord's Prayer: "Thy will be done." To experience this more completely, consult Joseph's painting, to which I've already referred, on page 54 of *Sound*.

LONG DANCING: VISIONING THE PEACE CHAMBER

Spirit persisted in unfolding Joseph's destiny as an agent of peace for forty-one years. At first subtle, the messages became more explicit. As we noted, Joseph had first envisioned the sound chambers at seven years old, in Picuris. Then, in 1942, he had just moved to Picuris. In dreaming, or existing as Nah, he saw the smiling grandmother, standing like an ecstatic mother hen in front of seven small, elliptical music houses. Next the chambers were one of the ten or fifteen scenarios he saw as the map in his Santa Fe office. During these years, he "had been through a period . . . of semi-madness in which I had a profound urge to move completely into a spiritual realm." He also recognized that this madness was associated with his need, his destiny, to "bring about a more spiritualized reality" (*House of Shattering Light* 130). The extraordinary energy that was infusing him needed to be shared and given form.

As he relates in *House of Shattering Light*, in the summer of 1981, shortly after receiving his vision of the map on his office wall, he walked in pilgrimage eighty miles to Chimayo, a recurrent ritual in his life. Walking, a way of plowing and planting, of becoming planted, is very important for Joseph. It became for the man what running had been for the boy. This planting of presence is evident in the meaning of its sounds: *ta-chi-who*; Life, walking/plowing, carries the presence of the Great Mystery. Walking is planting because, as Joseph explains, when we walk our energy field, our magnetic body, descends a foot or two into the earth, depending on one's physical magnetism. In other words, Life is unfolding/becoming/enacting the Vast Self. The walk gave the map a linear, sequential feel. He still, however, did not understand his relation to the chambers.

Spirit needed to act more dramatically. In 1983 while leading in a long dance on his land on the Ute reservation of his birth, Joseph understood more. In *Being and Vibration* he writes that the vision lasted only two or three seconds in perceptual reality time, so he had to slow it down and go back into the vision. He envisioned a luminous being of the subtle realm who then vanished, leaving a chamber, like the ones he had envisioned as a child, as well as on the map:

> I was shown people praying (directing our faith) and sing-ing (bonding our faith with the present) together in a sacred sound chamber resonating with light. The chamber was an oval structure of mud (matter carrying direction) and straw (ancient knowledge), partly underground (underworld) and partly above ground (middle world). It was a house of the sound of presentness, a structure built to reverberate sound. The melodious chanting of men (essence of expanding light) and women (essence of descending light) were a reflection of people whose spirits and voices resonated in absolute harmo-ny to balance the present, the future and the memory of how the cosmos is oriented through the use of sound. (148–49)

The luminous chamber had been created by the "mirth of the yellow people." It was an Edenic microcosm of love, harmony, and beauty, of absolute balance between man and woman, inside and outside, day and night, conscious and unconscious.

This was Joseph's third vision of the peace chamber. At first he treated the vision as a metaphor rather than a physical structure to be built outside of one's being. However, contemplating the vision, he realized that this was a collective, impersonal vision, something he needed to manifest for and with others. In *House* he describes his realization this way:

> Somehow the Vast Self was involved in the sound chamber, not just the individual self. I already knew that what we rec-ognized as the personal self is but an echo of the Vast Self, which is the eternal Self. Somehow I knew that the sound chamber had something to do with how the eternal self was involving all of our lives holistically, and that sound is another form of holism that is an ingredient of our physi-

cal well-being, our planetary well-being, our environmental well-being. (130)

In 1983 he had already begun to teach outside of New Mexico. Traveling in Europe and the United States, he pondered the metaphor; he sought the right place, holy ground, to build the first chamber. This proved to be a misinterpretation. The universe needed to remind him that every place was holy, the center of the universe, Campbell's world navel. And that the chambers were divine seeds that would enhance Earth's inherent sacredness.

Vast Self reminded him when he returned to Bernalillo. During an evening sweat lodge in his backyard (the sweat lodge is the purifying void which awakens clarity), he had another vision. This one, however, was not subtle; it was a directive. In the vision, he ascended in his *nah,* his subtle body of light. His ascent was immediate: from Earth to 'heaven.' To better appreciate Joseph's vision and ascent, one should know of Black Elk's Great vision, in which Black Elk, like Joseph, was taken up to a council of elders and given a directive.

Black Elk, who had been hearing distinct voices since he was five, was nine at the time, camped near the Little Big Horn River. A voice said, "It is time; now they are calling you." First his legs hurt, then he couldn't walk, and then be became ill, very badly swollen. Two men came down, slanting down from the clouds, headfirst like arrows. They told him that the Grandfathers were calling him and left, slanting upward. Without pain, Black Elk followed and climbed upon a small cloud that had descended for him, then carried him to the white world of clouds and thunder beings. After being introduced to forty-eight horses, twelve in each direction, the spokesperson, a bay horse, told him his "Grandfathers were having a council." A massive cloud changed into a tepee, and inside sat six men who "looked older than men can ever be—old like the hills, like stars" (Neihardt 18–21). These old men, the "Powers of the world," each initiated him with a spiritual gift, what is called in Sanskrit a 'siddhi.' (This reminds me of an anecdote that Joseph told me. Reflecting on the miraculous powers given to beings like Black Elk and Fool's

Crow, Joseph asked Spirit why he had not been given them. Spirit replied, "We've given you twenty, but you haven't used them.")

After exercising his revivifying powers in a series of tests ("ascents") that disclosed the future, Black Elk saw the fruits of his labor: "And I saw that the sacred hoop of my people was one of many hoops that made one circle, wide as daylight and as starlight, and in the center grew one mighty flowering tree to shelter all the children of one mother and father. And I saw that it was holy" (22-36). Then, he returned to the Grandfathers, the oldest of whom told him, "Grandson, all over the universe you have seen. Now you shall go back with power to the place from whence you came, and it shall happen yonder that hundreds shall be sacred, hundreds shall be flames. Behold." Soon he was back in his family's tepee with his parents surrounding him, elated he had arisen from his illness.

However, Black Elk, like Joseph, suffered from a sense of inadequacy. Though the Grandfathers continued to communicate with him, he did not enact the vision on Earth, for his people. He had not brought about on Earth what he had in heaven (as the Lord's Prayer implores). As a result, by the time he was sixteen, he was consumed by the vision, deathly afraid of the Grandfathers, unable to function normally, and anxious about his sanity. (Symptoms shared by Joseph.) Finally, a medicine man, Black Road, told him, "You must do your duty and perform this vision for your people upon earth. . . . Then the fear will leave you; but if you do not do this, something very bad will happen to you" (135). When it had been accomplished, he was healthy, the sick were healthy, and the people were happier, even the horses. Unfortunately, the results on this stone were short-lived. The virtual destruction of their perfect imperfect world was forthcoming (just as he had foreseen in the vision).

The tree (the stick, the tree at Picuris and Eden, the tree under which Buddha sat and to which Jesus and Wotan were attached) would also figure in Joseph's unfolding series of visions. As in the vision of Black Elk, it occurred after his initial ascent. But as noted earlier, Joseph was not carried to the elders; he instantaneously discovered himself standing amidst the elders, high above Earth. Though he had never been here, he recognized the council. The elders, who were sitting in a circle and draped in red blankets, asked him why he had not built the chambers. Searching for an explanation, then surrendering, he just said that he had not found the right place. As a response, they projected him back into his physical body, beside the sweat lodge. Just as the elder in the Ute sun dance had become a chamber, the circle of elders became a circle of luminous fire that descended to his yard, near the sweat lodge. Joseph, standing beside them, realized the flames would be the walls of the chamber.

Next, a smaller radiant disc, about six feet in diameter (similar to Black Elk's cloud), descended. Standing atop the disc was an eight-foot angel holding a brown child. The angel appeared as a typical Renaissance angel: androgynous, pale-skinned, white-robed, and winged. When the angel's feet touched Earth, he lowered, 'planted' the infant as a seed, two feet beneath the surface. Before disappearing, he told Joseph that the child was his to raise.

Joseph had not only been directed to act and given the energy to do so, he had been initiated, as Black Elk had, into the hierarchy of elders. In directing him to build the chamber of peace, they had made him a chamber of peace and announced to him that he would no longer have negativity. "No negativity," is the way Joseph refers to the initiation. He had been cleansed of what Buddhism refers to as the afflictive emotions of anger, aversion, and ignorance, from our addiction to pleasure, approval, attention, and importance. Most importantly, he had been cleansed of anger, the most disturbing, combative, regressive emotion.

> The next day I dug up my garden to begin building a chamber in spite of my wife's public contestation. In the vision of the sound chamber was an egg-shaped oval built half in and half out of the ground. It would sit where the earth and sky meet, to unite the masculine and feminine. By so doing, it would bring wholeness, harmony, and peace on an inner level to the individual, on a political level to all humanity, and

on a cosmic level to the universe. I knew in those moments immediately following the vision that the chamber was the circle of light, and the child had been planted inside the heart that all life everywhere might manifest its goodness. Insights are born similarly. (153)

For three or four days afterward, Joseph remained in an altered state; he "went a little crazy," in his own words, "because I was all filled with light. I could see through my bones and hear people talking from a distance." Hearing the conversations of truckers on CB radios and policemen in their automobiles miles away kept him awake at night. In desperation, he finally put his head in a mixing bowl from the kitchen. This stopped the receiving and allowed him silence (Personal Commmunication, February 2005).

In *House* he writes that about five years after he had built the chamber, he was in it receiving a massage when he slipped into his *nah* and saw a "five-year old child with brown skin, brown like the land, peeking around the corner of a house at me. Behind the child I saw an elderly man in a white robe with a long beard. Unlike the child, the elderly man was surrounded by a halo of light" (134). The child, pointing at Joseph asked the elder who Joseph was. The elder replied that Joseph was his "earthly father" and instructed the child to do whatever Joseph asked.

Two years later he was in the chamber performing a healing ceremony when he had another chamber-related vision. This time he saw the chamber rooting itself in the earth and then "ascending upward within the branches of a giant redwood. The redwood tree grew and grew, with the chamber sitting in a fork of its branches, until it had lifted the peace chamber a mile off the ground, to the same plane of existence" as the elders and the child and his guardian, who were standing there. Though still rooted physically, he traveled up psychically (as Carl Jung had) and "saw that there was, on that same plane, a light like a jet trail as it went" (134).

Joseph did his best to raise the child for eighteen years, building and inspiring peace chambers around the world. Though he said in *House* that profound peace will pervade

the Earth in 2021, he has since said that it may come earlier, perhaps 2016. Regardless, in 2005 he said that the ascendant peace chamber, fifteen to sixteen miles above Albuquerque, had become a crystal chamber, like the kiva beneath his first house in Hesperus. "The solar winds are already sending the crystal vibration and light of peace around the Earth. The solar winds are propagating the Earth with seeds of peace. The peace chambers both propagate the Earth and feed the crystal chamber" (Personal Communication, March 2005). He said that he, himself, had also been the heavenly child, the cleansed, reborn seed of peace, whose roots reached deeply into Earth. At the same time, he had been the elderly angel, wise yet innocent. The growth of the child was/is the growth of the tree, pervading all dimensions.

In a 2005 letter to Marchand, Joseph told the names of the peace child (who is Joseph):

> When the sound chamber child first arrived at the Bernalillo chamber it was an infant whose name was *Ooh-oh-ney*. After a year it became *Oh-cho-oh-ney*. He kept that name until he became five years old; then he became *Oh-cho-ney*, the second *oh* is dropped. At sixteen years of age he became *Oh-cho-ko-kway-neh*. His name changed again at twenty; now he is *Oh-cho-sue-may-neh*. At thirty years of age he becomes *Sue-may-neh*. At fifty-five he will become *Key-aah-ta-meh-nay* (Mother-Father Person). At seventy, eighty, ninety he will be *Slo-ley-oh-ney*.

Though Joseph has yet to translate most of these, I believe (based on Mother-Father Person) that the Tiwa sounds indicate the archetypal energies or principal ideas that all true humans actualize as they grow authentically.

ENCOUNTERING THE LORD OF THE WIND

As I have indicated several times, Joseph, though a being of all elements and directions, is a being of wind, the air element. This is obvious in his name, his running, his connection to the eagle,

and his training. Early on, Antonio directed him to catch the
wind, which he learned to do by coaxing whirlwinds, dust devils,
to enter a deerskin pouch. The deer is a hooved being, connected
to Earth, who has her antlers (*my-ah-neh*) in the sky.

Joseph also recounted another experience he had in his
first two years of training with the cacique. He and six young
boys were put in the kiva and tested on their capacity to invoke
the Lord of the Wind. They had all forgotten the songs and
directions. All the other boys failed. Joseph was scared, so he
just made up a ceremony, a song and a prayer, telling the being
he needed help, asking to be saved. The Lord of the Wind came
down through the hole in the top of the kiva. In the course
of his training, Joseph also received special directions from
this being, directions which updated the ceremonies that had
been previously revealed. In these cases, he was forthright
in correcting his elders, proving the verity of his intuition by
bringing the Lord of the Wind into the presence of the elders.

Joseph's most dramatic encounter with the Lord of the Wind,
however, occurred in a vision he had around 1986, when he
was sun dancing at the Southern Ute Indian tribal sun dance.
Joseph says that he was dancing "to purify and shatter." Shortly
after he began to dance to the center pole and back, Joseph saw
a light pass by on the outside of the corral. Then he noticed
it was a being. The being stirred the wind, spitting thunder
and dark clouds from its mouth. Then "he entered the corral
riding a golden horseless chariot. He was like a Greek soldier,
with gold armor, gold bands around his arms, except even his
hair was gold. He was like a Greek god of the sun [Phoebus]."
Joseph stared at him and he fell off his chariot (Personal
Communication, June 2001).

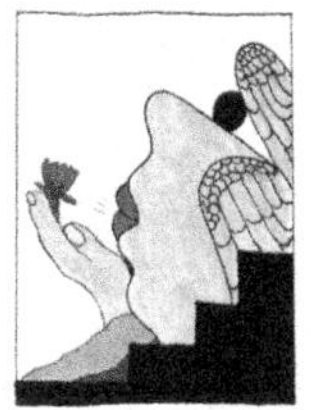

The being in the chariot, who knew Joseph had caused him
to fall, departed. And the rain and wind stopped. Wondering
what he was experiencing, Joseph consulted an old shaman
who was not dancing. The old man told him the being was The
Lord of the Wind who had come to test Joseph's mastery. The
whole arbor had been flooded. Organizers took all the sleeping
bags away to dry them. Everybody knew something magical was

happening because it was only raining in the corral. Though the night was quiet, Joseph knew that "the presence of the Lord of the Wind was still there."

"The second day, when the three hundred dancers began at the same time, the gale and rain returned. Only this time with cold hail, falling from high in the sky. This time the Lord of the Wind was driving a kind of bus that was finally crashed in the corral." Dust devils, whirlwinds were entering. The host medicine men couldn't see the being but had heard through the grapevine that Joseph was involved. Joseph relates that the medicine men were already wary of him because when he had danced there some ten years before he had caused torrential rains, brought Joseph said, by his deceased family members and relatives. As they had done ten years past, the shamans tried in vain to stop the storm. Everything was being destroyed. Suddenly, in the midst of the tumult, a leaf struck Joseph in the forehead, and Joseph said, "I want to stop the nonsense, non-sense." He split the syllables of "nonsense" as he spoke it. So he picked up his eagle wing from his spot on the circumference of the corral and walked toward the center pole, the axis which Joseph says is truth. He made light come out of his eagle wing. Then he held the wing out in front of him, and, starting at the bottom, he raised the wing, drawing the line of light upward along the pole and cut time. Adamantly he said, "I ask for truth." When he did that, "everything stopped. Two large trees that had flown through the door of the corral stopped in mid-air, just as they were about to strike each other. Puffs of smoke were suspended." With the stopping of time, Joseph's ordinary mind had stopped. So had everyone else's. When he thought to himself, "I stopped time," he saw the thought emerge from himself in an arc. "After the thoughts emerged, time healed itself, the two pieces that had been sliced, sewed themselves together. Then the trees dropped, and the dust clouds fell."

The corral was quiet. Joseph heard the Lord of the Wind say, "You have worked for truth. Acknowledge me." Joseph honored him, the being who had guided and empowered him since Picuris. After he did, the Lord disappeared, everyone cleared

out the corral, and the sun dance continued. As a result of this initiation, Joseph was given "the power to heal with the breath. To blow away sickness. Breath is the greatest power "—given to humans. We can call the Lord of the Wind, present within us as breath, by repeating '*Wah-oh*'" (Personal Communication 2001).

Envisioning the Blue Stone People Again and Ah-keh

In 1989, forty-seven years after first meeting the Blue-Stone People beside his grandmother's house, Joseph envisioned their extra-terrestrial origin: a purely impersonal vision. The occasion was a sun-moon dance, one of many Joseph led in Pennsylvania in the eighties and nineties. Just as he had when he was a young shepherd at La Boca, Joseph envisioned the subtle world, his awareness piercing the veil that separates the third and fourth dimensions. His vision had created a hole—a hole that was growing in diameter. Suddenly, his *nah* was in the sky, looking down on a vast mud plain that would one day become Picuris. In both *Being and Vibration* and *House of Shattering Light,* he recounts the descending of two kachinas, two supernatural beings, sitting in a luminous space ship that approached from the southeast.

Their ship approached the spot where his grandmother's house would eventually stand. The beings emerged from the ship as pure vibration and light and walked to a "sacred site for the new inhabitants who were to become the people high up in the mountains of north central Mexico" (*Being and Vibration* 26). The beings from space were male/female figures, about ten-feet tall, with white-washed, squared faces, white and black-striped bodies, and long flowing, black capes. Suddenly, the kachinas became the He-She-Stone People and energized the land and atmosphere. Joseph knew they had come to create the microcosm of Picuris.

For the Pueblo, kachinas, also spelled katsina and cachina, are supernatural beings, usually benevolent, who live in nature.

They bestow blessings, particularly rain, crops, and well being (Dutton, *American Indians of the Southwest* 40). Dutton explains that they function in three spiritual modes:

> First they are *spirit guides* of an anthropomorphic nature. Again they are masked, painted, and properly *costumed individuals* who appear in the village plazas and kivas as impersonators of the spiritual ones enacting esoteric rites and ceremonies. In another guise, they are *wooden figurines*—small representations of the life-size beings—by means of which Indian children become familiar with the katsinas as part of their religious training and cultural history. (40)

All Puebloans agree that the kachinas once ministered to the people, providing the energy necessary for balance and well-being. They also taught arts, industry, hunting, and above all, rain making. The people, however, fell spiritually asleep and no longer venerated the sacred guardians. The kachinas, therefore, refused to serve those who had forgotten them. But they did not abandon the people completely. They taught the awakened few some ceremonies, as well as the means of impersonation. Should the impersonators sincerely follow their instructions, the supernatural guides promised to become present in the masked participants and thereby bless the community. Dutton explains that the various kachina groups are controlled by a tribe's medicine societies, who meet in their corresponding medicine houses.

Describing the vision as the turning of pages in a book covering thousands of years, Joseph saw the rapid changing of the Picuris landscape. The vibration generated by the black and white striped kachinas was a seeding that germinated into vegetation, a river, meadows, trees, mountains, waters. From the mountain behind present-day Picuris, he saw water flow down toward the village, like arteries carrying blood from the heart. Suddenly, Painted Arrow's position changed, and he found himself to the southwest of Picuris, beside a fissure in the earth. A cloud emanated from the fissure; from within the cloud, sixteen people comprising three generations of ancestral Tiwans, appeared. They were the culminating fruit of the kachinas' seed.

Finally his grandmother's house appeared, emerging as if

from dawn. The vision stabilized with Joseph's envisioning
the house as it existed in ordinary time, occupied by his newly
arrived family. It convinced Joseph that the Picuris did not
emerge from a distant Sand Lake, that the sibapu was the pueblo
itself. The presence of the kachinas is embodied in the elements
which the two-legged people, who are also the elements, literally
and figuratively eat every day. With every breath, every ingesting,
every perception, Tiwans learned their sacred language of
metaphor revealed in Things.

In *Ceremonies* he describes a dream which revealed the
centrality of the tree to the unfolding of Picuris. Trees, *tslah-
ah-nay* in Tiwa, have long been used in ceremony by other
"ancient traditionalists" such as the Vikings and Celts, hence
the European and North American use of the evergreen at
Christmas. When the waters receded from the land of Picuris,
they exposed a lot of rocks. He saw winter arrive with snow, then
saw the snow melt and the summer heat come. The alternating
cold and heat of winter and summer broke down the rock into
sand. Finally, he saw a tree emerge from the sand, grow to
maturity and fall:

> . . . When it fell, I realized that that's how the land was im-
> bued with greatness. This first tree awakened the memory
> of greatness, because it is the essence of greatness. When it
> hit the ground, and as it started to rot, it gave us time. The
> rings in the tree tell us that time expands out from a single
> point. It doesn't expand inwardly—not in this dimension
> anyhow. Time begins with a seed of light, but once it goes
> out, it doesn't go back to the point of light until it breaks up
> into soil as humus. Then it goes back into the one, into the
> beginning. You can look at a stump or a cross-section of a
> tree and see how an insight might happen, beginning with
> a seed or a single flash of light and traveling out from there.
>
> . . . The tree is a symbol of how time is expanding and
> how we are expanding as a part of that greatness or expan-
> sion. It is the symbol of the movement and expansion of Di-
> vine Thought or Divine Essence. The tree is the most con-
> crete substance that we can see and touch that connects us
> to how greatness is expanding. (41–42)

121

The second vision that occurred dancing in Pennsylvania, involved Ah-keh, mythical prophet of the Picuris people who "connects us with all mystics, on all other planes of existence." Ah-keh, who is about four-feet tall and childlike, embodies the "innocence of the great beings." Ah-keh, aware of Joseph's work with the peace chambers, reprimanded Joseph because of the war and conflict in the world. He told Joseph about an electro-magnetic area near Picuris where lightning strikes. Then, Ah-keh transported Joseph to the spot. Because of this highly charged site, "Picuris is mystically connected to the Middle East." As a result, the "Ark of the Covenant sometimes moves from Israel to Picuris." He told Joseph that the Ark was there, at Picuris, but that it would soon return to the Holy Land. Via Ah-keh, Joseph was "connected to the illuminated souls, incarnated and not, of all times" (Personal Communication, June 2002).

Calling in the Thunder

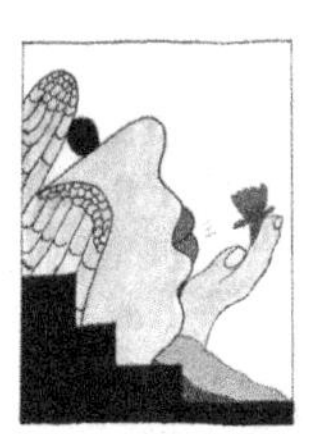

Joseph started and stopped rain on many occasions, in Europe and the United States, some of which he describes in his books. However, in *House* he describes a thunder-calling ceremony he undertook in 1990, the first since his high school days at Picuris. "A powerful inner voice was asking me to do a thunder-calling ceremony near my house in Colorado. I invited people to come to see it because that was what the ceremony was calling for" (171). Yet, he had no clan to help him, nor did he hold an official position with the Utes or the Picuris, so he had to recruit friends with whom to perform the ceremony the following July. Most importantly, he had to enlist the aid of relatives that had died. So, doing as he was taught, in January 1991, he asked the spirits to help him in the forthcoming summer.

On July 9, the day before the ceremony, he still didn't know if the spirits would help him bring rain. But that night he dreamed of Lucia and Agapito Martinez, his foster parents, who had died more than ten years before. "They were all dressed up in their regalia as if they were going to a feast" (172). Joseph asked them why they were dressed up, and "his foster mother said, 'Joseph, you haven't changed. You're still forgetting what you're supposed to do. I guess I have to come to remind you again. You're doing a ceremony tomorrow to bring in the thunder.' Of course, she was talking in Tiwa" (173). They told him they would start at two p.m. the next day.

So, the next day Joseph gathered the people and told them to line up. He instructed them to take stones from the river and lift them up to the sky and lower them, again and again. The sky was clear.

> Right at two o'clock low, rolling thunder drummed across the sky. We could hear it getting louder and louder, even though there were still no clouds in sight. After that first roll of thunder, I started the prayers, but I would break every three or four minutes. Whenever I stopped, and only when I stopped, there would be another roll of thunder. What's interesting about thunder beings is that they are very polite and they don't break in when you are talking. (174–75)

Joseph kept praying for all the directions and for all the people, all of life. Rain, "the Father Sun rain that makes awareness, began to fall. A circle of silver rain about twenty feet in diameter . . . was falling on us like light snow, . . . but there were no clouds in the sky yet" (175).

Once the rain fell in earnest, Joseph directed the eight participants to put down their rocks and go into the sound chamber. Joseph went atop the chamber and smoked a cigarette, honoring the directions. A participant accompanied him. When Joseph smoked, turning counter-clockwise, the rain diminished. When he turned back, clockwise, the rain increased. In following his intuition and calling in the rain, Joseph had applied age-old principles of his grandfather in a new situation. In doing so, he actualized another of Antonio's teachings: "What you need to do is something that I haven't done, something no one's done, because the whole idea is to increase the level of knowing, raise the level of consciousness" (178).

The latest step in Joseph's work for world peace has been "to announce the appearance of a new vibration in the cosmos" (*Sound* 35). This came about as a result of a vision on April 16, 2006, twenty-four years after the definitive peace chamber vision. On this day, while leading a dance in Australia, Joseph envisioned a Horn of Plenty. Above the dance arbor, a luminous cornucopia appeared, pouring blessings of fruit and vegetables upon the dance arbor, upon Earth.

At the same time, the "shape of the arbor changed from a circle into the spiral galaxy that we live in. From this I knew it was a galactic vision." In *Sound* he says that the spiral, *huh-leh-neh*, means germination, which means that the many-colored seeds that were spilling from the center of the galaxy would "germinate on Planet Earth as well as in this galaxy." First to fall from the Horn of Plenty was a blue seed, which was, at the same time, a five-pointed star, which symbolizes "personal gifts" to "all life on Mother Earth." "Spiraling in toward the center of our galaxy," the blue star brought "new energies," "changing everything on our planet. As it spirals back out from the center, new forms take shape." To Joseph the Horn of Plenty "is like a medicine bag . . . where the medicine man puts all his powers. Now the bag is open and it is spilling out its fruits into the galaxy" (35).

In the video, recently posted on *YouTube*, Joseph invokes the teachings of his people that "when mankind can't do something, the celestial powers, the celestial vibration, takes over." In this case he refers to the fact that we have not been able to solve, not really attempted to solve, our most pressing problems, particularly strife and war. His web site, created to herald the coming of *Sound*, announces that G-d "is going to take over" because "we humans have fooled around long enough" (www.josephrael.org/artwork.htm). He was shown and told that the time of abundance, of hope, of prosperity and peace is at hand, that we shall receive whatever we wish. If we want peace we will get peace. "As soon as we focus on a goal, the universe will take us in that direction" (www.josephrael.org/artwork.htm). Most importantly, in *Sound*, Joseph re-focuses on us. If we "pay attention, [we] will feel vibration shift to world peace." As well as the conflicts in our microcosms that preclude it. As for Joseph, he offers unbridled hope to humanity, having already "realized that my art was beginning to change, was being endowed with greater and greater levels of the vibration of peace for the whole world" (36).

Finally, though this vision is not another installment of the peace chamber visions, one can see it as a sort of fulfillment of that series. In his last chamber vision, Joseph saw the chamber miles above Albuquerque, in the arms of a Redwood tree, streaming light around the planet, carried by solar winds. Remember that the tree that grew from a seed, which was the child of peace, which grew into the giant tree. Seen as a cycle, the star fruit of the cornucopia is like the fruit/cones of the tree. The abundance of the cornucopia is a multiplication of the original blessings. It came from the heavens, needing to be nurtured by human hands, and it came back and comes back a hundred-fold, a million-fold, needing to be distributed by human hands and feet and breath. And, this fruit, according to the vision, spawned the seeds of future fruit, here and throughout the galaxy. So, it even cycles back into the vastness, the Vast Self. The stone of Earth somehow benefits the other nine stones. When teachable two-leggeds listen and work rightly. *Wa-Ma-Chi.*

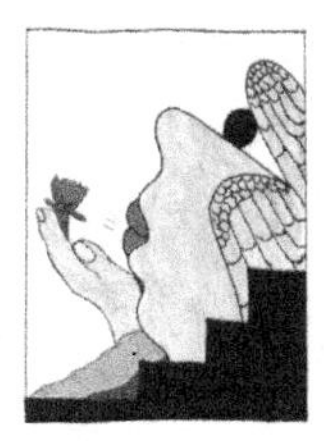

Retiring to his Hermitage:
The Hero Returns Full-Circle

In 1998 Joseph intended to retire to his hermitage, commencing the last chapter of his heroic Return. Such was his intention when he completed *House of Shattering Light*. He has not. For almost ten years, he continued conducting two mystery schools a year for his students. And he experienced the Horn of Plenty vision while leading a dance in Australia in 2006. Moreover, he has assisted his daughter and brother in other dances and performed healing sweats for those in need. More accurately, he semi-retired, slowed down, shifted his focus to meditation, and to beautifying the land.

In 1980 Joseph had been given a parcel of land by the Southern Ute tribe, given in the sense that he and his family can live there as long as they tend and protect the land. Though he still visits Picuris to participate in feast days and visit his father's family, he has increasingly committed himself to meditating and to helping the Southern Utes, centered around Ignacio. In particular, he has committed himself to assisting the young. In this sense he has come full circle. He has returned to the area where he was born, where 'he' chose his family and became a body, the first stone. Returned to the place his parents left because it had caused them calamity. Returned to the place from which he was thrust on his Call to Adventure. Returned as a Master of Both Worlds to a noble people who struggle (as we all do) to balance and integrate the ten worlds, the three dimensions and bodies, matter and spirit, business and ceremony, Caesar and G-d. To overcome duality.

Using Jesus and Krishna as his supreme examples, Campbell says that one becomes a master of two worlds, a dancer with a foot in eternity and time, by undergoing transfiguration, a metamorphosis by which one is both human and divine, and neither. Though Campbell speaks of the hero's ability to cross back and forth between the created and Uncreated, form and formlessness, he only does so to fit the linear framework of the journey. In reality, there is nothing to do, no one to become, and nowhere to go. The *Tao Te Ching* conveys this in saying that the wise ones, the ones who become the Tao, Being Itself, need no longer accomplish, for everything happens in their presence. When duality ceases, miracles occur. Yet, paradoxically, as long as one uses one's body, as householder or monk, one must act to survive and benefit others. Act both divinely and humanly, inspirationally and practically. And playfully. As elder/child. As Vast Self. As *Wa-Ma-Chi*: Breath, Matter, Movement.

Over the years, as Joseph spent less and less time traveling, he

has enacted his visions for his hermitage, given it the "quality of heaven is here now." His building near Hesperus is a wonderful parallel to Jung's building his "Tower" in Bollingen, which he originally intended to be a sort of African hut "where the fire, ringed by a few stones, burns in the middle" (*Memories, Dreams, and Reflections* 223). The first semi-permanent structure Joseph built was his kiva, half sunk into the ground, structured around an enormous crystal, the center of the circle of light. To the four directions, sit symbolic shrines and ritual objects. The circumference is ringed by tiles emblazoned with visionary shields, punctuated by symbols of the four directions. At one time, this sound chamber became the home of a large bull snake. Joseph later recalled:

> The bull snake was 6 feet long. She was yellow in color, and we met her because I had to get off of the car we were driving and walk, gently stomping my feet on the ground so that the vibrations that followed behind her would guide her off the road to safety. Later I found her tracks next to a rabbit hole next to the sound chamber where she decided to camp and stay and live for a while. We had a problem with the hantavirus, which is carried by the deer mouse. The mice left our area. She saved us from the virus and one day we saw her leaving while we said our goodbyes. (Personal Communication, May 2010)

Atop the kiva, the generator of subtle light, sits the house, built of wood by Joseph and friends, over the years. As Joseph generated more and more art from his light-filled studio, the house became a studio, teaming with his art. Envisioning it as an eventual gallery or museum, he meditated on the blueprints for another home, a hundred feet away. This structure, he realized, would reconcile the circle and the square, horizontally and vertically. Three years after the foundation was poured, it was completed, integrating the tribal gifts of his mother and father, of the Utes and Picuris Pueblo. Having moved into the new house, a living mandala, he has concentrated on constructing a green house to provide his family with vegetables year-round, so that through effort he might "complete the circle"

127

his family began at Shamisal (Grace/Greatness Where Sun Meets Heaven). "Work," as his grandfather told him, "is worship" (*Sound* 77).

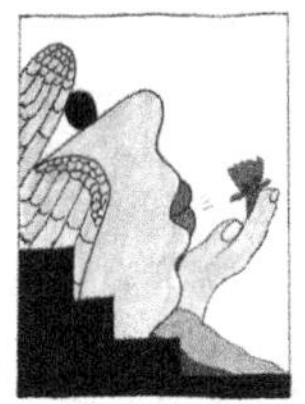

128

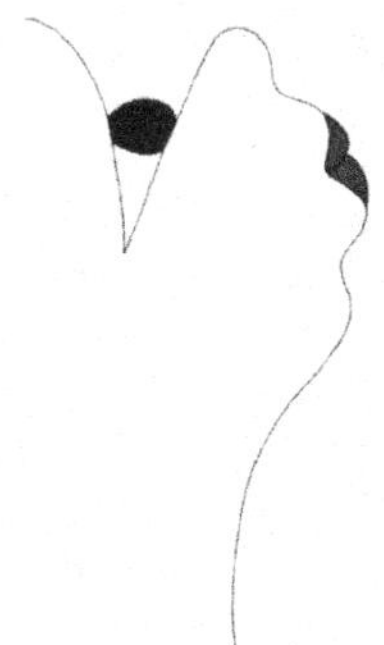

Entering the Mystic Universe
of Beautiful Painted Arrow

part two

130

THE WAY OF THE VAST SELF

In 1981 the Amerindian sage Joseph Rael had a vision in the
office of the Indian Health Service in Santa Fe. He saw a map
on the wall, a pattern of about fifteen scenarios, events with
which he would be involved over the next ten or fifteen years.
He knew the vision signaled the next stage of his life's work, the
sharing of native-based mystical teaching with non-natives. But
he did not know where to begin. He resigned from his full-time
position and resolved to make effort, the native way of achieving
clarity. He walked some eighty miles from Picuris Pueblo to
northern New Mexico; led a large group of people in a Long
Dance near Durango, Colorado; then, some months later, danced
the Sun Dance on the Ute Reservation in Ignacio, Colorado.

Beautiful Painted Arrow had been beset by conflict. He was a
university-educated, traditionally trained visionary; a Pueblo/Ute
half-breed bureaucrat with a smidgen of European; a medicine
man/healer often disregarded by natives he served but embraced
by pale skins seeking spiritual authenticity. The ceremonies
resolved this. He gave up efforts to found a holistic health
center at Picuris Pueblo, the ancestral home of his father, and
surrendered to the role of consultant, spiritual teacher at large.
Vision had shown him that humanity was his tribe.

In the late 1990s, after almost twenty years of world travel
and teaching, Beautiful Painted Arrow retired to land on the
Southern Ute reservation, to paint the myths of his peoples
and his visions. In general, people who have met Joseph or
read his books associate him with two activities that dominated
those years of travel: the leading of spiritual dances and the
establishing of peace/sound chambers. Though the activities
are rooted in the Southern Ute tradition of his mother and the
Picuris Pueblo tradition of his father, respectively, they have
unfolded directly from his visions and his interaction with the
contemporary world.

Somewhat overshadowed by these dynamic communal ceremonies are his profound contemplative teachings, teachings

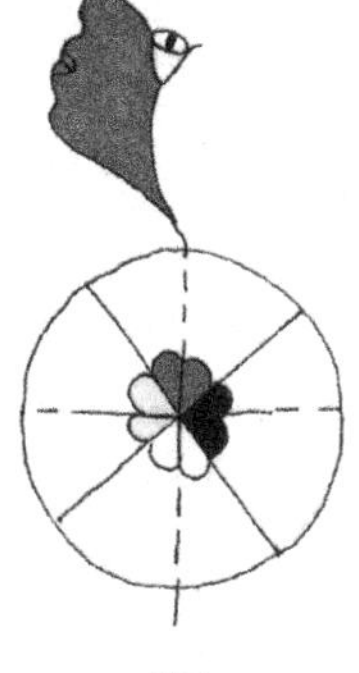

inspired by the Picuris mystery school, solitary hours spent in the kiva and the wilderness, and in ceremonial dancing. He has chronicled many of these experiences in *Sound: Native Teaching and Visionary Art, House of Shattering Light, Being and Vibration,* and *Beautiful Painted Arrow: A Medicine Story.*

Highlighting the meditative dimension of his work, this manual, Part Two, addresses this oversight. With this guide those who have never met him, as well as those who have, can establish a daily meditative practice, gradually developing his attunement and perspective, which accurately can be called the Way of the Vast Self.

Written in consultation with Joseph, this manual focuses on a rich array of breath, sound, light, and visualization techniques. All quotes are Joseph's exact words—from his books or our communications. The manual also includes some of the Tiwa sounds/metaphors necessary for entering the vibratory universe of Tiwa revelation. Tiwa, as Joseph continually stresses, is a "collection of sounds, not a language." And, it is a collection of verbs/actions/motions, not static things. And, while a pattern of sounds may refer to what Europeans consider an object, such as cup (*ti-uh*), Tiwas will also use that sound pattern to refer to the abdomen and to the action and archetype of cupping. Cupping is always cupping something else, which is also flowing and unfolding. Things are interrelated processes; all our relations (*kah-weh*).

Ti-uh is naturally related to *ti*. In *House of Shattering Light* Joseph writes that *ti* "means crystallized awareness, or awareness that is in the process of crystallizing and uncrystallizing"; it "means 'the essence of the power of crystallization that is influencing awareness' and that awareness is the awareness of holding something in" (125). *Ti* repeatedly occurs in the various ways that the Tiwa understand their (and all two-leggeds') work in the universe. The holding power of awareness, though not uniquely human, refers to our power to concentrate, to be one-pointed. It is, in fact, the basis of all spiritual practice and the only means by which beings can truly relate.

European languages are arbitrary words representing

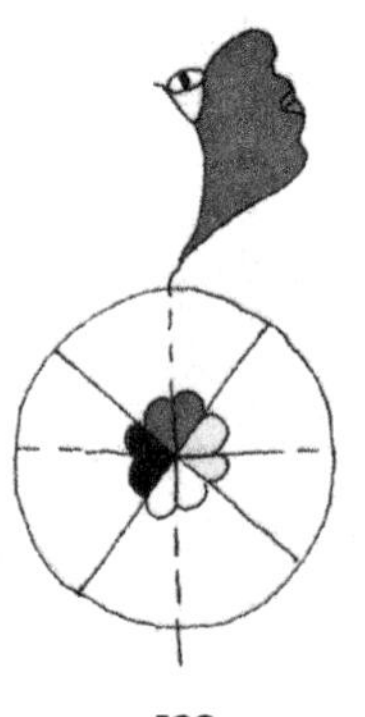

things and actions that can be realized as metaphors. Just as we did with cup. Tiwa sounds, learned from the natural world, originated as (and are still primarily understood as) vibrational qualities, not quantities/things. What we call 'things' are revelations of archetypal vibrations and meanings for traditionally taught Tiwa speakers. Before leaving the theme of sound and vibration, I note that Tiwa vowels are pronounced as the Spanish and French pronounce them rather than as the English and Americans pronounce them. A is pronounced "ah" (mama/pot), E is pronounced "eh" (day/weigh/grey), I is pronounced "ee" (fee/we/key), O is pronounced "oh" (low/dough/go), and U is pronounced "ou" (you/due/do).

In order to better appreciate these techniques, we shall describe them in the context of Joseph's own spiritual training and unfoldment as a medicine person and visionary. Spiritual practice cannot be divorced from perspective. So, we shall explain meditation techniques, what Buddhism terms 'skillful means,' in conjunction with the mystical teachings that laid the foundation for both his practice and perspective. Together, they act as a feather upon us. In Tiwa, feather, *kee-wah*, is that "which awakens potential possibilities." However, neither practice nor perspective is easy in Joseph's case. Those who have read his works or enjoyed his presence know the subtlety of his mystical understanding. (Not his thought; his understanding/experience.)

Reading Joseph's books, one realizes that many of his insights, intuitions, and capacities unfolded naturally, were spiritual gifts. They were also nurtured by a tradition and social structure thousands of years old, solely dedicated to preserving harmony between heaven and earth, finite and infinite, inner and outer worlds. Sometimes, despite his natural gifts and considerable effort, he would not experience the results predicted by his teachers and tradition. Usually, this occurred because he did not follow directions, the ceremonies needed updating, or he did not properly employ skillful means. Though Joseph had many unpremeditated spiritual experiences, he practiced very hard, undertook continual austerities, and made what most would consider phenomenal effort. As Joseph says, "effort brings

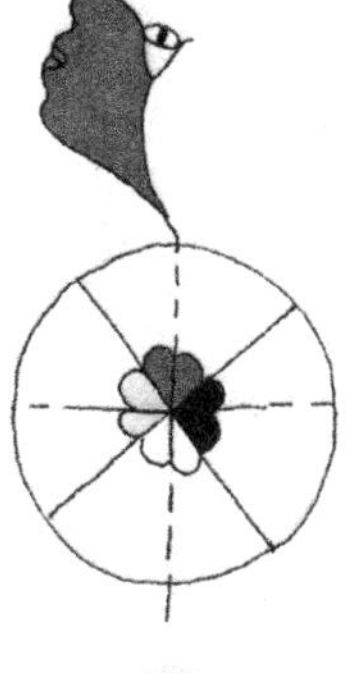

133

one closer to the supernatural."

Anyone who has studied or practiced comparative mysticism, more significantly, anyone who has had mystical experiences (intuitive realizations), will know that these teachings are profound—incredibly powerful in a beautiful way. Moreover, they are teachings and vibrations of this land, this continent, this Earth. Brought forth for this time by a contemporary sage. It is important to appreciate that the Pueblo and Ute traditions are orally transmitted, that youngsters in the Pueblo mystery schools learned by listening to metaphorical stories, imitating, practicing, intuiting, and experiencing. Alone, memorizing information only produces the illusion of spiritual growth.

Though this guide cannot convey Joseph's presence or substitute for his ancient mystery school, we hope it will aid sincere seekers of creation-based spirituality. Those who long to more fully experience the Great Spirit. From the references I've already made, you should understand that this book is just a companion to Joseph's books, particularly *Sound*, *House of Shattering Light*, and *Being and Vibration*, which offer teaching stories, visualizations, and sacred sounds. Nevertheless, implementing these practices will help you experience the teachings—even though so much of his recent teaching takes the form of mystical paintings, some of which you'll find in *Sound*.

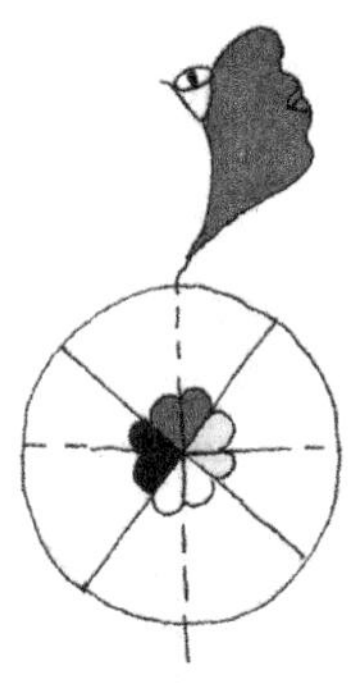

1. Living Naturally

Natural Law (A Prayer of Thanks)
We thank all the beings who came before us
That we can come into this moment and
Experience and enjoy all of the contributions
That have been made by
The two-leggeds,
The four-leggeds,
The wingeds,
The beings of water,
The plant people,
The rock people,
The sky people.
All of the peoples who came here to join us
In the naturalness of the natural law.
We come from a very ancientness of wisdom
That came out of truth,
And this truth is connected to the natural law of
Wa-Ma-Chi.

This prayer, spoken by Joseph and arranged by Norman
Marchand, orients us to our time and place, the impact of the
everlasting infinite on this very moment and point where our
feet touch Earth. You are an inverted triangle whose top is open.
Before practicing, you need to come under the natural law rather
than man-made law. To do this you must become natural, in all
its ramifications. When Joseph was young, the Tiwa still lived
a life of non-duality, in which spiritual and material life were
one. The people aimed to live from the inside out. Action was
understood to be prayer; work (*t'ah-lah*) was worship. In typical
non-dualistic fashion, work means "where God lives through
effort." Their language, Tiwa, is metaphoric, a vibrational vehicle
for communicating Reality, a vibrational vehicle they originally
learned by listening to nature through the subtle/inner ear.

Everything apparent and non-apparent was alive, and all was related (*ka-weh*). In order that the people would remember, their days were replete with ceremony, practice, story, and song.

Addressing Honors students at Saint Leo University in 2005, Joseph said this about life at Picuris:

> We were immersed in the moment. We didn't have mental health problems before modernity. We didn't know we were poor, ignorant, indigent, or overcrowded. We didn't have a word for poverty. We made do, and we responded to Spirit. We knew who we were and we tried to learn. We knew how to make effort, holy effort. Whatever we were doing or having was a blessing. We didn't make people's prejudices part of our emotional repertoire.
>
> We were verb people. We didn't have a curse word. Our language embodied innocence. Even bad was good in our culture. Life is about falling in love.

The Tiwa, and Pueblo in general, were a truly civilized people. This is ironic because the various invaders and most non-Indians (and many Indians) considered and still consider Amerindians/indigenous to have been barbarians and savages. Most people, sane people, realize this thought to have been egocentric and relativistic. Nevertheless, most Europeans, Americans, and first-world citizens would consider themselves to be civilized and indigenous peoples, non-educated, non-technologized people, to be inferior. This is a hoax, a great lie, and the cause of the horrific, deplorable condition of life on this planet.

A civilized society is a loving, compassionate, caring society that cultivates the well-being of its members, all its relations: humans, animals, plants, and elements. A civil person, as certain prophets have taught, tends to the needs of her vast family. Like the good shepherd, she will not rest until the last sheep, the weakest, little, sickly lamb, is safe within the fold. This is the only measure of a civilized society: the well-being of all. It evidences communion with the Creator. Mere training and indoctrination of the mind, at the expense of the emotions, intuition, and body, does not constitute education or civilization. In fact, they inhibit it. A person does not become a true human until her heart is 'open,' until she has become loving, compassionate, and generous.

Most two-leggeds (humans) live in an artificial world full of man-made things but empty of Spirit. We worship quantity, which can be perceived through the ordinary senses and reasoned with the ordinary mind, rather than quality, which can only be appreciated through the subtle senses/self, *nah* in Tiwa. Happiness, the most ineffable of qualities, the measure of what all consider the 'good' life, has been quantified as accumulation. The hideous illusion being that if we increase quantity (and power) to the 'nth degree, it becomes quality. That if we go real, real fast, we will enter timelessness, eternity. This, of course, cannot happen. Quantity will never become quality. A selfish person will never become a 'good' person, no matter how many so-called, apparently 'good' acts he performs. Quality, goodness, is a shift in consciousness, of one's condition of beingness. Unfortunately, we do not teach, encourage, or nurture this subtle dimension of beingness, the soul. The soul, *nah*, remains vestigial, dormant because we prefer to modify behavior, to offer a kit to salvation, which is really just success. And it will remain dormant as long as we accept a quantitative map to a qualitative heaven. As long as we imagine all we need to do is change the ordinary mind rather than lose it. And 'think' we can be reborn without awakening, 'dying' to every sort of ignorance.

Judeo-Christian theology, the so-called rational Enlightenment, and technology have manufactured an anorexic sacredness, an ersatz heaven that is out of our bodies (even our hearts), that excludes creation. A materialistic illusion/thought that we can obtain if we just give our money and allegiance to the right self-righteous entrepreneur. (Whereas the prophet/poet said one must lose life in order to gain it.) Instead of knowing spirituality as the balanced, integrated fullness of life (as did primal peoples and the early Greeks), we equate spirituality with repressive obeying. Our beauty/innocence has bitten the evil queen's poison apple. We exist in a spiritual coma.

According to Joseph, two-leggeds have two innate capacities: awareness and the power to manifest. However, we cultivate neither in our spiritual coma. If we wish to awaken awareness and the power to manifest (right action), we must work interiorly. The Utes, the Pueblo, all native peoples realized the action of grace and blessing (*who* in Tiwa), but they also understood that we must endeavor indefatigably to maintain and deepen our relationship to Great Spirit. Hence, their daily lives were replete with transformative ceremonies that required effort and sacrifice. We who live in a society antagonistic to awareness, innocence, and true conscience (as opposed to superego) may have to work twice as hard on our heroic quest to become truly human, real, authentic, and connected to all beings. Our quest 'advances' one way: with the accumulation of Awareness, *ti* (tee), Energy/Vibration/Light, *chi* (chee), and Love, *tu-tah*, (to-tah).

Wa is Transpersonal Consciousness/Light that descends into creation. (You can sense the descent as you pronounce it.) Joseph calls it the breath of Spirit and the energy of creating. We will use those terms for *wa*, as well as the terms, *Very Subtle Mind and Intelligence*. *Wa* is not transcendent energy, like the Sanskrit *Aum*, for instance. *Wa-chi-who* is a related term that means "consciousness of the Vast Self." It includes all three principle vibrations. (*Ti* becomes *chi*.) Together they represent inclusive consciousness, sometimes called Divine Mind, but a Divine Mind that is present, aware of Itself through the human. It witnesses all activity, all gross and subtle movement in and by the human being.

Ti, what Joseph calls "the power to crystallize Awareness," is also called One-pointedness, Concentration, Focusing, Big Mind, Attention, and Subtle Mind. In Tiwa, *ti* is primarily associated with the light of awareness whereas *chi* is associated with subtle energy, vibration, and light, as well as action. When pronouncing these two sounds, you can feel *ti* vibrate more on the upper palate and *chi* vibrate more through the lips and lower mouth. The energies of ti/chi correspond to what mystics call the subtle self or Higher Self, what the Tiwa call *nah*, and sometimes *soh*. *Soh* means "swallowing" and refers to the *nah*'s capacity to "drink light."

Westerners (left-brain dominant) rely on definition and

memory, assuming they know something when they know
a name that represents it. However, original, indigenous
Westerners rely on vibration. Moreover, sounds convey different
meanings depending on context. They often mean two or three
different actions simultaneously. And their meaning is nuanced
by their association with other sounds. (*Chi*, for instance,
can mean mind, beauty, light, energy, sound, and action,
depending on the sounds that surround it. Still, *chi* connotes
the manifestation of the subtle level upon the physical level.)
Remember the meaning of the sounds is in their vibration,
and try not to let the computer mind/left brain become fixated
on definition. If you experience this happening, just repeat the
sounds over and over until you resonate with the vibrations.
Then you'll begin to understand (stand under/carry).

Joseph says we are all experiencing *wa-chi-chi-who*, the search
for meaning, or—more true to Tiwa—becoming. We long to
become the presence (*who*) of the Great Spirit, *Wa-Ma-Chi*.
An even more true but 'mind-bending' English translation of
wah-chi-chi-who would be "The light that precedes creation's
becoming aware of Itself as the energy that crystallizes as
creation." Joseph has also spoken of *wa-chi-chi-who* as "Goodness
purifying the personal self—as above so below."

The latter description is important because it tells how we
become what we are in essence, the Vast Self: purifying the
personal self. Purifying the personal self through the *nah* so
we realize/become the Vast Self. It also contains the mystical
dictum "As above—so below." In European mysticism this
usually means that the Very Subtle world of the infinite beyond
is reflected or mirrored in the gross/sensate finite world of the
here and now, and vice versa.

Tiwa speakers say Grandfather Sky and Grandmother Earth
reflect each other, love each other, that Earth/Creation is a
metaphor for the hidden meanings of the subtle world. The
world perceived through the ordinary senses is an epiphany in
which the most esoteric realities are revealed. The Above and
Below (and everything in between) are nuanced expressions of
the same essence. They are the Vast Self. In European thought,

Tiwa experience could be called spiritual pantheism. All of this, Creation seen and unseen, is the pulsing, luminous, holy, sacred, Divine Presence. Can we, taught that God sits on a throne 'up, up there' overcome our dominant civilization's hatred for the so-called material world, its prejudice against the below, the under, the ground, the dirt, the sinful body/earth, the 'devil'?

The parables of the carpenter/prophet from Nazareth ("Last is first/first is last") have not cured institutional arrogance, egocentricity, and materialism. Alas, Europeans institutionalized the radical messiah's revelation. The revolutionary message of love has been twisted into a quest for self-improvement and abundance—egomania and greed. William Blake would say they have made it a force for duality, captured it in the churches. Can we, poisoned to worship superiority, self-importance, competitiveness, and artificiality, appreciate naturalness? Become like little children? Hildegard of Bingen, the great Catholic visionary, was a "feather carried on the breath of God."

Can we value becoming stones, leaves of grass, mere genes in the infinite web of the universe? The original teachings say we have/are a place (*ee-eh-mo:* awareness, placement, movement), collectively and individually. To discover this place, the teachings say we must become moving trees, deeply rooted via *ti/chi/who* into the Vast Self that we are. Interpenetrated by all the elemental beings, a home for all creatures. All relations in harmony. Can we, fixated on improving the image of the personal self, appreciate unlearning, dying before death? And, therefore, become spiritual children again?

In an impromptu teaching in a forest, some twenty years ago, Joseph ended an inspirational talk to a group of seekers with these words: "When we came, we chose a vow of poverty in order that we could see, and we knew that in order to see we had to listen, and in order to hear inwardly, we had to suffer in order that we could bring forth infinite possibilities."

Co-wen. It is good (because all that is being enhanced is beautiful).

II. Meeting Body/Essence: Pee-ah-who

In *Being and Vibration*, Joseph writes that "the true human is
someone who is aware, someone who is, moment by moment,
totally and completely merged with life"; "a true human is a
person who knows who he is because he listens to that inner
listening-working voice of effort" (67–68). To begin this, we
must work to commune with our bodies, because one's body is
one's revelation in the natural world. Rooting out the deleterious
effects of society begins at the physical level. In a simple
common-sense manner, we need to commune with our bodies
and nature. The body vehicle is what Joseph calls this "primary
world." For Tiwa, body is *tu-neh* (temple of Spirit/Vast Self) and
tu-tah (center, kiva, love, heart). It must be cared for and simply
'met' as we would meet a stranger.

"One of the first things the true human learns is to look at
life through the whole physical body" (68). For the body is the
presence of the Vast Self, the cumulative revelation of the infinite
archetypes of what Plato called the Forms. The body is also a
microcosm, a book/picture/map/miniature of the universe, the
ten worlds of the Tiwa that are really infinite. To contemplate the
Forms or archetypes expressed through individual body parts,
read "Metaphors of the Body" in *Being and Vibration*. Function
is the expression of principal idea: hair is "Spirit Connection of
the Heavens," knees are "Spirit of Completing cycles," hands are
"Spirit of manifesting" (158–59).

To meet the body and read its book, we must reinvest it with
energy: awareness and energy, *ti/chi*. We must once again, as
we were before our reliance on ordinary mind, become aware
of every sensation. To the Tiwa skin is *hai*, "life lifting us from
one level of consciousness to another." Skin, the entire body is
an extension of the ears. Relying on outer sight, without inner
or subtle sight, fools us. But listening with the entire body will
reveal the vibration of that surface and depth, appearance and
reality. In a later chapter, we will discuss physical mysteries in
the context of exploring the direction of the West on the medicine

wheel. Having a physical body is the miracle of being in this primary world. Ignoring body and relying on mind, we fall asleep and cease to experience this miracle of perceptual reality.

With this body, this micro-Earth, we experience through the five senses. This is the only reality in which this occurs. How and why have we taken this for granted and forsaken this direct sensate relationship with reality for the indirect relationship via thought? Knowing the name of a so-called thing, remembering a previous encounter with a similar thing, is not knowing or experiencing that phenomenon in the here and now, the present. So in order to become natural, to begin to live, we must practice being present in and through the micro-body/universe right now. This breath.

In fact, many mystics begin this awakening by watching the breath, sensing it enter and exit the body, causing various anatomical nuances as it does. In the instant of presence, of applying *ti* to sensations, time (which is a construct of thought) disappears. To become natural, Joseph expands the practice of presence: "To live naturally is to train oneself to live every day by practicing being present in mind, body, and spirit. Every living moment is a gift of life. Treat every single moment as if it were your last. Live from a place of honor, respect. Keep joyous. Wonder all the time. Always keep a child-like curiosity." We will discuss ways to implement this in succeeding chapters.

Once we meet the body (*tu-neh*) and are awakened to its miraculousness, we will appreciate its myriad ways of perceiving, which we cumulatively call instinct. We can literally consult the body for healing at all levels. In fact, it's already telling us everything we need to know to become real, but we don't want to hear. We will also encounter our essence, which natives often refer to as a primary and secondary animal, and the starting position on the medicine wheel. Jung refers to essence as a combination of the functions of intuition, intellect, emotion, and sensation. Alchemy and Asian medicine refer to essence as a mixture of primary and secondary elements, similar to astrology.

In Tiwa, *pee-ah-who* is being who you are, essence, "clothing yourself with your song, your music." The sounds of *pee-ah-who* tune us to primordial nature, our beginning place, as well as the archetype that some mystics call eternal being. Repeating these Tiwa sounds as a sacred phrase or mantra will tune us to our foundation and potential, awaken essence, the uncut/ unpolished stone of our eternal being. Joseph also suggests that one can lovingly repeat *chaah*. Draw the vibration out on the exhalation, as the very sound of your breath. Inhale, repeating it silently. *Chaah* is a very important Tiwa vibration with many connotations, all of which relate to singing. *Chaah* is "the song of now, the moment; it is the descending of the beauty of the heavens so we can have spiritual clarity; it is our going back to our original purity." Joseph teaches that we should commemorate the discovery with ceremony, one that incorporates song, dance, and shield-making. Indulge your being body with this vibration until it is the very sound of your breath.

Encountering and understanding essence is absolutely necessary. It is the unavoidable first step to knowing oneself. Real life, real growth is the expansion, integration, and balancing of functions/elements: the cutting and polishing of the rough stone. Not the accumulation of information: the one-sided muscling-up of mind/intellect. Only when you have met essence and gradually become it, will you discover your primary, fundamental relationship to life. We can only relate directly to life, all our relations (*ka-weh*), through *pee-ah-who*. Watch, listen, sense, taste, smell. Spend a weekend alone, camping in nature. Joseph even talks of fasting and spending days in a dark closet with the nature of your body. Get to know your body being intimately. Alone. Cry to the Universe for a vision, *weh-seh*. (Consult later chapters about crying for a vision and vision questing.) Send a voice that the doors of perception will open: *show-peh*. (*Show-peh*, "open the door," can be repeated as a mantra/prayer on the breath's inhalation and exhalation to take the next step into the unknown. Sense the openness of *show* and the penetration of *peh*.) Sing, dance, run, swim, sleep. Disregard mind. Experience directly.

Above all, Joseph, a visionary, advocates listening (with the entire body) to open the inner and outer doors:

> Listening is understanding the mystery of vibration because listening has to do with the inner vibration of the descending intelligence of the moment. Meditators become silent so that they can go to true vibration, which becomes the audible workings of vibration, of which ideas are made.
>
> Inner listeners, or people who are continually listening to life as it is unfolding, are true humans because they are picking up vibrational messages before the messages become crystallized energy or perceptual forms that can then be articulated by the brain. (67)

What primary animal/animals are revealing themselves in your being/body? What does the being/body really want/need? What does it avoid? What makes it powerful and magnetic? What depletes its energy and vigor? If you truly 'listen' with every sense, you will discover and become essence. And ask questions. Become an attentive question. Often, you can expedite this essentializing by remembering the natural inclinations of your being/body before the mind took over and you were indoctrinated and exposed to external suggestion, coercion, influence, and advertising. Not a single force in society values essence, wants you to be real. Being real, you escape commercialization. You follow the essential needs, not the herd. You become authentic, relatively free.

I write, 'relatively free' because essence is raw, limited. At the fundamental level, we have a primary and secondary animal/ element. But at a deeper, recessed level, we are all directions, functions, animals, elements. And growth (*wa-chi-chi-who*), life Itself, means exploring and developing. Life necessitates the integration of opposites, the discovery of napping capacities. Too much and too little of any element means limitation and disharmony. Too much Earth is stubbornness and sloth. Too much Water is affection and submissiveness. Too much fire is aggression and domination. Too much air is aloofness and irresponsibility. Life is all. We are each all. Allness is in order. Hence the spinning around and leaping across the medicine wheel.

Discovering and becoming underlying essence is related to

our communing with nature and Earth. Becoming absolutely intertwined in Grandmother Spider's (*Pah-ai-yah*) web. You must retreat from the concrete, practice physically what we will later practice in meditation with the elements. Your body is the miniature of the three worlds of Sky, Earth, and all creation in between. Joseph teaches that we are maps, maps containing all potentialities. Nature relates directly to essence, *pee-ah-who*. We relate to nature/universe only via essence and evolved essence. And that relationship is unique. No one else's history will help us discover and nurture it.

Again, this is why mind-dominated people continue to ignore and destroy creation, including their own bodies. Mind thinks it does not need body. But even mind needs body to exist in this primary world. Immersing your being in nature, even a park, extricating your being from technology and artificiality, awakens essence. Remember, you must re-inhabit your body to be alive and grow. Walk and sit on earth/Earth and its covering. Remove your shoes.

Practice what Whitman writes in *Leaves of Grass*. Release the repressed child. Play, *eh-pee-ah*. *Eh-pee-ah* means "God is here making." The Tiwa metaphor for *eh-pee-ah* is "strengthening oneself. When we are playing, we are . . . making the self what it is becoming" (69). Commune. Relax. Let your aura/energy field expand and merge. Experience all with all senses. Hold a tree, lean on a tree, climb a tree, breathe with a tree. Lose yourself in sky. Lie on the shore. Bury yourself in sand. Float in a lake. Run in the rain. Shower in a waterfall. Drink the sun. Build a fire. Fly a kite. Be a kite. Play like a child with no intention and no purpose. (As Carl Jung did to recover his creativity.) No gain and no achievement. As often as you possibly can. And then realize all this is you too.

We must imagine the primary, indigenous peoples who were their environment, who were their relations. The land provided their needs. They manifested as tribes in certain places, with certain elemental features. Though food was sometimes scarce, their diet was perfect. Nature gave them what they needed. They were nature. And if nature did not provide what they needed,

147

such as rain to grow corn, they were shown ceremonies to come back into primordial balance.

Not only are we not essential, many of us have lost our primal, tribal relation to place, geography, the seasons, the sun and moon. We are alienated from the land of our essence. And everywhere we have destroyed land in order to inhabit urbia and suburbia. How can we learn what to eat when? How do we rediscover the essential rhythms and elements of place, in addition to the rhythms of body? How do we integrate them? How do we introduce the natural into the artificial? We must build from scratch, bit by bit. We are like an unhealed wound. We must clear away the infected flesh first. Then introduce healthy, natural activities and ways.

In his first pamphlet, *Healing*, published in 1981, Joseph explains the use of shrines and landmarks to orient the body and environment. Remember, we are each *tu-tah*, center, kiva, love. Experience the cup (*ti-uh*) as we inhale; the throne as we exhale. We experience this through sensing the body and conscious breathing. We enhance it by discovering how all the directions of the universe originate from and return to this Center. We are the moving Center, but our homes, our nests, are stationary. Orient your home with the cardinal directions, first with the East and West. Know where the sun rises and sets, even if you can't see it from inside. Then add North and South. Mark these in your home, with a plant, a crystal, a stone, a shell, something natural. These, then become shrines. Orient yourself to the shrines, the Directions just as primal people do. If you live in a home, you can build shrines or place stones around your house, extending the sacred ground of your subtle body.

148

Next, you can orient the directions of your home to your surrounding environment. You can place these up to twenty miles away from your home, your dwelling center. If you don't place them, you can find natural phenomena nearly equidistant from your home in the four directions. Then, you need to "feed" them, invest them with your awareness and occasional presence, maybe even saying a prayer or leaving some tobacco, sage, or corn meal. Such a geographical orientation (map/

medicine wheel) approximates the holy planning and lifestyle of the pueblo, whose entire physicality unfolds in a sacred context. Every pueblo is permeated and surrounded by shrines, kivas, and mountains which mark, energize, and protect the gross and subtle bodies of the people, individually and collectively. You are the holy microcosmic map of the holy home, the holy village, the holy Earth, the holy universe. Order. As Above so Below, as Inner so Outer.

III. Discovering One's Animal/ Animals

For native and awakened peoples, natural phenomena are metaphors, epiphanies or archetypes—pure meaningfulness. This spiritual sensitivity is particularly heightened among the Tiwa, for it is embedded in their language, which they learned from nature. Your primary body is the point (*pee*) or the arrow, which is the soul (*kai-pee-ah-neh*). Your arrowhead or point is composed of all four elements, but you will have one major, one minor, and two peripheral elements. The elements manifest in concrete and subtle forms, throughout creation. We will discuss this more deeply when we experience the elements.

Knowing that animals are the perfect embodiment of essence will help you discover yours. And, while some animals have qualities of several elements (like the horse which has aspects of all four), humans have all elements in infinite combinations (though they are naturally imbalanced). Humans are born raw. Potential. And soon most of the so-called civilized ones become unnatural, artificial. To realize potential, humans must unlearn in order to become raw again, so they can undergo arduous preparation and cooking, for a long time, over a low heat. Finding the predominant animal archetypes that comprise your raw essence will jumpstart your becoming. Remember that the animals/elements are reflected both in your physical and metaphysical or subtle body (as pure archetypes).

Your animal/animals will have natural style and needs. The more unnatural you have become, the more you will have to remember your natural inclinations as a child. What did you wear, eat, do? Did you dig holes, climb trees, flood the bathroom, fly kites, start fires? Wrestle, run, sing, whistle, purr, cuddle, jump? Were you diurnal or nocturnal? You will sort out all this confusion if you practice presence in the body. It will guide you. It is the focal point of the entire creation. You can, however, be aware of certain guidelines. The more your being body grows (incorporates, integrates, balances), the more difficulty you will have identifying original essence. Joseph clearly came into this world as an air being, an arrow/eagle, but those who experience him sense all the elements in plenitude. Remember *chaah*: Your soul is a song (the universe is polyphonic); go back to original purity; become the eternal beauty descending into spiritual clarity.

Also, at any given time, a certain element/direction will be most challenging for you, but at the same time, will give you the most energy when you've learned to embrace and incorporate it. You can see this subtlely and overtly in every aspect of your life, particularly in human relationships. Also, you will always have an abundance of original essence, too much for your own good. So, you will always tend to rely on it, or lead with it, as in card games, because it is your strong suit. Especially when you are exhausted or out of balance. For instance, Air types will always be challenged by Earth issues. Always be tested to take responsibility, make a stand, hold one's ground, stay put. Under pressure or under the weather, they will tend to fantasize, 'blow-off,' avoid, escape. Essence will always involve one's primary strength/gift and one's liability.

Living according to essence, you will be rooted, able to truly grow—actually, pressured to grow by the Universe. Jesus the Prophet referred to this as building one's house on rock rather than sand. And also as sowing seeds in good soil, under the sun and rain. Your essence will know what it needs to eat, what it needs to do, and when it needs to do nothing. But remember, it has natural inclinations that are inevitably unbalancing. Once you are rooted in essence, the next step is to sense where you are headed, which is always the direction/element/animal opposite beginning essence. Yet, you may already have leaped into that opposite and begun to explore the opposite of your secondary direction/element/animal. And so forth, multi-dimensionally. Being always grows toward balancing essence and evolving essence. Level upon level. World after world.

Raise some tomatoes. Plant sage. If you can't start a garden, eat less processed food, food with fewer chemicals. Ingest less processed air and water, our primary foods. Implement a balanced diet and manner in every sense. Act and rest. Right act and rest. Inhale and exhale fully and deeply. Act, make effort, but don't abuse the body. Sleep but do not become lazy and slothful. Work physically so the body is tired enough to sleep. Wake before sunrise. And you should certainly monitor whatever you put in your body. Every food is a medicine/ poison, depending on circumstances, as well as your animal/animals. Begin to appreciate the essence of foods and additives by fasting for two or three days and then experiencing the quality of your intake. Organic tobacco. Tea. Coffee. Salt. Pepper. Sugar. Chocolate. Juice. Alcohol. Ingest one substance at a time. Listen with the entire being body. Sense its essence and its effect on your evolving essence and eternal being, which Jung called Self.

Experience the effect of landscapes, buildings, trees, flowers, weather, animals and other people. Everything is an expression of the elements. And sensing through presence will open to intuition, immediate knowing beyond mind, despite experience and facts. Every moment is an encounter of infinite essences. Not living in a sacred, natural community like Picuris of old, we are challenged to grow, to not just get old. We must learn the perennial wisdom from within. We must be our own guardians and elders. With so much resistance, so much inauthenticity and ignorance, we must dedicate ourselves to the natural life in order to become real. We must recreate our own Eden before the fall. Within and then around us. The Self/Vast Self, the eternal being, will naturally impose reality upon illusion, ignorance, and pretence. By being, by doing nothing. *Pee-ah-who. Pee-ah-who.* On the breath, in and out of the chest. How the Vast Self is uniquely present in/as you.

These contemplative practices that follow are embedded in or suggested by Joseph's teachings. In time, establish a pattern, like in eating. Meditation is subtle food. Practice in early morning and evening. Sit on the floor with your back straight but not stiff. Sensing that your head is suspended from the sky helps. It encourages the flow of *chi* along the spine. Sit in a chair or lean against a tree if you must. But make the chair a wooden one, one that was once alive. In fact, Joseph has suggested that we imagine ourselves to be a tree: "Like a tree we sit straight and high in God's greatness." He has also suggested repeating *thlii* to enhance our treeness. "Wood equals wisdom."

You will see that some of the practices are better suited to morning; others to night. Some accumulate energy. Some pull energy inward; some expand energy outward, in one or all directions. Some direct energy upward and some downward. Some do not direct at all. They work. But you may not notice a change initially. They must be implemented in the spirit of adventure. Partake according to your taste. In hope of being less rather than more. Emptiness (the fount of *ti/chi* and presence/ *who*) is essential to becoming natural and appreciating this revelation. Paradoxically, we are never so full, so much our Self (the Vast Self), as when we cease to exist. "The true measure of our success in life is how much of, or the degree of nothingness (emptiness) we can achieve" (*Being and Vibration* 181).

In general, unless one is on retreat or keeping vigil, practices which direct energy downward and outward should be performed in morning, afternoon, and perhaps early evening. Day, sun time, is for outer action and achievement. Practices that direct energy inward and upward are best performed at night or very early morning. Since energy naturally moves in and up in evening/ moon time, this accords with nature/Tao and prepares us for restful sleep and inner transformation. Evening is generally the time of prayer and receptivity.

IV. Wiping Clear the Walls

Visualization/creative imagination has finally been recognized in our culture as a means of transformation, healing, creativity, and intuition. In order to visualize successfully, you will need to develop concentration and to image colors and shapes with the imagination. We know this involves the right brain, the belittled half of our biocomputer. More than just the right brain, you must strengthen the subtle mind and impose it on the gross, personal mind, sometimes called 'monkey' mind. Your subtle mind (cornerstone of *nah*) must watch and eventually curtail automatic thought through noticing. Tiwans refer to this as *ah-tschlu*: "Doing with full attention." This will happen naturally when awareness (*ti*) is clear and locked in to the body. When your brain-wave activity shifts into the Theta range, associated with choiceless awareness. If you are obsessed by certain thoughts, Joseph suggests that repeating *pi-ya* drives habitual thought into the depth of the heart, gateway to *nah*.

In order to prepare ourselves for practice, our consciousness must become kiva walls. In Tiwa, kiva walls are *nah-pooh*, meaning "wiping clean the screen so that wisdom can be projected for the person watching." We can visualize the sides of our skull as the walls. First, visualize your skull as hollow, filled with clear light, like an empty stage. You clear out the clutter in the room/stage with the breathing (*hah*). Conscious breathing strengthens awareness, visualization, and energy.

Luminous Skull

154

Inhale descending light through the top of your head, which is like a cup (*ti-uh*). Then exhale that light out in all directions. You will strengthen subtle mind and disperse random thought. You can also practice 'blue sky mind' by visualizing clear, cool blue sky inside the head, and eventually all around. You simply breathe away any thought clouds that appear. Onto that blue-sky horizon/canvas, you can project/paint anything.

You can also build upon the luminous skull practice by

visualizing radiant arrows emerging from the illuminated center. This practice strengthens what Joseph calls Intent, *poh-ceh* in Tiwa. *Poh-ceh* is "blowing breath with eyes that see." Again inhale descending light (*waa*) into the empty skull (through the nostrils). This time, when you exhale (through the mouth), blow luminous arrows of *ti* through your empty eye sockets. Breathing through the nostrils is the sky breath. (You can sense the breath circulate higher in your head.) Breathing through the mouth is the Earth breath. (You can sense it circulating in the lower skull and throat.) You can also send a third luminous arrow through your forehead. In Chinese alchemy, the energy center between and just above the eyebrows is called the yi. Yi is the Chinese name for *ti*. Sending light and breath through this area heightens awareness, one-pointed concentration.

Once awareness establishes openness, you can summon up virtually any image. Holding the image demands concentration. The next stage is contemplation. When consciousness becomes contemplation, you can interact with the object (actual or imagined). Your faculty of intuition can reveal new, unnoticed aspects of the image you have invoked. For instance, if you're concentrating on a mountain, you may see mountain goats and trees upon it, or caves. If you're concentrating on a red, four-petaled rose, four more petals may appear, or a butterfly may arrive, or the rose may change color. This signals contemplation. It is a kind of subtle dance between subject and object, a sort of mutual disclosure. You can even ask the image/being what something means and receive an answer. Contemplation (which grows from one-pointed awareness) allows us to commune with the universe, to consciously share at the subtle, archetypal level.

When our consciousness is locked into the serene level of contemplation, we can also receive rather than project. Instead of creating, concentrating upon, and interacting with an image, we can also just maintain open awareness, without focusing. In this state of consciousness we receive *ah-who*. *Ah-who* is the "breath of highest inspiration which is washing us." *Ah-who* enters us as we inhale. If we're in silent, open awareness. Wiping clear the walls is the foundation of all practice and can be utilized at all times of day.

v. Realizing the Three Worlds

Although Joseph had visions as a young child living on the Southern Ute Reservation in Colorado, his spiritual training began when he arrived at Picuris Pueblo at age six. Picuris was not only a school for learning the mysteries taught by elders; it was a mystery school itself. The closest examples we have in Western culture would be the great Gothic cathedrals such as Chartres, which contained sacred art and symbols, and were constructed as spiritual metaphors. However, people lived in and on Picuris, which was built according to revelation. Living there as a child, coming in as an outsider, Joseph was able to appreciate the sacred structure, vibrations and symbols.

The pueblo was constructed in accordance with spiritual principles. Homes, prayer chambers, shrines, cemeteries, fields, and paths were oriented with the sacred landscape and cardinal directions, realized as spiritual powers by primal peoples. The people were sacred energy among sacred energy:

> Because we lived as energy, we began to understand that everything in each designated location was the resonating vibration of the play of principal ideas. The holy shrines were placed there because the vibrational essence of those holy sites would enhance the psyche of community and of each individual within community. The vibration would bind us to a love relationship, a knowing that life was in love with us, that we held the living life within our lives. This knowing kept me loyal to my beloved landscape. (*Being and Vibration* 21)

The village was composed of three different levels: the central square/circle, the higher level with a few homes and kiva, and the highest level with many more homes and fields.

Walking *(taa-chi-who)* on the path connecting the three levels, Joseph realized he was traversing and connecting the three levels: Under world, Middle world, Upper world. Picuris is a microcosm: as Above, so Below; as Outside, so Inside.

The Underworld is below the Earth's skin. It is the womb realm from which the Pueblo emerged and the womb in which

they, like many animals, once burrowed their homes and still
burrow their prayer chambers. Middle world stretches from
the skin to the sky, from surface to mountain top. This is the
creature realm, from plants, to the crawlers, to the finned, to the
four-legged, to the wingeds. The Upper world is the infinite sky
realm of the subtle, angelic beings, touched by mountaintops
and eagles.

Just as Picuris is a microcosm, our body being (which is the
Vast Self) is a microcosm containing the three worlds. The three
worlds also correspond to the abdomen, chest, and head. The
lower/underworld can be experienced from the navel down to
the sacral plexus at the bottom of the spine, and from there into
the Earth. We are an 'open system.' The lower world extends
infinitely below. We can begin to experience this world by
coordinating concentration, creative imagination, and breath.

Breathing

Sit with your spine straight but relaxed, on the floor or in
a wooden chair. Take a long in-breath, feel your abdomen
expanding. In Tiwa, the abdomen is *ti-uh*, the same sounds as
cup. In the abdominal cup "awareness and time come together."
The cup is an excellent image/metaphor. Chinese alchemy
recognizes the same phenomenon. Ancient Taoist practitioners
called the navel area the crucible, the gathering capacity for the
subtle energy coursing through the microcosm of the body, the
energy also called *chi*. (Though in both traditions the *chi* sound
means subtle energy that can be directed inside and outside, in
Tiwa mysticism *chi* can have many more meanings depending
on its context.)

Exhale naturally. With every inhalation, relax and further
expand the abdomen. Fill your cup with *chi*. With every
exhalation begin to send stress and tension down through
the bottom of the spine; release all limitation and dis-ease to
the depths of the Earth. At a certain point, you may sense or
visualize the dis-ease as a murky cloud or automobile exhaust.
With each new inhalation bring *ti* (and thereby *chi*) into the

abdomen. The focus of *ti*, especially when coordinated with breathing, creates *chi*.

You can further refine this practice by visualizing the Earth's surface at the navel and the navel as the entrance to the lower world, the womb from which the Pueblo people emerged. Like Indian sages, and Greek figures like Orpheus and Hermes, you enter the opening on the inhalation and descend a path of light as you exhale. Descending energy/consciousness is *hli-o* in Tiwa. With succeeding exhalations, you deepen and widen the light. The lower world is associated with the infrared part of the spectrum. So you can enhance this practice by filling the abdomen with orange-red-burgundy light. When it is relaxed and charged, it should glow like the sun or the inside of a furnace.

BELOW

Many mystics associate the abdomen with power, sexuality, sensuality, instinct, and the unconscious. You can address the presence of the Underworld, also called the Below and Grandmother Earth. In Tiwa, She is *Naah-aah-uu-kwill*. You can address Her with the following words: "I/we send a voice to Grandmother Below, *Naah-ah-uu-kwill*. I/we invoke Her blessing of sustenance and protection." If you say this silently, repeat the first part (sending) as you exhale, and the second part (invoking) as you inhale. You may also combine the two sentences (and subsequent invocations) into one: "I/we send a voice to Grandmother Below, *Naah-ah-uu-kwill*, invoking Her blessing of sustenance and protection."

158

MIDDLE

Middle world is associated with the chest and stretches from the solar plexus to the base of the neck. To enliven and explore this world, inhale through the solar plexus (the area below the ribs) and exhale through the chest. With each inhalation, fill the solar plexus with more *chi*; with each exhalation release tension, stress, and dis-ease through the chest. The middle world

corresponds to the middle of the spectrum, so inhale yellow sun
into the solar plexus up to the sternum and exhale green from
the sternum to the base of the neck.

Mystics associated the middle realm with sympathy, love,
generosity, compassion. The center of the middle is the
Center of the Universe, the beginning and end, the first and
seventh direction. Physiologically, this hub/axis (which is also
circumference, *haah-ley*) is behind the sternum. You can address
the direction of the Center by saying: "I/we send a voice to the
Center which is also the Circumference, *Pii-ini-aah-ii.* I/we
invoke Its blessing of Unity."

Upper

The Upper world extends from the chin up through the top of
the head. Inhale through the forehead and exhale through the
top of the head. The neck is a bridge connecting the Middle/
chest world to the Upper world. The world of pure feeling with
the world of pure thinking/Awareness. While inhaling, keep
filling the skull with *ti* and exhaling dis-ease from the top of the
head, which you can visualize as a chimney releasing smoke.
You may start to sense heightened, sharpened awareness. Once
the exhalation clarifies, you will experience consciousness rising
to the transpersonal level. Rising, rising energy/consciousness
is *we-ley.* The Upper world is also known as the Above, Sky, and
Grandfather. You can address the Above by saying: "I/we send a
voice to Grandfather Above, *Pa-peh-tah.* I/we invoke His blessing
of wisdom."

Sense how your awareness is co-extensive with beyond-
the-beyond consciousness/Intelligence. Like Lower World, the
Upper world extends infinitely. Your head is like a cup (with a
hatch in the bottom). Explore all the organs of the head, all the
nuances of the brain as you inhale. You can continue until you
sense the exhalation becoming luminous and fresh. Or until
you are relaxed, more aware, or energized. If you wish, you
can illuminate your eyes and your glance as you exhale. Joseph
teaches that the eyes are channels for "the washing lights." Or

you can shift to using color. The head corresponds to the ultra-violet edge of the spectrum: light blue and violet.

LINK THE THREE

If you want to link all three worlds together, you can inhale up red/orange in the bottom, then yellow/green in the chest, then blue/violet in the head, then white above the head. Then you can exhale downward visualizing violet/blue in the head, then green/yellow in the chest, then orange/red in the abdomen, then burgundy below. A nuance of this practice would be to visualize the energy/color swirling around in each of the worlds before guiding them up and down. You might visualize the worlds as pools, eddies, or lakes connected by a river. Don't let the pools become stagnant. Allow them to flow into each other, energize each other and communicate.

This simple but profound practice connects and purifies sensing, feeling, and seeing, and opens us to intuition and inspiration. You also know the invocations of the first three directions—Center, Above, and Below: *Pii-ini-aah-ii, Paah-peh-tah*, and *Naah-aah-uu-kwill*. This is the Tiwa trinity, the first three forces that form the vertical axis, the unity that created the initial duality. If you are sitting or standing, you can pray with the names by silently breathing *Pii-ini-aah-ii* behind the sternum; inhaling into the beyond and exhaling down with *Paah-peh-tah*, and exhaling down into the below and inhaling up with *Naah-aah-uu-kwill*. A more difficult concentration involves centering yourself in *Pii-ini-aah-ii* and exhaling down and up at the same time, experiencing the spreading of your energy field, the splitting of the poles; then inhaling and experiencing the convergence of the poles, the empowering of the Center.

The full practice, up and down, is best done in morning and afternoon. At night, one can benefit from moving energy upward, the first half of the practice.

VI. Housing the Shattering Light

Joseph's first spiritual teacher was his paternal Grandmother Rael, with whom his family lived for over a year. The house, located just inside the pueblo, on the far side of the river, was constructed of adobe, a mixture of straw, mud, and micaceous clay. Though box-like, the adobe's outer walls were slightly rounded. The myriad specks of mica in the clay reflected the sun's golden rays, causing the home to glitter.

Telling him that her adobe home represented the first house, Grandmother introduced the perception of the *house of shattering light*. As a container or shell, what some mystics call a capacity and identify with the element of ether or space, her house was a metaphor for existence on Earth, what Joseph calls our *primary* world. Literally made of glittering earth, her house reflected the physical body, which is crystallized light, and the subtle, auric body that interpenetrates it.

In *House of Shattering Light*, Joseph says in Tiwa body is *tu-nay*, which means "to crystallize the power of carrying the experiences of the Vast Self in a pure clarity of awareness" (76). The subtle auric body that penetrates it is the *nah*, the Tiwa equivalent of higher self or soul. *Nah*, at a finer level, is also the "pure clarity of awareness" that fixes the "carrying of the experiences of the Vast Self."

The Vast Self is the Great Spirit, Oversoul, Absolute, or Divine, with specific primal, Tiwa nuances. The Vast Self is not just transcendent. We, crystallized creation, are the presence of the Vast Self; humans just generally lack the awareness of the *nah*. Without the pure clarity of awareness they exist in duality, thinking body/Earth is other than the Vast Self. Thereby not allowing the Vast Self to experience Itself through them.

In fact, Vast Self is not *just* any thing. It is Every Thing and No Thing, infinite and finite, constant metamorphosis and circulation. Circulation from the Void, which is purely potential, uncreated, pre-existent to all that we perceive with the subtle and gross senses. Joseph teaches that the Void is really not empty; it is an energy so pure, so clear, that we cannot see it. To be more precise, The Vast Self is not a noun or thing at all but a verb. An action, an 'ing' that is beyond our understanding but not our experience. The Tiwa name for the Vast Self revealing in/as manifestation is *Wa-Ma-Chi*. The *wa* that ever becomes *ma*, that becomes *chi*, that becomes silent Non-existence, that becomes *wa*.

Grandmother taught that every thing in the primary world of the physical universe will dissolve, dismantle, die. Solidity and permanence are illusory; everything apparent is shattering, right now. The adobe of the body is weathering into its constituents, and our subtle light body doesn't have to go to the world of light because it's already there. We simultaneously exist and non-exist, and are every subtle state in between.

In this sense, the house is the slice of white light, the white stripes of the koshares, the sacred clowns. Joseph likens the house to a moment in which we exist (really *Wa-Ma-Chi* exists) that allows us to change before we and the moment slip back into the black of non-existence (the koshares' black stripes). In Tiwa, the Pueblo tricksters are *ah-wa-yeh-ne*, "shaking up, circulating, interpenetrating, dying before death."

Understanding the metaphor of the house of shattering light allows us to understand the relativity of time, creativity, choice, and responsibility, all in the context of inherent (egocentric/personal) non-existence. Joseph also illustrates this with the metaphor of the strobe light. When it flashes on, experience the ray of existence: Intelligence, awareness, aura, and crystallization. When it disappears, between inhalation and exhalation and inhalation, experience non-existence, spiritual death.

So, the house of the body, which the ordinary senses and mind experience as solid, is the crystallized presence of the *Wa-Ma-Chi*, and the subtle light that interpenetrates it is the *nah*. And the energy/light that connects these two aspects of our being is awareness. Utilizing awareness (*ti*) and the creative imagination (capacities mystics associate with the subtle mind), we can experience the house of shattering light.

Square Breathing

This practice is best done in the morning. Face East, the
direction of the rising sun. Sitting cross-legged and straight
on the floor as Joseph did or in a straight-backed chair, we can
follow his grandmother's instruction, tasting her consciousness.
In Tiwa, sitting means "being greatness." At the same time,
our frame of bones and flesh and the imaginary adobe that
surrounds us are both the shimmering house.

First feel the expansion of abdomen and chest as you inhale
and relax and you exhale. You create space, a capacity within the
trunk. This is *in-spansion.* If you are not breathing with your
abdomen but your throat as many do, activate your diaphragm,
the breathing muscle. Extend the diaphragm, lengthening and
slowing the breath. When you are comfortable centering your
breath in the diaphragm, balance your breath by inhaling in
four counts, then exhaling four counts, each count being about a
second in duration. This is known as 'square' breathing.

Four Counts

Learn to breathe naturally, as you did when a baby, by first
expanding the lower abdomen(1), then the stomach(2), then the
chest(3), then the throat(4). You can literally say one, two, three,
four mentally. By consciously doing so, you will draw fresh
energy into the contracted recesses of the body. Also, conscious
energy, the light of awareness (*ti*) will penetrate the unconscious.

As you exhale, also in four counts, you will pump out
stagnant, stressed energy that has gathered in the abdomen.
Pause for a second, one beat, between inhalation and exhalation.
You can count four to one as you exhale. Begin your count
and concentration in the lower abdomen, just as you did the
inhalation. Initiating inhalation and exhalation in abdomen, we
fix the soul, the spiritual child, the *nah,* in the spiritual womb.

As you exhale from the bottom up, pushing carbon dioxide
out the nostrils, the house of shattering light—your awareness,
energy field or aura—spreads outward (*wu-leh-neh*). With each

163

succeeding inhalation and exhalation, you in-spand your center (increasing your capacity to contain and receive) and expand your subtle body (increasing your capacity to give and express).

Noting that we are also the house of shattering light in which we sit, expand exhalation to and then beyond the shimmering walls of the squared adobe, discovering inside yourself the space of the room as you inhale. Once you are at ease with balancing the breath, further refine your breathing by smoothening it. Imagine that when you breathe, you stroke a violin bow, making it even and constant. When you have done this, make your breathing even finer, more subtle. When your breath has become balanced, slow, smooth, fine, and luminous it will become a tool of intuition. It will also become a 360-degree shield of protection.

In order to experience this shield, we must extend all four sides of the house, as well as the roof and the floor. Breathing luminously in front is much easier than expanding and in-spanding the breath in the other directions.

Full House

To experience the full house, you must isolate the dimensions. After becoming comfortable breathing to and from the sun, rotate your breath sun-wise from front, to right, to back, to left in four successive breaths. After you send and receive the breath to East, South, West, and North in four successive breaths, rotate around in one breath, devoting one count to each direction. Envisioning your breath, the house of shattering light, as a lighthouse of radiant awareness can help. Next, inhale moon-wise, from front, left, back, and right (East, North, West, and South). Rotate the inhalation and exhalation back and forth, remembering to keep the breath, aware, balanced, slow, smooth, and subtle.

Next, you can imagine the breath expanding and in-spanding the breath to all sides simultaneously as you exhale/inhale. Then, you can add exhaling and inhaling above the head, into Grandfather Sky, the transcendent aspect of the Vast Self. Exhale and press awareness/aura into Intelligence, the clear white light 'beyond the beyond.' Your exhalation ascends above the head as if it climbs a luminous staircase, like Jacob in the Bible. Pause a beat; then inhale downward, drawing the transcendent light into the depth of the solar plexus. Joseph teaches that descending light is our spiritual law.

Next, exhale and inhale with the earth, the immanent aspect of the Vast Self. Sink your luminous roots as you exhale, penetrating golden Grandmother Earth. As you inhale from 'below the below,' draw the magnetism of creation into your center. In Tiwa mysticism, ascending light is our natural law. After this, you can try exhaling/inhaling upward and downward simultaneously. When you're ready, you can use creative imagination to extend the entire house outward at once, all flanks, all six directions. You are a luminous pulsing cube. The seventh and final direction is the Center, the cardiac plexus/heart from which the breath emits and to which it returns.

With practice, you will experience your luminous breath extending to the sun and stars at the speed of light, 186,000 miles per second. As you inhale, you will draw in the light of the stars, as well as all the subtle levels. Balancing the inhalation and exhalation not only integrates receptivity and activity, but inner and outer life. You will also experience that, after a slight pause, they flow into, become each other. That the inside is outside and the outside is inside. In its own way, becoming the house of shattering light is the contemplative equivalent of the sun dance, or Joseph's sun-moon dance, in which one dances to and from the central tree/cosmic axis, the spine. Here we do it with the breath, a practice that tries us more psychologically than physically.

Dancing Sun

If you want to skip all the previous inner work, just envision the horizontal sides of your shimmering, shattering house dancing in (*tu-yuh-ah-ney*) and out (*wu-leh-ney*) from your heart center as you inhale and exhale. Each side is a dancer, dancing in harmony. Collectively they, you, become a sun, a cubic/crystal-centered sun. Remember, practice cannot create what doesn't happen. It enhances it. This practice allows you to experience the four directions of breath: Upward (*we-ley*), Downward (*hli-o*), Outward (*wu-leh-ney*), and Inward *(tu-yuh-ah-ney)*.

This is a morning and afternoon practice.

VII. Becoming the Kiva

Though the adobe home was the domain of women, the feminine, it was the shape of men, the masculine. In the home, experiencing their 'squareness,' women experience their inner male. However, the kiva, the ancient Pueblo ceremonial chamber, is round, the feminine. When men enter the kiva, actually or imaginatively, they experience their roundness, their inner female, themselves as time: everchanging and flowing.

Pueblo life was not only created to enhance awareness and relatedness; it was created to enhance balance, integration of male and female qualities, sun and moon, the summer and winter moieties in the tribe. In fact, when Tiwa become elders they are no longer known as men or women but women-men. If the Pueblo sacred system of life has worked they will have become spiritually androgynous. They will have experienced the spiritual wedding of Magpietail Boy and Yellow Corn Woman that Joseph describes in *Beautiful Painted Arrow*. The inner spiritual marriage of autonomy, action, instinct, and mentality to relatedness, receptivity, intuition, and emotion.

Before the Pueblo and their ancestors, the Anasazi, lived in square adobes, they lived underground in pit houses. According to Joseph, the pit houses represented the underground womb in which the Pueblo lived before they emerged into the above-ground world we now inhabit, what Pueblo call the middle world (beneath the infinite heavens). The pit houses then, replicated the Pueblo's existence as pure intelligence (*wa*), when they lived under the crystalline surface of the legendary Sand Lake. Before the primal female deities of Blue Corn Woman and White Corn Woman birthed humanity.

In time, perhaps working toward a balance with father sky consciousness, and the masculine energy in general, the Pueblo built adobe homes above ground, sometimes several stories high, and kept the pits as ceremonial chambers in which they could experience original Corn-Mother consciousness, identify with Great Spirit. In time they became the extraordinary circular chambers we see in Anasazi sites such Chaco Canyon, Mesa Verde, and Aztec. In time some kivas were built half-under/ half-above ground, straddling both lower worlds. Some kivas, incorporating both male and female shapes, blended the square and circle.

The kivas at Picuris are both below ground and half-above/ half-below. All have a *sibapu*, an emergence hole, in the center of the floor. Above the *sibapu* is the sky hole. Descending the sky hole is the wooden ladder, the spiritual axis, the spine connecting heaven and earth. As Joseph wrote in *Being and Vibration*, "Going underground was a metaphor for entering the perfected self" (60). Simply said, we enter the kiva to be reborn.

The Tiwa call themselves *Tuu-taah-teh-nay* and *Pii-tah*, which Joseph translates as "where the center of life is, or where the kiva is the center" (*House of Shattering Light* 48). Identifying themselves with the emptiness and darkness of the womb, the people call themselves "the No-form creating the form." Paradoxically, Joseph states that they both don't exist and exist in states of non-existence. "Non-existence gives validity to existence" (48). Joseph was seven when he was taken into the kiva by Antonio Simbola, Pel-qui-weh, spiritual chief of Picuris and leader of the thunder-calling clan. Joseph's profound experiences in the kiva are described in *House of Shattering Light*. The kiva is a place of heightened receptivity in which the inner, subtle senses awaken. The specific Tiwa vibration for kiva is *tau-lee-uu-tah*, "point of light that acknowledges abundance." The place/condition for expanding clarity. Understanding and visualizing the kiva, even without being able to physically enter one, helps us better understand that we do not exist, Joseph's most fundamental and difficult mystical teaching.

We spoke about non-existence at the beginning of the shattering light meditation. In the context of that meditation, we are the strobe light: We exist as light during the inhalation and exhalation; we don't exist between inhalations and exhalations and vice versa. (When we inhale, the light turns within until it disappears.) The keys to understanding non-existence are egolessness and emptiness.

Egolessness means not being governed by personal desires—desires for pleasure, approval, attention, importance, and superiority. Collectively, these egocentric impulses comprise what is known as self, small self, gross self, ego, me. Joseph calls this aspect of us the personal self. It is governed by ordinary or gross mind. Beings fixated in personal consciousness are said to be 'asleep.' Awareness (subtle mind) is not yet independent. Mystics say it is 'identified' with its content. When we are spiritually asleep, we do not see our motives and reactions; we believe we are just our sensations, emotions, and thoughts. And if we are somewhat aware of our automatic behavior, we lack conscience (subtle emotion) to realize it is destructive. This psycho-spiritual limitation can only be lessened by grace, longing, and long-term witnessing. Most importantly, one must realize (via conscience) the destructiveness of egocentricity and long to lessen (die to) egocentricity, self-image (persona), and undesirable aspects (shadow).

Emptiness, a major focus of Tibetan Buddhism, is best experienced when we descend the ladder of consciousness into the darkness of our inner kiva, our inner space. When we do this, we are Magpietail Boy, seeking the realization of our wife, Yellow Corn Woman, who dwells with the wizards in original consciousness (*wa-chi-who*). Emptiness is fostered by giving-away, a practice built into everyday native life. Giving-away, we do not cling; we create inner space. We guard against clinging and attaching to the material.

The practice is best done at night. First imagine yourself in the high arid landscapes of the Southwest. You can imagine sunset, firelight, or moonlight. You might burn sage. Antonio Simbola burned sage in the kivas to purify and heat the space. Sage (*taah-uh-lo*) means "to clear a pathway to divine self." Descend a ladder and sit on the floor, in the center of the kiva, facing west. The Tiwa name for sitting is *laa-aa-ii-eh*, which means "bringing clarity to awareness."

When you are comfortable in the cool, dry darkness, begin the square breath, as described in the first practice. Send the breath in all directions, 360 degrees. Slow, balance, smoothen, and refine the breath. Exhale into blackness. Inhale blackness. Expand your breath until you become the kiva: black, empty, silent, and still, peaceful. Merge with, become the Vast Self. Though it is not the aim, you may experience subtle light, sound, or energy around you or reflecting off the kiva's invisible walls. Remember, walls are *naah-pooh* in Tiwa: "wiping clean the screen so that wisdom can be projected." You can end the practice here, repeating it as often as you wish. Or you can proceed to the next stage.

In this stage you are the kiva. The hole in the top of the kiva, through which the ladder descends, is the top of your head. The ladder is your spine. The *sibapu* is the bottom of your spine. You will descend the ladder of the spine on the breath. Concentrate high above your head, in the sky, transcendent consciousness. From a point high above the head inhale downward through the top of the head, continuing down to the solar plexus. Pause and then exhale down through the bottom of the spine.

Center your breath in the abdomen and gradually begin the square abdominal breathing pattern. As you inhale down, you can count one in the head, two in the neck, three in the chest, and four in the solar plexus. Pause one count in the solar plexus, and then exhale four behind the navel, three in the groin, two in the bottom of the spine, and one in the earth. Continue this concentration until you feel grounded in the underworld and sense a hollow column of energy around the spine.

The next step involves expanding that inner column and experiencing the kiva within. Your skin, the outer shell of crystallized light, is the circumference of the kiva. Temporarily abandon the square breath and accentuate the inhalation, expanding within, inspanding. After a long inhalation, hold the breath, experiencing the emptiness within the solar plexus, abdomen, and chest. Exhale naturally. Continue to lengthen the inhalation, lengthen the time you hold your breath, and exhale naturally. With every inbreath, with every inspansion, experience inner opening, the breaking of bands of stress, anxiety, and egocentricity. During the holding of the breath experience emptiness, hollowness, the void, silence, stillness. All within.

Gradually balance the breath and return to the slow, smooth, refined square (4/1/4) breath.

SACRED WITHINNESS

With continued practice, you will experience the sacred withinness of the kiva/circle, the womb of creation, the unlimited black hole, the hidden aspect of the Vast Self. Not only will you experience emptiness and non-existence, and become aware of your subtle senses, you will be able to perform spiritual practices within your inner space, just as Joseph did inside the kiva. The next step is to coordinate these breathing practices, to integrate the male, square house and the female, round kiva within.

Sacred withinness is best practiced in early evening or early morning. At night energy leaves the container. If you follow this with a more extroverted practice, you can do this in morning or afternoon. Or anytime you feel the need to turn within and regain your center. Remember, once you become kiva, all practices take place within emptiness, even if they rise into the beyond the beyond.

As a boy, one of Joseph's kiva practices was to sit in the kiva and enter various colors, all of which are archetypal energies. (He describes this in *House of Shattering Light* and *Being and Vibration*.) Black is "seeing that which we have been looking for and haven't found yet" (*Being and Vibration* 116). "Breath and blackness are the same thing because Spirit is in the breath of nightimeness" (115). It is also the "power of the void, or the No-form, to speak through into the form—in essence, the power to create." Yellow "[opens] new doorways of opportunity" (*House of Shattering Light* 43) "Yellow is the symbol of openness—openess to another realm that you have not been able to access up to this point. . . . White is used to break a pattern or readjust something in your life." White has the power to overcome obstacles, to break molds. Red brings "satisfactory completion" (*Being and Vibration* 116–17). It infuses us with courage, physical power, and assures fulfillment. Blue empowers us to venture into unknown territory (*House of Shattering Light* 43).

VIII. *Reconciling through Listening: The Woman and the Wolf*

Before young Picuris girls and boys were able to practice reconciliation of their male (square) and female (circle) natures, their unconscious was primed by their elders (male/female ones). The storytellers (*key-ah-tah-meh-nay*) gathered the children in kivas to listen to the ancient, archetypal stories, much the same way that Euro/American children listen, or used to listen, to fairy tales. When Euro/American children hear "Once upon a time," they know that the story is not a rational narrative aimed at the ordinary mind, but a timeless, irrational tale aimed at the metaphoric subtle mind of the unconscious. Tales also planted the pattern of sacred vibration into the empty centers of its listeners. (For the Tiwa the skin of the entire body is an extension of the ears. The entire body listens.) Sacred tales, metaphors, nurture becoming rather than success or societal acceptance.

Tiwa elders told stories in the month following the winter solstice, during the coldest time of the year, when the mind is clear. They would begin stories with *chu-ha-men-ten*. In Tiwa, which is a collection of sounds received from nature, the Vast Self, *chu-ha-men-ten* literally means "at the sand place." The sand place is the legendary place where the Pueblo first emerged from the dark underworld womb. Every grain of sand is a crystal; hence the sand place is primordial, crystalline Intelligence, transcendent mind. To experience the radiant consciousness of *chu-ha-men-ten*, enter the kiva of your being and sound the vibrations, without thought, swallowing the vibrations deeper and deeper into the chest abdomen. Sense the tones and overtones in the abdomen, chest, throat, and head—the resonating chambers of the body. This will in turn awaken the subtle, metaphoric mind.

In *The Power of Myth*, Joseph Campbell calls this the mystical function of myth:

> Myth opens the world to the dimension of mystery, to the

realization of the mystery that underlies all forms. If you lose that, you don't have a mythology. If mystery is manifest through all things, the universe becomes, as it were, a holy picture. You are always addressing the transcendent mystery through the conditions of your actual world. (38–39)

The story "Magpietail Boy and His Wife" (Yellow Corn Woman) is the fundamental Tiwa becoming/integration myth. If we are able to listen like little children, it will initiate in us, as unnatural as we are, the integration of our square and circle natures. Imagine that the Wise Woman/Man elder (*kap-ah-neh*) in you is telling the innocent, teachable child in you this story. Yellow Corn Woman is the realized circle, the woman who has become whole, the Vast Self. She, along with Blue Corn Woman, is one of the original deities in the underworld womb. Magpietail Boy often represents the mischievous trickster. Here, the elegant black and white bird represents this and more. He represents spiritual sleep and unawareness. The animus that seeks illusory mastery of the outer world. As a boy, an 'uncircled' square, he is a purposeless player, in all the connotations of the word. This metaphoric tale conveys the inner circling of the square, transformation through spiritual marriage. The story was summarized and interpreted in Part One. Please read Joseph's original telling and interpretation of the story in *Beautiful Painted Arrow: Stories and Teachings from the Native American Tradition.*

While "Magpietail Boy and His Wife" tells about a man's quest for wholeness, "The Woman and the Wolf" tells about a woman's quest. First I'll tell it conventionally, as Joseph recounted it at a Mystery School. Then I'll discuss it, applying some of Joseph's translation from the original Tiwa. In a letter Joseph wrote, "study the Tiwa words and you will see that the story is more about the higher universal Intelligence that is constantly gathering our natural essence inside the essence of an Earthly home.

Once upon a time the people were dwelling at Picuris Pueblo. The women, after it got dark, were to remain inside their houses.

And one woman in the night had no water. She took the water jar and went down to Painon to get water. As she was pouring the water with her gourd, a Wolf came to her. "What are you doing?" he said.

"I am pouring water," the woman said to the Wolf.

"Get on my back, then," the Wolf said to her.

"I am already about to take the water to my house," said the woman.

"Get on my back, I said to you, or I will eat you up right here."

The woman became afraid, left the jar and got on the Wolf's back. And the Wolf took the woman up to the mountains. When he had brought her to the mountaintop, the Wolf went northeast, northwest, southwest, and southeast, to call the other wolves. The woman climbed a tall piñon tree.

Her husband, when his wife did not come up from below quickly, yelled as a signal from the top of the house. And shortly men with their weapons arrived.

When the old wolf arrived from summoning the other wolves, the woman was sitting in the top of the piñon tree.

The men all gathered for a search. And then about midnight, one man found the woman. The man gave a yell. After the rest came they took the woman home again. The woman was scolded very much by the men. And this is why the women, after it gets dark, do not go forth from inside the houses alone, for something might happen to them.

First, the story begins, as all Picuris stories, "where the sand place sits," where each granule is a universe. There is also the understanding, based on the original Tiwa, that we are participants as well as listeners: "Life does not belong to us, rather we belong to life, and we are participating in many, many stories, yet we exist in only one of them, in each moment." Picuris is "where the heart of drinking light lives."

The women are the houses, which they own and maintain. They are the capacities, the receptive containers, the kivas. Women are the "power to descend to many levels of vibrations," "to explore new psychic territories." Women, in the story and life, represent withinness and belowness. Joseph commented that "the people need to know who they are, where they came from, and so the women's staying inside of their houses meant to protect the holy journey of the people." This, of course, also keeps women in their place, as representatives of a single principle.

The home lacks water, which is light, which is "awareness." Therefore, she took the jar ("To have the powers to look into the deeper levels of consciousness, inner knowing") and went down ("loving warmth"). Wolf, which means "spiritual power" or "angel of food" arrived to "heal her." We understand that they are spiritual food for each other.

He asked her to get on his back, to be carried by him to another level of consciousness. Wolf is the wild, the untamed, the undomestic, the animus.

After resisting, stating that she is fulfilling her role of "throwing the light of awareness," "lifting up the child of beauty," she acquiesces after he threatens her. She climbs upon him, "food that is prepared and has been served," and is nourished by his taking her up toward the mountain, the Above, Grandfather Sky. The Wolf's calling the wolves of the Directions, the "other foods" that will nourish her.

The woman climbed the tree, ascending into the Above, balancing the Below, which she is. When his wife did not come from below (which she is and what she expects him to be), "he stepped into the role of a chief and yelled as a signal." In the meantime, Wolf ("below, above ground") returned to find the woman ("a shaft of light/wisdom that descends") at the top of the pinyon, having reconciled/integrated the opposites.

The men assembled and searched ("the dark light of the night"). One of the men found her at midnight (the height of the unknown) and yelled out to the others. They brought the woman down ("to repeatedly fall into the realms of the unexpected") and home; then they scolded her. This is woman (light/awareness); they stay inside (are kept inside); something might happen to them. They might respond to the call to adventure, receive spiritual food, experience spiritual marriage (tame and wild, house and forest, day and night, known and unknown), and become spiritually free, a boon to all her relations.

This story offers a parallel to the Arapaho story told by Campbell, in which a young girl chases a porcupine for its quills and experiences spiritual/alchemical marriage. She chases it up a tree that keeps growing and growing into the highest heavens (like Jacob's ladder). Eventually the porcupine reveals itself to be a handsome brave. As the Beauty's/Belle's Beast reveals itself to be a prince.

Approach stories, myths, such as these as you would dreams. As the characters, animate and inanimate, are us, parts of us. Contemplate your life as a quest. Tell your own story.

(To understand more of this story's psychological and mythological implications, read Pinkola Estes' *Women Who Run with the Wolves*.)

IX. Reconciling Square and Circle

Listening is receiving ancient wisdom/vibration, intuiting guidance and inspiration, inhaling fresh energy. It leads to contemplation and understanding. Now we, like the Picuris children, can better bring about the inner marriage of square and circle. Practicing house of shattering light accentuates the outbreath, our expansive, extroverted, angled, active, solar, radiant, archetypal male nature. Practicing the kiva accentuates the inbreath, our inspansive, introverted, arched, receptive, lunar, dark, archetypal female nature. After practicing them separately, we can integrate the 'house' and the kiva in a single paired inhalation and exhalation.

{BREATH} Start by exaggerating the inhalation, the exhalation, and the holding within and without. For example, you might inhale for eight seconds, hold for sixteen seconds, exhale for eight seconds, and hold for sixteen. The kiva breath comes first, inwardness gives birth to outwardness. After exaggerating for some time, developing a strong sense of inwardness and outwardness, shorten the duration of breathing and holding to the four/one/four square breath. Again, after having become slow and balanced, the breath becomes smooth and subtle.

As you exhale, envision the awareness/energy/light of your shattering house stretching over the Earth and into the galaxy, in four, then six directions. As you inhale, experience the hollow center, the seventh direction, the extraordinary inwardness, inspansion as the subtle light of the aura converts to dark energy of its source. Some mystics call this the indwelling of God. Your solar plexus, and by extension your entire body, becomes the silent, still potentiality 'before the beginning.'

Each time you exhale, you give birth to the cosmos like the sun of suns. You experience *taah-keh*, the Tiwa vibration for the big bang. A new square/house extends beyond the circle. Each time you inhale, creation infolds into what physicist David Bohm calls the implicate state. The empty Center/circle has widened.

In Tiwa, the inner space or black hole (that holds all potential galaxies) is *pooh-meh*. Existence and Nonexistence flow into and become each other. Mystics paradoxically say the Center is the Circumference.

This may be a good time to consider posture and the placement of your hands. Joseph sat cross-legged on the floor of his grandmother's house. In ceremonies, he usually sits cross-legged or kneels. He teaches that kneeling means "bringing being into completion." Though enduring discomfort is a way of making effort, you can also practice sitting in a wooden chair or standing. If you sit in a chair or stand, realize that your legs and feet are your trunk and roots, the extension of the energy center at the bottom of your spine, associated your sacral plexus. In Tiwa, standing means "questing."

The hands are wands of *chi*, energy/light. They direct the *chi* that wells and circulates in your chest and flows through your arms and wrists. Sky (transcendent) energy descends into the chest (cardiac plexus), circulates around, and continues descending through the trunk into the Earth. Earth energy ascends into the chest, circulates around, and continues ascending through the top of the head into sky.

If you place your palms downward, they will direct the energy circulating in the chest downward, tending to lower your center of gravity, making you more 'grounded' or immanent. If you turn your palms upward, they will direct energy skyward, tending to elevate your center of gravity, making you more 'spaced out,' transcendent. If you interlace your fingers, you enhance the integration of the energy circulating on the left (lunar) and right (solar) sides of the body. If you put the knuckles of one hand in the palm of the other and tilt them toward or against your abdomen, you direct the energy into the midsection. This helps with the concentration on abdominal breathing and the beginning of emptiness.

You can also move the hands/arms to direct energy. For instance, you can direct Earth energy upward by attentively raising the palms while you inhale, all the while visualizing the ascending energy and sensing the connection of the palms with the cardiac plexus. You can draw energy down from sky by using the same concentration and exhaling while you pull down your arms, palms down. You can accentuate expansion (the house of shattering light), by spreading the palms outward from the chest while exhaling, all the while visualizing the infinite extension of the aura. And you can pull energy from outer space into inner space (kiva) by inhaling as you pull the palms toward and against the solar plexus.

The in and out waving of the palms can be done in conjunction with the paired kiva (circle)/house (square) practice discussed at the beginning of this chapter. The paired upward and downward waving of the palms will be discussed during the explanation of the tree meditation.

If you experiment with the hands as wands, you can enhance your experience by first placing your palms against your chest. Put your right palm above your sternum to the right. Put your left palm on the left side of the chest, just opposite the right. The four fingers of one hand will lie upon the other. Begin the square breath, inhaling up from the Earth and down through the sky simultaneously. When you count one, start the inhalation. When you count two, draw the breath/energy/light into the head and lower abdomen. When you count three, draw the breath into the neck and solar plexus. When you count four, draw breath from above and below into the chest, behind your hands. Pause one count, and then exhale from your cardiac plexus/heart center into your palms. After a few breaths, the energy/light of heart and palms will merge. This will make the palms more effective wands.

179

Voice

Though we will describe sound practices in another chapter, you can further enhance this light/energy practice by lowering the pitch of your voice and humming into the cardiac plexus/palms. In addition, you can press the lips tighter, increase the force of the breath, direct the vibration within and below, and 'swallow' (*soh*/soul) the vibration. It now becomes a light and vibration practice. Subtle energy manifests as both light and vibration. As awareness becomes more subtle, as the inner senses unfold, one can experience both phenomena. After you hum a while (after inhaling up and down), you can sound/swallow, the *aah* sound. *Aah* is both the sound for breath and the sound of the heart.

This balancing, integrating practice is for morning and afternoon.

X. Becoming the Medicine Wheel

Joseph says that the Tiwa didn't formally teach the medicine
wheel, probably the most widely known aspect of Amerindian
mysticism. As a boy he heard elders say that one person was
a northerner, that another was of the south. Though he heard
persons associated with the four cardinal directions, he and
other young 'becomers,' students of the mysteries, were left to
realize the medicine wheel by themselves, the same way they
grew to understand the meanings of the stories they were told
each year, in the depth of winter.

Joseph's teachers, particularly Antonio Simbola, didn't want
his students to get stuck in mental forms. The medicine teachers
were cultivating insight, 'inseeing' (*oh–oh-ney*) among their
students. One could also say that Antonio was trying to 'heat up'
Joseph's house/kiva. In Tiwa, 'heating up' is *leh-lee-ah*, which
means "to bring up ancient wisdom into conscious knowing."
Sometimes, bringing up ancient teachings means retrieving
that which has been lost or forgotten. In Joseph's early life, it
often meant receiving 'updates,' being told how he and the elders
should do practices in the present.

Ceremonies only work to the degree they are inspired,
relevant, attuned to the needs of time and place, to the way
heaven and Earth impact each other in the moment. Tradition
and inspiration/revelation continually dance/wrestle within
mystics and their mystery schools. Relevance also accounts for
the difference in teachings like the medicine wheel between
tribes. Though American natives (and primal peoples worldwide)
generally acknowledge the 'powers' of the four/seven directions,
they often assign the directions different attributes, colors, and
animal archetypes. Joseph explains that each tribe embodies a
different vibration due to their specific language and location.
(The Tiwa acquired their language by listening to the vibrations
of nature, the crystallization of the Vast Self.) Moreover, the Vast
Self is what gave the original vibrations of all languages to all
people, and each tribe/people/language has its own purpose.

Painted Arrow's insights on the medicine wheel began in the kiva. The most notable occasion occurred when Antonio sent him into the kiva for a special ceremony that Picuris perform once every hundred years. *In House of Shattering Light,* Joseph recalls his being alone in the sacred space for weeks, attended by a lady who brought him a corn-based diet and removed his chamber pot. Mostly, Joseph says, he was fed by subtle energies/ beings of sound and light that entered the kiva.

Sitting at the center of the ceremonial chamber, he realized he was the center of the circle, the medicine wheel, the universe, the heart. He also realized the directions were the sound/light beings manifesting against the silent darkness. The heart, the hub of darkness, is a flash of light that becomes a star as we exhale.

> As it lights up the darkness, this light . . . realizes that it is really wisdom that is coming into conscious thought. But it doesn't realize it until the light goes out as far as it can and then hits the banks. . . . Finally it reaches the bank. It can't go any farther because it has run out of steam. In coming back, it carries life-sustaining energy because when this flash of light originates, it is asking for one thing, abundance of life. (*Being and Vibration* 84)

Joseph also uses the sound metaphor of a being (the heart), who stands at the center of a canyon and shouts. Her voice strikes the walls of the canyon/kiva and echoes back. The walls are not just the spread of the luminous breath, our wings, they are the known, that of which we are conscious. They represent the inner walls of the kiva, which represent the frontier of awareness, the known. The flash from the heart pushes out the metaphorical kiva walls, extends perception.

The abundance that the inhalation brings back from the new frontier is pure energy, energy that we perceive as thought, feeling, sensation, and intuition. When the inbreath enters the heart center, it endows it with energy/wisdom. The light disappears as the energy is ingested and digested. The heart, recharged, explodes in the void. The big bang begins again. The directions of Above (*Pa-peh-tah*) and Below (*Naah-aah-uu-kwill*), contribute pure energy to the ever deepening/expanding heart center. The Center (*Pii-ini-aah-ii*) which is the circumference (*Haah-ley*).

Joseph realized that corridors exist within the circle, corridors that relate to the mental, emotional, sensate/physical, intuitive/spiritual energies. These corridors of energy that extend from and to the heart center are the directions of East, South, West, and North respectively. In *Being and Vibration* Joseph describes how, while on retreat in the desert (another metaphor for emptiness), he experienced the colors of the Directions (sometimes referred to as archangels or elements): "Then, after a few days, I ceased to be aware of thirst and heat and cold. I became aware of vibrations from the sand and the plants around me. I noticed that each of these had their own specific qualities of vibration, their own natural resonances. I then became aware of the vibrations of colors, vibrations not audible, but sensible" (114).

Joseph realized that the East (Mental) is Yellow, South (Emotional) is White, West (Physical) is Black, and North (Spiritual) is Red. We'll treat the directions one-by-one, from East to North. Joseph's realization corresponds to Carl Jung's designating the four psychological functions as Thinking, Feeling, Sensing, and Intuition. For a more comprehensive explanation, refer to Painted Arrow's books. In a later chapter, we'll consider his teaching of the sounding of the vowels for the directions.

What does the East's being the Mental direction mean? The East is the direction of pure mind. Pure mind means that the biocomputer, our facility of ideas, analysis, definition, and memory is operating properly, that we are truly rational. If we are truly rational, we don't rationalize, don't allow prejudice and bias to influence thought. The pure yellow light/energy of East can purify us of these obscurations. At a deeper level, when we invoke the pure energy of East, we are calling upon awareness/*ti* to make us see, to free the faculty of thought from these obscurations. Joseph often calls East the direction of wisdom. Wisdom arises from awareness' capacity to purify thought.

Actually the descending light of Intelligence/*wa* flows into awareness/*ti*, flows into mind. Kabbalists would utter a prayer for pure seeing as they concentrated on the Y or YHVH.

EAST

When Joseph spent days in the Picuris kiva of the thunder callers, with and without Antonio, he entered into the colors of the directions as they appeared on the walls of the kiva. As Joseph did and does, imagine yourself in the kiva and face East. Begin breathing the square breath. Visualize pure yellow in front of you. Visualize walking into the yellow. Walk into the yellow with your breath as you exhale. Inhale the yellow into you as you inhale. Your inhalation is the East's exhalation. Remember we have a reciprocal relationship with all life, all directions, all relations. Continue this breath/bath until nothing exists but yellow. Continue breathing/being yellow until yellow becomes clear, white light.

If you have trouble contemplating and becoming yellow, you have a deficiency. So you need to gather, literally and figuratively yellow objects and beings, and gradually saturate your being with the pure color. Await the sun as it rises over the eastern horizon. Another way to accelerate your becoming of the colors/ directions is to inhale the color through the top of your head, once you are sitting in the kiva, facing East. You are an empty vase being poured into, inhaling yellow, indeed, all the colors or the directions and spectrum. Exhale the pure yellow through all pores, all directions. This will increase your capacity to become East.

In Tiwa, East is *Tso-leh-neh*. Joseph's invocation of the Power/ Archangel of the East is: "I/we send a voice to the East, Tso-leh-neh. I/we invoke the yellow blessing which opens the doors of perception to the spiritual light." If you would rather connect the two sentences, you can say, "I/we send a voice to the East, *Tso-leh-neh,* invoking the yellow blessing which opens the doors of perception to the spiritual light." Whichever form you use, choose either "I" or "We," whichever feels best. If you do this silently, the sending occurs on the exhalation. It proceeds through the various gates of the Earth, the solar system, and galaxy, forever. The invocation occurs on the inhalation, which returns from the infinite distance. You can also repeat the sounds as a mantra, inside the kiva of your being, inside your chest. This will overpower thought and saturate your being with sound. You will become the Eastern vibration.

Joseph also suggests that we immerse ourselves in a different direction/color every day: visualizing, contemplating, invoking. So, become yellow for a day, for a week. You will notice all the subtleties of yellow in your environment. Then become the next color/direction. Until your palette is complete and the colors manifest spontaneously, depending on need.

South

Next, still in the kiva, concentrate on the South—for ten minutes, for a day, for a week. All the while breathing the square breath. South is the purity of the emotions, of our emotional nature or body. Essentially, South is our lovingness, our capacity to give and receive love. Ultimately, South is our capacity to become love. South's color is white, a color associated in many traditions with love of the infinite, unconditional love, rather than personal love. While East is the opening and purification of the mind, on all levels, South is the opening and purification of emotions.

Facing South, we address the heart, wishing to be purified of like and dislike, resentment, and self pity. See the white southern wall of the kiva. Visualize walking into the white as Joseph did. Walk into it with your breath as you exhale. Breathe the white into yourself as you inhale. Inhale white through the top of your head. To be emotionally alive is to experience the pain of others. To feel the suffering that is inherent in birth, life, and death. We open to compassion for all sentient beings. We pray to die into love of all our relations, of the ineffable Great Mystery. Continue the practice until you become the color, and until the color becomes clear light.

Paa-tuh-hey is the sound of South. Sound *Paa-tuh-hey* in the kiva of your being, in your chest. Sense the movement of sound, how you resonate as you inhale and exhale. Joseph's invocation of the South is: "I/we send a voice to the South, *Paa-tuh-hey*. I/we invoke the blessing of the house of white light that cleanses the emotions." (Remember, you can join these two sentences.) If you say this silently, you exhale as you send through the archangel of the South, to the far reaches of the universe, and inhale as you invoke the blessings. Repeat the sounds until you become them; they become you.

WEST

West is the direction of the Physical, of our instinctive nature and of the Earth. When we honor the West, we wish for physical health and magnetism, for purification from disease and stress. For our reconnection to Earth, upon and in which we walk.

Facing the West, visualize the West wall of the kiva as Black. Walk into Black, breathe into Black, inhale Black down through the top of your head. Honor the Black/physical and the vehicle of soul, *sooh*. And beyond that as the presence of the Vast Self (*who*).

Who-kweh is the sound of West. Sitting in the kiva, facing West, vibrate the sounds aloud. Once you sense yourself vibrating, repeat the sound silently on the inhalation and exhalation. The invocation of the West is: "I/we send a voice to the West, *Who-kweh*. I/we invoke the black blessing that purifies our body with the breath of innocence." As with the other invocations, say this aloud and silently. When saying it silently, send on the exhalation; receive on the inhalation.

NORTH

North is the direction of the Spiritual or Intuitive body. Its color is red, and its Tiwa vibration is *Pai-eh-ney*. When we address the being/archangel of the North, we wish for the purification of intuition, for direct spiritual guidance. The red energy of the North burns away egocentricity, our separation from Great Spirit, from the Vast Self, which is center and circumference. Joseph says that the red breath of the North overcomes fear, the fear that arises from separation.

Sit facing North. Perceive the red wall that extends infinitely to the North. Walk into the red. Walk into red with your breath as you exhale. Draw it into yourself as you inhale. Draw it down through your crown as you inhale. Fill yourself with it, and exhale it until only red exists. Continue until you pass from red into the clear white light.

Invoke *Pai-eh-ney* aloud. Resonate that energy/vibration of pure red in all your resonating chambers: abdomen, chest, throat, head. When you are charged with energy/vibration, repeat it silently on your breath. Then invoke North: "I/we send a voice to the North, *Pai-eh-ney*. I/we invoke the red blessing that dissolves duality and fear." You can then pray to North silently on the breath. When you have honored the North/*Pai-eh-ney*, you can honor Above/*Pa-peh-tah*, Below/*Naah-aah-uu-kwill*, and Center/*Pii-ini-aah-ii* as you did in the practice of the three worlds.

In honoring the directions, you always begin in the kiva of your inner space and end with the inside's becoming the outside, with the kiva's becoming the world. Of course, we experience this profound mystical state according to our capacity. Yet, as our individual breath gradually aligns itself with the breaths of the directions, we become Being, the Vast Self from which all directions emerge and to which all return. Purification by the directions, and the balancing of our bodies/functions that results, allows us to experience Center/circumference to a greater degree. Presence (*who*) grows, becomes through/as us. This does not seem possible, but Vast Self, *Wa-Ma-Chi* in Tiwa, is not static. *Wa-Ma-Chi* is forever *Wa-Ma-Chi-ing*.

Perform this practice and series of invocations all times during the day. If you perform it in evening, just honor the directions. You do not want to draw them in, to empower the being body in evening before sleep.

XI. Becoming the Elements: Climbing Mountain

Variations of this meditation/concentration are daily practice for various shamanistically connected paths, meaning mystical paths rooted in the immanent aliveness and holiness of creation, every form's being revelation. Understanding the elements is the basis of Indian, Tibetan, Chinese and ancient Greek medicine. A vestige of elemental medicine can be found in the medieval science of the humours, as well as alchemy and astrology. According to the ancients/indigenous, the elements exist in subtle and gross forms.

They compose material life, all bodies and structures, including internal organs, processes, functions, systems, personality, colors, and sounds. For instance Fire is associated with volcanoes, fire, sun, heat/dryness, oxidation, digestion, the small intestine and heart, force, determination/anger, courage, aggression, domination, orange-red, trumpet, roar, hiss, thunder. Elements also exist in combination. For instance, fire functioning behind Wind manifests as intense winds, such as gales and tornadoes. Generally, we have one primary and one secondary element. Or according to native Amerindians, such as the Cheyenne, we have a beginning place and an initial direction, from which we move around the medicine wheel, eventually becoming the totality (seven directions).

One practices the element breaths/concentrations in order to purify and magnetize the subtle elements/ingredients of our being. Earth is densest; Ether (Space) is finest. Some say Ether, sometimes referred to as Awareness, is the source of the other four elements. Tibetans (Bon and Buddhists) practice the elements (constituents) in order to prepare for death, the elements' disengaging from the physical body or sheath. The 'departing' of the four elements from the physical body constitutes the first four stages of death (followed by the graduated dissolution of consciousness). In this practice, however, the elements are not dissolving into one another. We magnetize them, balance them, gradually transmute one into the other, from denser to finer, then 'backwards.' It is still a practice of spiritual death, detachment, and disengagement. We'll engage in this practice of the elements by visualizing our ascent and descent of a mountain. The mountain of Te, the mountain that became Joseph.

Begin by visualizing a city at sunset. The city represents your forgetfulness, your physical/psychic/emotional pollution, as well as our herd tendency, habituation, persona. In a word it represents *old*, the alchemic 'materia prima.' Walk out of the city to a river. Remember, by walking you become more aware. You can even sense Earth because your energy/aura penetrates the concrete. You cross a footbridge (Magpietail Boy's tail) heading to the forest on the other side, toward a magnificent mountain. The side you have left is the unnatural side. You have entered the natural. The river/bridge is the symbolic transition to the *new*.

You pass through the forest, relaxing, shedding vestiges of the city, becoming ever more aware. You merge with massive oaks, redwoods, all sorts of roots, trees, animals, and insects. Your being/body breathes nature; your natural self is evoked and strengthened. Your breath slows and regulates itself. You are calm, not aggravated or anxious. Your evening eyes emerge. All senses become keen.

As darkness sets in, you arrive at the base of a mountain. You search around some large boulders at the base for a cave. The boulders are igneous rock: heavy, dense, iron-like. You find the cave and burn some sacred sage or tobacco at the entrance, just as Te did with Joseph when they spent the night in the cave and Joseph underwent initiation. Maybe some bats will fly out. When the smoke has purified the cave, enter, descending. Find your spot in the cave in a back corner. Sense around with your limbs. Stop. At this point, you can lie down on your back and surrender to Earth. Deeply relax, feel your heaviness and sense that your breath is the breath of Earth. You are a bear hibernating. A snake. Revel in the darkness. Feel the loving security of the cave and Earth, this natural kiva. You are spending the night in the cave, but you are so full of energy from merging with the Vast Self that you cannot sleep.

Sit up and begin breathing in the nose and out the nose, balancing inhalation/exhalation with an easy count, perhaps 4 beats IN, 1 pause, 4 OUT. Breathe abdominally, allowing the breath to start and end in abdomen. (One might breathe abdominally before initiating this practice.) We visualize *gold* (or *copper*, which is more grounded), first entering and exiting the feet, hands, and bottom of spine, then penetrating the entire body as we breathe in a balanced, smooth manner. We merge more deeply with the rock people; become the base of the mountain, rooted in the earth. Upon inhaling we receive gold energy/light from Grandmother Earth; upon exhaling radiate it.

Next, silently repeat the Tiwa sounds *nah-weh*.

After about ten breaths, notice the light of dawn entering the cave. Sing the Tiwa Sunrise Song or make up your own song to the archangel of the sun (*to-le-ne*). When you sense strength/rootedness/stability/responsibility, you are ready to end your mini-hibernation and climb upwards. For the upward climb, you might become a mountain goat, an animal Joseph often saw upon the mountain. You have hooves. Large shoulders. And great horns. A bighorn sheep, a mountain goat. You are *gold/copper*.

You find the trail, passing through boulders. The trail up leads through grass, meadows, flowers. The sun rises. You hear the trickling of water and continue joyously. You see a rivulet, a stream. You follow it, smelling the freshness of water. It becomes larger. It leads you to a pool on the mountainside. A small waterfall cascades into the pool. It is brilliant, translucent *emerald*. You hear frogs and see rainbow trout swimming. You remove your clothes and wade into the pool, experiencing baptism. You immerse yourself. You can become an otter or fish. You play. You swim under the waterfall. You become *green*. You are Green Otter. Thoroughly cleansed inside and out. You breathe rhythmically *in* nose and *out* mouth, the green magnetism flowing through and over the head, neck, chest, and legs. You are emotionally purified, unburdened from wounds of the heart. You are renewed with compassion, kindness, mercy. You repeat *paah. Paah.* Once energized, smoothened, fluid you emerge, return to the path, and seek the sun to dry.

The sun is reaching its zenith. You find a large illuminated rock and lie upon it, sunning yourself. You inhale the heat from the rock and the rays, sensing the warmth and the radiance. Once you are warmed, concentrate on the radiance. You begin to breathe *in* the mouth and *out* the nose. Concentrate the inhalation around the navel; you feel yourself glowing inside with *orange-red*. When you exhale you pull concentration up to the chest, which fills with yellow radiance. Continue this breathing, creating heat, converting it to radiance, like the sun. You have the power to become a mountain lion (*mo-sa-neh*). Whatever you become, even if you stay human, you become orange-red, powerful, glowing, active, determined, creative. *Peeah* is fire. When you are ready, return to the path.

The path leads upward. The landscape becomes sparse, some heather or sage here and there. You hear and sense the wind. Listening to it, you seek an overhanging ledge. You notice the vast blue sky. You stand on the ledge breathing *out* through mouth, *in* through mouth. Rhythmically, gently, balanced. Your breath merges with sky, which passes through you and all. At this point you can become an eagle/hawk, feeling the breeze (breath of planet) passing through your feathers. You are Blue Eagle, the eagle of subtlety, fineness, grace: *woo-hah*. You are the wings/wind, lifted from the ledge. You enter into and become blue sky. Then you become the clear white light that pervades the sky. You inhale and exhale through the nose and mouth together (pressing tip of tongue to roof of mouth). Allow your breath to become finer and finer, becoming pure awareness. You can silently breathe *waaw*.

You return to the ledge and gradually descend, reversing the metamorphosis of the elements, experiencing the various landscapes, eventually returning to your 'regular' life, refreshed, renewed, empowered, relatively enlightened. The city becomes illuminated.

In several of his books, Joseph describes becoming an eagle as he raced/flew down the mountain into the Picuris center. This marked his initiation as a thunder caller, one whose being flies (extends) into sky to draw the blessing (rain/light/wa) of Sky onto

Earth. You can come down as any and all beings, for you, as Vast Self, contain all. You become the mythical sphinx or dragon, all elements interplaying.

This is a very important, fundamental practice. Once you learn it, you should perform it as the first practice every morning, after saluting the sun. This practice also brings benefit in afternoon. You can do it in evening as long as you stop the practice midway, with the ether/space concentration. Done this way, it prepares the soul for rest.

XII. *Saluting Sun*

One of the simplest yet most profound practices you can perform
is to salute the rising sun. Primal peoples recognized the sun
as the sustainer of life, a symbol of the Great Spirit, and an
Intelligent being, or beingness on the subtle level. William Blake
saw the angel of the sun, as did the Zoroastrian magi who called
sun Prince Hurashq. Remember, every form of beingness, all
living things, are realized in Tiwa to be epiphanies, the revelation
of spiritual realities and principle ideas, archetypes.

In Tiwa, sun (gross dimension), the lord of sun (subtle level
dimension), and solar Intelligence (very subtle dimension) are
all known as *to-le-neh*. (Remember that each of us function
simultaneously in these dimensions.) We salute this beingness
or the sun, and ourselves as well, by stationing ourselves to face
the sun before it rises. The communion between sun (and moon)
and native peoples is so deep that some peoples believe that the
need is reciprocal, that sun needs two-leggeds to greet/welcome
it, along with all the other diurnal creatures. Every dawn, we
are born anew. We embrace the day, a slice of light between two
nights.

If you know the Tiwa sun chant, start to sing it to sun before
it rises. Continue singing this chant until sun has fully risen
over the horizon. You can look directly at the sun when it first
rises. This will allow your eyes to soak in the ultraviolet, subtle
light. This excites the photons in your eyes. They transmit the
light along the optic nerve into the brain. You accentuate this
drinking of light by inhaling consciously. The physical body
drinks vitamin D. And the eyes perform photosynthesis, turning
light into energy, *chi/nah*. The *nah* drinks (*soh*) subtle and very
subtle light. This will enhance your capacity to see subtle bodies/
beings. It also enhances what mystics call the 'glance,' the
casting of subtle light, *poh-ceh*, "blowing breath with eyes that
see." The awareness capacity of the eyes is also conveyed by the
Tiwa sounds *cheh-eh-ney.*

After you bathe the dimensions of your being in the sun,

inhaling and exhaling, squint your eyes or offset your glance so you are not looking directly into the sun, but around it. You can even block the physical sun with your hand and rotate you glance just off the edge of the orb. Over time, you can increase your gazing into the sun; it is a good way to make effort. You can also put your palms up to *to-le-ne* and inhale and exhale. The hands are healing and empowering wands of *chi*. Then you can expose the top of your head, the subtle region associated with intelligence and transcendent consciousness.

You can even turn around with your back toward sun and bend up and down, sensing the rays of *chi/to-le-ne* upon your back, along which *chi* ascends and descends.

While your entire being, all your energy centers, will be charged and illuminated by the sun, certain areas will be particularly affected. Spend time exposing them to the sun or imagined sun, inhaling its presence into them. These are the navel, the heart/center, and the forehead, which is connected to your crown. (Corresponding to the three worlds.) In succession, inhale the sun or imagined sun into your forehead, sternum, and navel. Illumined by sun, they will express the solar aspects of awareness, radiance, and power respectively. Then exhale out of them in reverse order. You can do this with a 3-in/3-out breath. Or you can add the crown of your head or the bottom of your spine to the sequence and create a square-breath rhythm. As a variation to this practice, you can isolate each of these three centers, breathing light/energy/power in and out of each area, utilizing the square breath. As another variation, you can inhale and exhale out of all three centers (worlds) at the same time, drawing infinitely in, radiating infinitely out. Ending your practice by exhaling the presence, you *to-le-ne*. Radiating, blessing, beautifying, loving unconditionally.

You can also chant, attentively repeat, two three-syllable Tiwa 'names' while honoring the dawn. One, *to-le-ne*, you already know. The other is *oh-tol-lo*, the sounds corresponding to brain. The similarity of the sounds indicates an inner link between brain and sun on the subtle level. A good time to sound *oh-tol-lo* is when you are drinking light through the eyes into the brain and when you bend down pointing the crown of the head (your subtle-feathered headdress). Remember, *to-le-ne* appears solid but is really a star of swirling gases/energy. And like us, like all configurations, it will unravel, its constituent elements returning to the gross, subtle, and very subtle dimensions. Until the dimensions contract again in rebirth.

In addition to these solar practices, Joseph teaches that you can place a crystal in a bowl of water and expose it overnight to the rising sun. After sunrise, drink the energy-infused water.

Butterfly is *tschla-tschlo*. The two parts are the sounds of the butterfly's wings moving up and down. *Tschla* wings up; *tchlo* wings down. You can practice this standing, facing any direction. But the best direction is East, for at least two reasons. *Tschla-tschlo* are beings of air, and East is the direction of air. You can think of butterflies as having double air, and eagles, who are their more mighty, intense cousins, as having a dose of fire. Another reason is that butterflies do not produce heat. They rely on the sun to heat them and to produce energy in their bodies. One can often see them presenting their wings to sun, *to-le-neh*, for the three levels of light. They are solar collectors.

So, stand to the East, facing the actual sun if you can. Stretch your arms out to each side. The two parts of each of your wings connect above and below your outstretched arms. Each of your wings has an upper and lower half, connected above and below your arms. The upper half of your wings is your *tschla* part, the lower half is your *tschlo* parts. Close your eyes; sense and envision this. Butterflies incarnate the beauty, subtlety, and fragility of air. Perhaps you are a yellow Sulphur, the color of East. But you try all colors and all patterns of colors. Maybe, if your consciousness is strong, intuition will show you patterns and colors.

Your anatomical structure also relates to three energies, three energies that relate to what we will later call the three worlds. Butterflies don't have feet. So you are not really grounded. Your lower wings relate to Earth, physical magnetism. They connect to your lower body, your sacral plexus at the bottom of the spine, which inhales and exhales physical magnetism. Your arms, in between, connect to your heart, through which you inhale and exhale *chi*, life energy. And your upper wings connect to upper chest and neck. They reach up into the very subtle energy associated with the top of the head. Imagine that the *tschla-tschlo* wings connect in the middle of the chest.

So, you can stand, maintaining your concentration, and

silently inhale *tschla* and exhale *tschlo*. Or you can move your wings up as you inhale *tschla* and lower them as you exhale *tchlo*. Or you imagine your wings as energy collectors and radiators. Inhale *tschla* and draw down/in very subtle energy from above. Continue to inhale *tschlo* and draw earth/physical magnetism from below. Then pause and exhale while repeating *tschla-tschlo* silently. *Chi* will naturally enter and exit your middle where the wings overlap. If you fly off in your imagination, enjoy.

You can do this practice anytime. If you do it in evening, visualize yourself/butterfly ascending into the Upper world. You are carried by *tschla*.

XIV. Merging with Grandmother Earth

One of the most important, fundamental practices we can make is to lie with our backs on Earth. Just as we did in childhood innocence. Feeling soil and grass, gazing at trees, mountaintops, and sky. This is particularly important to understanding and experiencing Joseph's teaching and presence because the Pueblo are of the Earth. They emerged, were birthed from the underworld (after being planted from above) and lived in pit houses before turning their pit houses into kivas. As a vibration, the Tiwa are Earth looking up. Not only looking up, but often building up several stories toward Sky.

Western civilization's denigration and de-sacralization of Earth and body and worship of ordinary mind have made this communion very difficult. Without re-establishing this communion, this link with our own instinct, we cannot appreciate Joseph. The body is a holy extension of the Vast Self. But until awareness begins to function through the senses, we will continue to be fractured, alienated, and isolated. We must develop what William Blake called four-fold vision, which permits us to see the eternal in the temporal, spiritual forms in material objects. Moreover, what Blake said of seeing, can be applied to all senses.

Lying on the back allows us to receive, inhale the vibration of Earth, to allow its magnetism to flow and merge with our physical magnetism. As we exhale, most of our energy radiates through the front. We are much more likely to receive through the back where we are less protected. Perhaps we can shed what Blake called Experience and experience newfound Innocence. In Tiwa this is *moo-hu*, "manifesting in a sense of grace." We also become *o-hee-o*, "innocence in a state of teachability."

Inhale through the nose (the Earth breath). Experience how, as you inhale, Earth rises (*weh-ley*), exhales into you. In your personal consciousness, you are the doer; you are pulling Earth into you. In your subtle, higher consciousness (*nah*), you are the receiver. As you begin to experience very subtle consciousness, the Vast Self, you and Earth are one, One Breath.

When you exhale downward (*hlee-o*) into Earth, relax, let go. Allow gravity to overwhelm you. Allow Earth Grandmother to embrace you and take your stress, anxiety, and dis-ease. Your exhaling is Her inhaling. Inhale and exhale deeply and slowly at first. But gradually surrender and relax. Focus all your awareness through your senses. Your body and energy field will blend with the Earth's. Earth's rhythm is slow, steady, and smooth. Notice how Earth is in love with sky. How She reaches up while you inhale and draws Him downward while you exhale. You will be incredibly relaxed, yet solid and empowered with energy. Remember, when you are relaxed and open, you are filled with subtle energy. Notice everything.

Once you have experienced merging with Grandmother, try reversing the breathing pattern. This will allow you to experience Her yearning for Sky, for Him. As you exhale, experience the total thrust of Earth up through you (you are Her) to the Above. Then, as you/She inhales, feel Her pull Sky downward, into Herself. And while She pulls downward, He reaches/pushes down to Her. Above and Below long to overcome apparent duality created by the Big Bang. The Breath of Center, however, keeps equilibrium.

This is a morning and afternoon practice.

This practice is taught by Joseph. It is a practice that reveals essence and evolving essence. Assume a meditation posture, wipe clear the walls, and enter kiva-consciousness. Visualize night, the black light of void, of the unconscious. You are standing on a plain, looking for a hole, a burrow, a tunnel. This is your navel. Try this practice both as a pure visualization and as a descent into your lower world, your lower abdomen.

Be patient. Find the entrance to the Underworld with your feet, your hands, or your inner sight. Inhale through nose, expanding the abdomen, especially the lower abdomen. Exhale through the mouth and enter the portal. Keep expanding as you inhale, creating space below. Exhaling, sensing your way below. Apply square breathing as your carefully follow the tunnel. You may need to invoke your mole, snake, or groundhog nature, an Earth aspect of yourself that loves to tunnel and dig, that exults in the depths of Earth. You are effectively descending through a hollow root.

Once your breath becomes balanced, smooth, and subtle, look for an opening into internal vastness. You are exploring the unconscious, the instinctual impulses and energies of body. Find yourself near the shore of subterranean water, a grotto. With your awareness, *ti*, perceive the cavern, the presence of animals. Some of them will be around you. Some may even be touching you or in your lap. You may even perceive yourself as an animal or series of animals. Breathe with the animals. They are the energies, the archetypes that infuse essence and form the potentialities of evolved essence or Self.

After breathing with them for some time, noticing all you can with all inner senses, prepare to ascend. Tell the animals you are ascending, that you are inviting them to ascend with you. As part of you. Those that readily accompany you are aspects already incorporated. Others may need convincing, or even coercion. You may need to swim out to coax or carry a dolphin, otter, or alligator. Those that you perceive but cannot bring up are looming on the edge of your being, not quite embraced or incorporated. They await your effort and realization. Ascend with your tribe as you inhale through mouth. As you exhale through the nose, you emerge from the hole into daylight, into consciousness. You have introduced awareness into the unconscious and brought its power and mystery into consciousness.

This practice is best performed in early morning or early evening. In morning, you ascend to face the day and create. In evening your being/consciousness/light ascends into the beyond (as you inhale).

XVI. Walking

Joseph wove the inner and outer worlds through walking *(taa-chi-who)*. The three sounds are the vibration of stepping forward *(taa)*, the back foot's rubbing against the front *(chi)*, and the second's stepping forward *(who)*. One way to express the principle idea of walking in English is "Time and Purity, Beauty and Awareness of God's light." Joseph has also offered the concentration, "The Father in beauty is walking with me and carrying me." In *House of Shattering Light*, he talks about realizing that when a person walks, she is plowing because plow is *taa*. (Westerners also have the figure of speech 'planting the foot.') By walking/plowing, we are becoming aware.

Joseph is emphatic about this. Walking we become more and more aware *(ti)*. Even if we walk unconsciously, inattentively, without sensing our soles penetrating Grandmother Earth, the Vast Self. Joseph relates the archetypal act of walking to the Tiwa principle of *tai-eh-neh*. *Tai-eh-neh* conveys that the people are vibration and their work is to create. And that walking is, in itself, an act of creation, as well as acquiring knowledge. *Tai-eh-neh* means "We are doers in states of placement so that the holy self *(naa)* will place itself among the heavenly planes."

We can, however, enhance becoming Awareness (and the possibility of Awareness' becoming Intelligence and the Vast Self's realizing It is walking on Itself) if we walk attentively and breathe through our feet. First this is enhanced by the Picuris teaching that we don't walk on Grandmother; we walk *in* Grandmother. This is where plowing and planting *(kah)* come in. When we step, our subtle body, our energy/light *(chi)* penetrates/plows a foot or two beneath the skin of Earth. We thereby plant whatever energy is flowing down through us into Earth. And we draw up energy/awareness from the embodied Vast Self into our version of the Vast Self. If we can become aware of this, just a little bit, the Presence *(who)* will happen.

In *Being and Vibration*, Joseph describes this magical (but natural) interpenetration this way:

> In walking, when our foot impacts with [into] the ground, the descending light marries ascending light in the sound of our foot on [into] the earth, nourishing our whole bodies. The sound which starts at the foot travels then to all of the other body parts and shakes the old ways alive and implants the new. It is as if we have moved from "as above so below." This chant (nowness) sings of the energy which bonds the past, present, and future. This is sound energy, and it heals as it comes upon the energy that is lifting us awake. *Taa*— walkingness of the purifying father—gives us clarity of mind. *Chi*—alerts us to the "cold truth that knows," which then awakens the physical body for creative activity. *Hu* [*Who*] carries us next into the unknown. (183)

To begin to experience walking/plowing/planting/beautifying, you should slow your walk and sense the energy extending from your feet, as well as the entire physical body. As you put a foot down to caress/marry Earth, you exhale descending light into Earth. Pause; inhale. The ascending light courses up through your energy field, sole, foot, leg, trunk. Then shift your weight and put down the other foot, exhaling. Your limbs are hollow conduits. This is, of course, a very slow method of locomotion. (Remember that mysticism/awakening values quality over quantity.) But it is a powerful way of developing Awareness/ Presence *(ti/chi/who)*. You may begin to experience yourself as the bridge between Grandfather Sky and Grandmother Earth, your whole being/body as the Middle World. Like trees. Walking trees. Every time you step/exhale, the descending energy penetrates deeper and deeper through your luminous roots. With every inhalation, ascending energy shoots up from the roots, through the trunk, into the Sky beyond.

After you've experienced this, try repeating *ta—chi—who* as you take three steps, one syllable for each step, maintaining the marrying/intercourse attentiveness. You can direct the vibration of the syllable to the point of contact. This will also enhance your realization of sound. What vibration shines? Whatever shines vibrates. If you start on your left foot, for instance, you inhale, internally saying *ta*. When the right sole impacts the Earth, you say *chi*. And when the left kisses again, you say *who*. When you come back with the right, your fourth step, you pause the breath.

When you step with the left again, you say *ta*. Aloud. Then *chi* with the right, and *who* with the second left. And with the final right, you pause the breath again. After awhile, a number of sets, you can switch and start the silent inhalation/spoken exhalation of *ta-chi-who* on the right foot. Remember to try and maintain awareness of the ascending and descending energies as you inhale and exhale. You should also practice *ta(1)-chi(2)-who(3)–pause(4)* silently, on both inhalation and exhalation. This will make it more natural and allow you to deepen the link between vibration, breath, and movement.

You can simplify this silent, mantra breathing practice eliminating the pause. Just keep inhaling and exhaling for four steps, saying nothing on the fourth step of each set. This will allow a more natural rhythm. You can also add another *chi* in the middle, and then you will have a syllable for each of the four steps as you alternate inhalation and exhalation. *Ta-chi-chi-hu* means "the Father in beauty is walking and talking with me and carrying me." Speech, subtle movement of vibration, is sacred. Just as the silence from which it emerges. You can also practice *wa-chi-chi-who* in the same manner, using the square breath. Because in walking we are "becoming."

With practice, you will be able to maintain the consciousness of a walking tree even when walking at a faster pace. For a slight variation, you might experiment with the way you place your foot into Earth, stepping heel-ball, then ball-heel. How do the styles compare?

Sometimes human trees realize their breath is the Breath of the Vast Self, circulating through them/creation as they move their lungs. Or have their lungs moved by the Breath. When they exhale, Sky is really exhaling down and Earth is really inhaling down. And when they inhale, Sky is really inhaling up and Earth is really exhaling up. Or sometimes they experience the reverse. When they inhale, Earth is pulling/inhaling down and Sky is exhaling down. And when the human tree exhales, Earth is exhaling up and Sky is inhaling. Sounds complicated. Being breathed. Very simple really, for only One Vast Self is ever becoming into and out of existence. Though two-legged trees contain the three worlds, they are also the moving rainbow bridge connecting Sky/Above and Earth/Below.

XVII. *TREENESS*

In Tiwa trees *(tslah-ah-nay)* are wisdom. We are walking trees.
We can experience our treeness through a concentration similar
to the mountain. They ascend and spread. But trees are obviously
not as formidable and solid as mountains. They are more flexible.
Water and sap flows through them. In Chinese medicine, wood
is one of the five elements. Trees embody *lo* (descending), *la*
(ascending), and *le* (spreading). They are rooted, draw minerals
and energy from the manifest Vast Self. But they also draw
warm light from the sun, producing sugar and chlorophyll. They
produce green energy (upper heart energy that characterizes
the Middle World), as well as oxygen. They take our exhaust
(carbon dioxide) and sustain us, in many ways. Clearly, we have
a profound spiritual kinship with trees and can learn much from
them.

In both *Ceremonies* and *Sound,* Joseph describes a dream that
revealed the centrality of the tree to the unfolding of creation.
When the waters receded from the land of Picuris, they exposed
a lot of rocks. He saw winter arrive with snow, then saw the snow
melt and the summer heat come. The alternating cold and heat
of winter and summer broke down the rock into sand. Finally, he
saw a tree emerge from the sand, grow to maturity and fall.

> . . . When it fell, I realized that that's how the land was im-
> bued with greatness. This first tree awakened the memory
> of greatness, because it is the essence of greatness. When it
> hit the ground, and as it started to rot, it gave us time. The
> rings in the tree tell us that time expands out from a single
> point. It doesn't expand inwardly—not in this dimension
> anyhow. Time begins with a seed of light, but once it goes
> out, it doesn't go back to the point of light until it breaks up
> into soil as humus. Then it goes back into the one, into the
> beginning. You can look at a stump or a cross-section of a
> tree and see how an insight might happen, beginning with
> a seed or a single flash of light and traveling out from there.
> . . . The tree is a symbol of how time is expanding and

how we are expanding as a part of that greatness or expansion. It is the symbol of the movement and expansion of Divine Thought or Divine Essence. The tree is the most concrete substance that we can see and touch that connects us to how greatness is expanding. (*Ceremonies* 41–42; *Sound* 88–89)

This practice of becoming tree is best done standing. Exhale straight down your spine, through your hollow middle. Keep exhaling deep into the center of Grandmother Earth. In the center of Grandmother, in her womb, you will find a sphere/pool of golden light. Tap into that sphere of liquid gold. Just inhale naturally for a while, stressing your inhalation that taps into the energy center of Earth.

Once you sense this well (you can also consider it a well), visualize drawing this yellow energy up through your long, thick roots. Draw it all the way up to your heart center (the sternum). Begin the square breath. Inspand the rising light in the heart. You can visualize your heart center as a heart, a six-pointed star, a diamond, or the center of a Celtic cross. Don't let the light/energy expand out of your chest. Let it inspand, swirl around in your chest, relaxing, cleansing, releasing resentment and grief, transforming pain.

Eventually, spread your arms, your branches, exhaling out to the sides. So your exhalation sends energy down, your inbreath brings energy/sap to the chest, and a second exhalation sends it out through your arms. You can spread your fingers; they are smaller branches and twigs. The golden light energy will ascend from the heart of Earth, through your roots, up your trunk, and out your arms and fingers. Visualize your brown crust, your bark. It is a thick skin that surrounds your roots and your entire body. The next inhalation will draw the light/energy/sap up from the heart, into the head. Then, it transpires into Sky. You can now complete the tree by realizing the upper tree, adding branches from the side of the head.

Once you experience Earth, roots, heart, head, and branches, start to add lots of smaller green branches and leaves sprouting from your arms in all directions. You are essentially three colors:

brown on the outer trunk (like Earth), gold inside (like Earth), and green all around. You are also using two square breaths: exhale down to center Earth, inhale up to tree heart, exhale to arm branches, inhale to top branches. This is the basic tree meditation. You can experiment with lots of tree types. This type is based on a redwood archetype, the tree Joseph saw in one of his peace chamber visions, which we shall discuss later. However, another stage exists.

This meditation builds on the first stage. It really only works once you have developed connectedness between Earth, roots, trunk, and branches. It amplifies the experience/realization of tree greatness. Inhale the cool, clear white descending light that becomes presence *(wa-chi-who)* from infinite Sky. Inhale through the nostrils, the Sky breath. Draw that light down through the leaves/branches stretching up from the crown of the head. Fill the cup of head, the cup of chest, and cup of abdomen, and bring the energy to the base of the spine. Pause; then exhale down through the roots, expanding fully into Earth, Vast Self. Pause one count. Then inhale up through the mouth, pulling golden sap up the roots, trunk to heart, where the branches connect. Pause one; then, through nostrils, exhale energy/sap through branches. Everything becomes green. Try to extend the branches/leaves out and up far. This is the tree's aura. You can shift from greenness to radiance. The fingers and fingerlets of tree are pure green, and its aura extends far beyond those. Pause and savor.

The next time you inhale, be aware inhaling the sun's aura, its subtle light. It is also being inhaled by the leaves, primarily the ones all around. So you are inhaling two levels of light: Very Subtle Light and Subtle Light. In fact, we are really inhaling at least three levels of light because we are also inhaling the warmer physical light of the sun, the light we perceive through our ordinary senses. So the tree inhales three energies/lights: Very Subtle, Subtle, Gross/Physical. It transfers all three of these to Earth. Recharging, feeding, reinvigorating. Then as it exhales, it produces electro-magnetic magnetism energy, auric energy/ light that radiates around the trunk and branches, and ultraviolet energy that passes above the head into the Very Subtle Upper-World level.

Another variation of this practice is to add flower and fruit, of many colors and shapes. All represent archetypal energies, colors, and shapes. To accentuate the experience, make the flowers or fruits very large, so you can more fully experience their/your nature. You can also produce a series of fruit and flowers (like lotuses), blossoming/fruiting along the column of the trunk. These various fruits/flowers would correspond to the colors of the spectrum we—as they—do in the arrow meditation. For instance, you could put a big cherry below, a peach just below the navel, and orange in the solar plexus, a lemon in the heart, a green plum in the upper chest, a blueberry around the eyes, and a violet plum in the forehead. This seems a little funny. You might prefer flowers or gemstones, a common practice among Eastern mystics.

Remember the total growth of treeness/soul. The farmer, *oh-kaa-meh-neh* ("the essence of childlike innocence of the highest goodness that sits"), plants the seed in the manifestation of Vast Self, Earth. Sustained by all elements and energies, it germinates and ascends to Sky, spreading, drinking all levels of Light. It is (we are) "going up" *(weh-leh-who)*. *Weh-leh-who* means Great Spirit (concerted action of Earth/Sky) is connecting us to the highest potential of the heavens in childlike innocence. In our emptiness/innocence, we become the longing of the Earth for Sky and vice versa. In turn, as the tree matures, it radiates light/energy/oxygen/greatness. Producing flowers, nuts, cones. Without Light, greatness perishes. Without trees we perish.

You can add a simple sound practice to this by sounding *lo, le, la*. With *lo* concentrate on the downward rooting, with *le* concentrate on the horizontal spreading around the chest, and with *la* concentrate on the ascent.

You can do this practice anytime. If you do it in morning or afternoon, bring the light/sap down from the high heavens and end the practice concentrating on the outspread limbs and leaves. If you do it in evening, end by concentrating on the sap/light's rising into the upper world.

XVIII. *Becoming the Painted Arrow*

Shortly after arriving at Picuris, Joseph was given the name
Tsloot-ta-koi, which generally translates in English as Beautiful
Painted Arrow. Like Tiwa sounds in general, the syllables are
onomatopoetic. Joseph immediately loved the sounds because he
could "hear the sound of an arrow being released from the bow,
flying through the air, hitting its target" (*House of Shattering
Light* 37–38). His name also implies rainbow, double rainbow,
in fact. The bent wood is one rainbow; the string is the other.
Altogether, this makes three: the arrow, the bow, and the string.
Maybe they represent the rainbows of the three worlds.

He could hear and visualize the arrow flying, painting beauty
everywhere. The arrow flew everywhere he cast his breath,
everywhere he extended his concentration. Our energy field, our
subtle body, extends everywhere we concentrate. Our subtler
shells extend further. (But they don't have to extend far physically
because at the subtle level we are a connected web of light.)
When Painted Arrow began traveling to teach (in about 1980),
the arrow(s) of his being (his aura) traveled in time and space,
eventually around the world, several times.

Painted Arrow also speaks of the painted arrow as a magical
arrow that was only used by hunters in emergency, if they were
lost for instance. They could shoot the magic arrow for miles
back to their camp or village. A medicine person would retrieve
the arrow and create a rainbow bridge, which would transport
the hunter home.

In this concentration, visualize the arrow sticking vertically
into the Earth. Begin this practice with the same orientation as
the Three Worlds' practice. Visualize the arrow as the spectrum
of visible (and invisible) light. The top of the arrow represents
the ultraviolet end of the spectrum; the bottom, the infrared.
The butt of the arrow (with the nock) pointing directly upward
is violet. The tip of the arrow, penetrating Earth is red, bright
cardinal red. Energies extend beyond the visible spectrum,
infinitely up and down into Grandfather Sky/*Pa-peh-tah* and

Grandmother Earth/*Naah-aah-uu-kwill.*

In this practice, you, the human two-legged, are essentially the bridge connecting Earth and Sky. This practice is best experienced while standing. Your hair, the feathers at the top of the arrow, represent the violet energy that penetrates the Upper World. Your feet, which sink at least a foot beneath the surface, are the red arrow point. Your heart/center/cardiac plexus/*Pii-ini-aah-ii* is the middle of the arrow: yellow-green.

Extend your exhalation downward into Earth/red. Then pull inhalation upward, through your head, into Sky/violet/clear light. For a while, exaggerate your breathing along the vertical axis of the arrow. Practicing will stretch you, straightening your spine. You will begin to feel energy course along the axis of the three Directions. In time, start the 4/1/4 square breath. And slow, shorten, and make subtle your breathing. As you do this, begin to introduce the other colors of the spectrum: a salmon/pink color between red and orange, and blue between green and violet. You will have a total of seven colors.

From the Under World, breathe up (inhaling) red, salmon, orange, yellow, green, blue, violet. From the Upper World, reverse the visualization. Gradually, balance your inhalation and exhalation by your concentration on the colors; forget counting.

By practicing the arrow, you ground yourself in the three worlds and all the subtle dimensions in between. You will also strengthen the vertical circulation/flow of energies Above to Below to Above to Below. Every time the breath passes the heart, it empowers the Center, the origin that both holds the two poles together and keeps them separate. We are all three Directions. By concentrating in this way, we magnify our vertical rainbow, beautifying the universe.

The rainbow arrow is also the prayer stick *(paho)*, the lance, the flowering stick, and the staff. The arrow is particularly powerful because of its arrow tip that fixes the soul into this world of crystallized light. Many Westerners are not grounded; they are spaced out, alienated from creation, uncommitted to fulfilling their purpose, becoming. The arrow, with its tip *(pee)* fixed deep within creation, commits us to breathing and acting through the body, allowing energies to fully flow. The arrow point/body is *pee-ah*: "Rootedness that holds our light." Contemplate this. Sound it. *Pee-ah*: "Rootedness that holds our light (of soul, *kai-pia-neh*) while we're in body." And body is crystallization of light/song. So we can make ourselves, all our relations, all worlds, whole. The descended arrow symbolizes the lightning bolt, the medicine person, the messenger who brings revelation and beauty.

You can perform this any time. If you perform it in morning or afternoon, end with energy moving downward, or downward and outward through the middle of the yellow-green range. If you perform it at night, focus on the breath's rising up through the ultraviolet feathers.

XIX. *Becoming Mountain*

A variation of the arrow meditation is the mountain meditation. Both concentrations bridge the inner and outer levels. However, the arrow meditation accentuates the descent of the Sky to Earth, the cold, white light's unfolding from ultraviolet to infrared. The mountain accentuates the rising of the earth, the whole upward thrust of the Below into the beyond, the love of Earth for Sky. You can practice this standing or sitting. But if you sit cross-legged, your body will form a sort of pyramid/mountain.

Begin by exhaling downward, sending your energy roots into the center of Earth, the Vast Self. The mountain is the Vast Self rising. So you must merge with the Below. This means that you practice 'dropping' your center of gravity, energizing and expanding the energy center at the bottom of the spine (sacral plexus). Remember every time you exhale, you relax and release all tension, stress, and dis-ease. When you inhale, expand the lower abdomen and groin. Fill your basement/kiva with fresh magnetism from below. When you inhale, the below pushes/exhales up. Don't let the rising energy rise above the navel. Concentrate on emptying/descending when you exhale and inspanding/recharging when you inhale.

When you start to feel grounded and heavy, an extension of the Earth's center, introduce the square breath. Then pull the ascending energy up the abdomen, making the abdomen swell. This is the wide rising of the mountain. Geologically, it is the sliding of one plate upon another. Continue to merge with Earth as you exhale, and swell/spread/rise as you inhale. You can visualize your midsection rising toward the blue sky. Try to visualize a mountain like Mt. Fuji, symmetrical and triangular. (If you 'see' asymmetrical growth, note the imbalance.) When you get to the peak, visualize snow around the peak. This is the white light beyond the ultraviolet edge of the spectrum. This is where Earth pierces Sky. But don't abandon your descent concentration. The mountain is the rising of the whole Earth.

This practice will make you grounded, strong, and formidable.

Though the mountain is Earth and represents the earth element, it is illuminated earth. It is not stuck, not 'heavy.' It is dynamic. It is kissed, blessed by the clear, white light: the snow that melts down its sides and blesses and refreshes all of life. This is why humans really want to climb mountains. They just don't know that the real climb is internal. A person with illuminated earth would be an ideal chief or leader. She would exude spiritual responsibility.

If you want to introduce light into this practice, you should use the color copper or gold. This is the color of illuminated earth, brown that has been penetrated by the cold descending light. You can visualize the entire Earth below as this color, before and after you draw it up as the mountain. Mountain in Tiwa means center, the golden heart. You can sense the wideness of the mountain around your chest. This is its generosity.

The Pueblo are people of the Earth, the manifest Vast Self. They emerged from the Earth's womb. They continued to live in it, then pray in it. Then they started to build higher, on top of mesas, constructing adobe of three or four stories. Eventually, they started building the kivas half above ground. And their ancestors, the Anasazi, lived on high plateaus and built sophisticated villages in creviced mountainsides. This movement shows the Earth's longing for Sky.

Joseph's mother's people are Utes, people of the mountain. After Joseph came to Picuris, he spent a lot of time in the mountains while he was trained by Antonio/Te and other elders. Te lived on the side of the mountain, above the village. He told Painted Arrow he preferred the mountain because the people were losing their connection with the Sky. They were out of balance. They had become too earthy, too material.

Upon the mountain, Joseph was the heart, the ascending and expanding Center. Antonio, called Te in *Beautiful Painted Arrow: A Medicine Story*, symbolizes mountain-ness: the Earth's longing for Sky. Joseph lived for long periods of time in the father mountains, with and without Antonio. Just as he spent intervals in the mother kivas. Mountain ceremonies involved staying in a cave, fetching special herbs and ingredients, and running up and down the slopes, to and from the village. In addition, Joseph often hunted game and sought solace there. If you read *Beautiful Painted Arrow: A Medicine Story*, you'll realize the entire story revolves around the mountain, from beginning to end. His initial climb, his staying there, and his eventual return symbolize the spiritual journey of his first thirty years.

You can do this practice any time. If you do it at night, you should emphasize the upwardness of the mountain, the peak that penetrates night sky. At the end you are no longer Earth thrusting up, just the beyondness.

XX. Connecting Sky and Earth, Mountain and Kiva, Above and Below

Joseph has integrated his Ute/mountain nature and Pueblo/kiva nature. Though most of us do not have such a dramatic genealogical split, we, nevertheless, have this vertical, split nature. Our Grandfather/Above/Sky/mountain nature is transcendent. It causes our energy to rise. Physicists call this buoyancy. Buoyancy orients us out of life into the beyond. On the other hand, our Grandmother/Below/Earth/kiva nature is immanent. It is governed by gravity. It pulls us down. Through our energy flows up and down the body (as we have read and practiced), it tends to well in certain areas, in the upper or lower body. When energy rises, the voice rises and we walk on the balls of our feet. When it descends, our voice descends and we shuffle our feet. Each of us has a center of gravity.

As we learned in previous practices, these two loving poles are balanced by and in the heart. We have already done a mountain meditation. This frees our lower half from stagnation. The tree meditation does this as well, but introduces circulation. The arrow practice is similar to the tree practice, but it is more vertical and emphasizes more circulation. And the walking meditation connects us dynamically with Earth, linking the vertical with the horizontal.

More than any other practice, this practice focuses on reconciling the opposites. Geographically, Joseph experienced the vertical poles when he traveled in mountains, caverns, canyons, caves, and kivas. However, a number of times, Joseph (his *nah*) has traveled in vision to the upper and lower worlds. His most dramatic ascents occurred when he was brought up to be told by elders where to build the first chamber and when, seven years later, he went up again to see where the first chamber had gone. The most dramatic descents occurred when Jesus took him to the underworld and when he hung head-down in a hole and was initiated by the same council of elders as a being of peace.

Like many natives, Joseph often sought visions in holes, as well as kivas.

The following practice can help us integrate our vertical extreme. Kneel on the earth or a carpet, or sit in a wooden chair. But as Joseph often did, you must concentrate on the practice and forget your body. We do this practice to bring about a breakthrough. To jolt our energies back into circulation. To juxtapose and knit apparent opposites. To oppose positive and negative poles.

Before you begin to bow, visualize a mountain in front of you, with its icy peak above your head. And visualize a hole, a kiva, a cavern below it. They both direct energy infinitely, in opposite directions. At a stage during the practice, you become the mountain/cavern; you no longer see them before you. Turn your head and eyes upward; inhale, aiming beyond the beyond. Then bow from the waist, exhaling, aiming below the below.

Once you overcome your resistance, maybe after one hundred or two hundred repetitions, you will start to gain *chi*. Though you will experience periodic obstacles and resistances, you will undoubtedly cross thresholds. As I said, at a certain point, you can consciously shift into experiencing yourself as mountain and cavern. Or you will suddenly slip into non-duality. A simple, powerful way to aid this is to superimpose an upward and a downward pointing triangle (forming a diamond) over your body. The two meet in the sternum. As you continue the diamond stretches and stretches. Try to stay focused, keeping the joint base of the triangles in the heart. Before starting, it is good to decide to do a certain number of repetitions or to continue for a certain time until an alarm goes off. This will help you make effort and counteract laziness and the mind. You can always go longer. Allow yourself to hit the floor, but don't do so intentionally. The effect is akin to falling, to hitting the pole during the sun-moon dance.

If you wish to introduce sound, use the sounds associated with the growth of the tree. Repeat *la* as you rise and *lo* as you bow. Do this as long as you wish. Eventually, just repeat them both silently, *la* while inhaling and *lo* while exhaling. Mystics sometimes speak of stretching the heart, love, to include heaven and Earth. When we do the house of shattering light practice, we experience its horizontal expansion *(le)*. This infinite, mysterious encompassing love refers to what Joseph calls *qu-weh-yah-who*.

This is a morning and afternoon practice.

XXI. *Receiving Inspiration*

In order to better understand inspiration, *ni*, you should read
Sound. One cannot overemphasize the importance of inspiration
in Beautiful Painted Arrow's teaching. He teaches that all
the potentialities of the soul, which is itself the vehicle of the
Vast Self, manifest through inspiration. He also says that we
shouldn't act unless inspired. He means the major undertakings,
the themes or octaves of our lives, not daily tasks that are figured
by the ordinary mind. We should, in fact, live downward and
from inside/out. From the light descending the central axis that
becomes the four-sided house of shattering light when marrying
Earth.

In Christian terminology this would mean "Thy will be
done." Soul expresses Oversoul. Actualizing the will of *Wa-
Ma-Chi*. We know we are inspired when we have been filled
with enthusiasm, the breath of Great Spirit. Enthusiasm
literally means to be inspired by G-d or that G-d within one. We
perceive this mentally, emotionally, and physically. It is clearly
not the desperation, anxiety, and excitement of the body/mind
in isolation. "To be inspired means to have the Breath of Life
give us life. Life, God, breathes life into us. And now we have
spiritual bodies. So in other words we have to go back to our own
breath to find Breath—the Breath of Inspiration" (*The Way of
Inspiration* 40–41).

Once again, as always, breath is the key. Re-finding the
natural breath. Regaining the natural, innocent, complete breath
of childhood. Only now it is conscious and more inclusive.
Joseph says that we must "let go of our blocks" (*The Way of
Inspiration* 41, *Sound* 192). One way that he teaches is to dance
while fasting, even dancing in one's closet. Dancing shakes
us up; we become a rattle. It also links us with Earth and
empties the body of stress and energy, exhausting the physical,
emotional, and mental bodies. Opening the straw of our being.
Creating a vacuum. Calling second, third, fourth, fifth wind
from Vast Self.

The primary, day-to-day blockage is what Blake called Experience. Our conditioning, egocentricity, and ordinary mind. To be inspired we must be in a place of innocence so we can drink light, *soh*. Remember that *soh* is another name for soul, light drinking. In Joseph's painting, these are the *pa-ne-ne*, the innocent faces glancing upward in bliss. Contemplating his paintings is enough to inspire the innocent.

Two general ways to prepare for inspiration are to vigilantly guard against habit in general and to make effort. Being aware, witnessing, watching thoughts, emotions, and sensations is effort, in itself. In particular, doing the opposite of your habitual tendency opens you up. This is cultivating the sacred clown *(kosare/koshare)* archetype. The koshares are the backward/forwards, the Magpietail boys, the tricksters of the pueblo. They constantly reverse habit, tradition, and morés. They also walk the way of blame, counteracting our fixation on approval. They dismantle repression, one of the great deadeners.

Here, we concentrate on the way of meditation to disengage ordinary thinking and open the energy pathways. Then, if we are fortunate, we can 'raise' *ti/chi* to embrace the very subtle level. Doing so, we might 'catch' *wa*, the descending breath/light/energy of Intelligence that creates every moment anew, out of Nothingess.

If we can receive *wa*, it will penetrate our subtle (consciousness/conscience) and gross (personal) natures. *Wa* aligns us. Reconnects us to sacred body, sacred Earth, asleep in materialism (as Blake has written). The essential condition is emptiness, 'kivaness.'

220

Inspiration comes from the space of divine emptiness and manifests itself in the space of manifestation. Inspiration comes only when it can come forth into a realm of manifestations where there are no mental, emotional, spiritual, or physical presences. There has to be emptiness, only then can manifestation grasp it. (*Sound* 194)

Inspiration wants to manifest; the hidden treasure wants to become known, as some mystics say. But manifestation, the Vast Self, is hungry for inspiration. Starving for inspiration. Humans are just not upholding the covenant, our work of being and connecting the worlds, of *Wa-Ma-Chi*-ing.

Practices involving *ni* are best done at night. To prepare ourselves for inspiration for inspiration, we should sit or stand facing Northward, specifically Northeastward. It is at this line, midway between North and East on the wheel, that Winter becomes Spring. Joseph says that at this precise interval between the Spiritual and Mental energies inspiration descends into manifestation. In *Ceremonies* and *Sound,* he correlates this to the descent of the kachinas into Earth at the place that would become Picuris. Two images are helpful in becoming empty and, perhaps, enthusiastic.

The first is the 'T,' a cross in which the crossbar has 'risen,' indicating the subtle body's attunement and receptivity to the very subtle. 'T' indicates that we have climbed the mountain and are camping at the pinnacle. Effort, gross and subtle, moves us up. Breath moves us up. *Weh-leh-who* moves us/soul up into pure innocence and receptivity. Your spine is the vertical axis, the pole, the arrow, the staff (which we hope will flower). The horizontal bar corresponds to the three worlds, levels of energy, very subtle, subtle, and gross. The crossbar indicates our center of gravity. If the crossbar crosses at the navel or below, we're stuck in the gross/personal/lower world. If it crosses between the navel and the forehead, we're stuck in the subtle/middle world. If it crosses from the forehead upward, we're stuck in the Upper world. Some people are stuck in this world. And being stuck in any realm is imbalanced and counterproductive. *Wa-Ma-Chi*-ing stops.

Sitting or standing straight but not stiffly, accentuate the inhalation through the nostrils. You might sense where the cross bar is. As you inhale upward through the chimney/straw/ hollow bone of your middle, lift the crossbar. Hold your breath above your head a few times. And exhale naturally, through your mouth. Every time you exhale, release stress, anxiety, and thoughts. Ease the crossbar into the violet realms. At a certain point, repeat *weh-leh-who* as you inhale.

"*Weh-le-who* means to go up. *Weh* means to give. *Leh* means the horizontal plane. *Who* gives us a sense of being carried. It gives us a sense of the connection to the vastness, to the heavenly planes. *Who* means God is carrying us, or God is carrying the highest action that is being taken. This is connecting us to the highest potential of the heavenly planes, and it is giving us the place of childlike innocence in which we are simply conduits of energy at the core of existence – energy that is moving through us without any effort on our part and nourishing our souls. (*Ceremonies* 84, *Sound* 126)

Repeat *weh-le-who* silently as you inhale. Occasionally, repeat it as you hold your breath, concentrating above your head. The bar is your crown, your fountain. The rungs of the bar actually are luminous steps, a ladder that ascends infinitely. When you begin to taste peace, bliss, and 'consciousness-without-an-object,' you are *pa-ne-ne*.

The next image is the cup, or chalice. The cup is just a little more ordinary, more natural, made of clay. Like us, nothing special. Ordinary/extraordinary. Joseph teaches that cup is *ti*, the energy of awareness, as well as *kola-oh-omo*: "beauty that defines itself to the deepest recesses of the infinite self, that carries with it power of teachability and has eyes to see" (*Sound* 195). Once the bar has been raised, lifted by the infinite, it no longer exists; the grid ends. It/we are just the luminous rays of the cross. Or the empty cup. After you have inhaled and held your breath above the head, sense what sort of a cup you are. What color? What material? What shape? Repeat *kola-oh-omo* silently as you inhale and exhale. This will help you sense the nature of soul, how *Wa-Ma-Chi* works through you.

Next, inhale downward through the nostrils and exhale through the mouth. You are, effectively, performing the water breath. If you are not attuned to the upper world, you should continue practicing the bar/crown concentration. As you perform the water breath, welcome the descent of *Wa*, the liquid light of intelligence. Repeat *wa* silently as you inhale, drinking light with your entire being. Also letting it wash you inside and out. This is the first stage of inspiration that Joseph calls *weh-mu*, the "incoming of meaning" (*The Way of Inspiration* 15). Remember that the Above doesn't end, and we don't suddenly begin. We, Life, are a continuum. The three worlds are just an orientation in perceptual reality.

After experiencing *wa*, you can repeat *tsclo-ii* on the inhalation. When you exhale, be aware of yourself as cup, that which is filled. *Tsclo-ii* combines, childlike innocence, descending light, and awareness. It means "rain that is falling on parched landscape" (*Sound* 157). Parched means empty. Ready. Longing. Rain is light in Tiwa metaphysics. Your cup is catching rain. In the same passage, Joseph suggests you can also say *tah-tsclo-ii-eh*, "I am the one that's in a state of nurturing—a state of awareness, a state of innocence, a state of descending light."

Once you feel purified and full, begin to repeat *nah-mo-low-ney* as you exhale. Continue to repeat *tah-tsclo-ii-eh* while inhaling. *Nah-mo-low-mey* is "*nah* descending into lower recesses of self, so they (recesses) can place themselves in heaven." *Wa*, having merged with *nah*, descends into the lower recesses of the unconscious, the underworld, which embrace heaven. In other words, they become illuminated. As above so below. This is a very powerful practice that can prepare you for epiphany, realization, revelation. If we can learn to inhale and exhale (be inhaled and exhaled), we become a child of the moment. The slice of light.

This an early morning practice and day practice. In the morning it should be followed by a practice that ushers energy outward, something solar-like. At night the cup rests, and the light *(wa)* recedes/ascends into no-thing. Silence.

Sounding Tiwa sounds, syllables and 'words,' is greatly enhanced by our capacity to be a kiva. Or, as we shall learn in the next practice, to be a peace chamber. First, practice the inner kiva meditation. Discover yourself to be the hollow center of the universe. Begin by humming, swallowing *(soh)* the vibration down into the middle world, your chest, even the cavern of your abdomen. Then, sound the vowels, A (AH), E (EH), I (EE) O (OH), U (OU), as they are pronounced in Latin languages. Joseph associates the archetypal vowels sounds with the cardinal directions. For a more in-depth explanation of the vowels and directions, consult Joseph's *Being and Vibration.*

A/AH is the sound for the East. In Tiwa, AH means "to wash"; it washes. AH purifies, baptizes. Face the East as you swallow AH, vibrating it within the chest. Inhale through the mouth and repeat AH silently as you draw breath/energy into the center of the kiva. You can repeat AH once for each exhalation. You can repeat it over and over as you exhale. Massage your insides with its vibration. Singers project; chanters 'inject.' Wash yourself of previous actions, reactions, moments. Do this until you become AH. Once your microcosm becomes a bell/gong, the vibration will radiate, washing not only the East, but all directions.

Face South. Sound E/EH within. You will notice that this sound will not descend as deeply as AH. Nevertheless, swallow the sound, keep it within so the kiva resounds. In Tiwa, EH vibrates relationship. Your relationship with yourself (self, Self, and Vast Self), as well as all of beingness, visible and invisible. Consciously repeat EH again and again. Allow it to permeate every space, every pore. Permeating the kiva/macrocosm, it will touch all worlds.

Face West. Sound I/EE. EE vibrates awareness, insight. EE naturally vibrates in the head. Sound it there. Allow the sound to empty the skull, fill it with light. Move the vibration into the throat and the chest. Even the abdomen. The vibration will follow your focus. Listen for overtones. You can create overtones, higher octaves of sound, with all vowels, but producing them is easiest with EE. Again fill all spaces, even the seemingly solid body parts (that are essentially space). When you become this vibration, face North.

Facing North, sound O/OH. OH is the condition of eternal innocence, openness, wonder. OH also vibrates placement; we can feel this within because the OH sound descends most deeply into the inner space. When we are placed, we are exactly who we are, in sincerity and authenticity. Being who we are, we assume our "place," without illusion or pretension. We surrender to the Overwill and can potentially fulfill our purpose/destiny. Understand this by becoming it through vibrating.

Remain sitting toward the North. Begin vibrating U/UU. UU is the vibrating essence of carrying. If we have found and become our place, then we can be carried. UU, which vibrates naturally in the back of the throat, is an introverted sound. Consume the sound. Be consumed by it. UU takes us to the center of the circle, the first and last direction. It accentuates the emptiness of the center. No me, no intention, no need. The open void into which Above and Below dissolve. Here, as this vibration, we can carry our relations literally and figuratively, as a parent carries a child. The empty center, the sun of the sun of the sun, is responsible for all the universe, carrying them. We, as little suns, carry according to our capacity.

Once you have sounded all the vowels individually, sound them, staccato and legato. Make all the sounds in one exhalation. Sound them distinctly, and sound them smoothly so they blend, one into another. Sound them again and again. You can try rotating your head sunwise, following the directions from east, to south, to west, north. Repeating UU in the center. UU will stabilize you in the center, along the central axis. Concentrating the UU there will prevent you from getting dizzy.

You can even turn your body around the directions of the compass, saying each sound as you face the corresponding direction. Remember to 'sneak' the UU sound in between OH and AH, concentrating in the center, the heart. Another option is to say the UU silently within as you inhale. This centers you very powerfully. Also, rather than rotating your head or body, you can simply face East and project the vowel sounds from within the kiva, out along the rays of the medicine wheel, in the four directions. So, you become like a rotating Tibetan prayer wheel. While sitting centered and still, you send AH infinitely Eastward through your front, EH infinitely Southward through your right side, EE infinitely Westward through your back, OH infinitely Northward through your left side, and UU infinitely within. This practice can truly transform you. Help you to experience yourself as pure vibration/light. Remember, you must surrender yourself to vibration. Practice attentively, again and again. Enter the subtle vibrational world of *nah*. Notice all the nuances. Sense and listen.

Do these in daytime. In evening you can perform them silently on breath, ending on inhalation. But don't do them at night because you might be too energized to sleep. If you wish to sleep.

XXIII. *The Child of Peace*

If you skipped the Peace-Chamber visions in Part One, I'll summarize them here so you don't need to refer back when practicing. In 1981, Joseph envisioned a map on his office, in the Indian Health Service. Among the various scenes projected, Joseph saw natives suffering on reservations and a peace *(key-ah-teh)* chamber. He didn't connect these two snapshots until he sun danced on the Southern Ute reservation in 1983. While dancing, all the while fasting from food and water, Beautiful Painted Arrow saw a messenger from the *nah* world, the angelic world. Suddenly, the messenger metamorphosed into an oval-shaped chamber. Inside the chamber, women and men were chanting. Later, he linked the oval chamber to his map vision, as well as to a vision of a woman he had had when he was seven. Then, in 1942, he had just moved to Picuris. In dreaming, as *nah*, he saw a smiling grandmother, standing like an ecstatic mother hen in front of seven small, elliptical music houses.

Joseph's directive was clear. Since he was seven, Vast Self had been preparing him to build sound chambers. Not traditional kivas. And not among Indians but non-Indians. This realization led him to understand how he could address the scene of suffering natives. Building the sound chambers, he would raise and refine the vibration of non-natives, who would aid the native people's their ancestors had decimated. The non-natives might even awaken to their own ignorance in destroying native life.

In 1983 Joseph had already begun to teach outside of New Mexico. He pondered the metaphor as he traveled, teaching. Traveling in Europe and the United States, he sought the right place, holy ground, to build the first chamber. This proved to be a misinterpretation. The universe needed to remind him that every place was holy, the center of the universe. And that the chambers were divine seeds that would enhance Earth's inherent sacredness. Give Earth what it needs from humanity.

Vast Self reminded him when he returned to Bernalillo. During an evening sweat lodge in his backyard (the sweat lodge is the purifying void which awakens clarity), he had another vision. This one, however, was not subtle; it was a directive. In the vision, he ascended in his *nah*.

Suddenly, he was high above Earth, standing amid a council of Native American elders. They directed him to build the first chamber and called it a chamber of peace. Just as the elder in the Ute sun dance had become a chamber, the circle of elders became a circle of fiery light that descended to his yard, near the sweat lodge. Joseph, standing beside them, realized the flames would be the walls of the chamber.

Next, a smaller radiant disc, about six feet in diameter, descended. On top, holding an infant, was an eight-foot angel. When the angel's feet touched Earth, he lowered, 'planted' the infant as a seed, two feet beneath the surface. Before disappearing, he told Joseph that the child was his to raise. In the forthcoming practice, we shall see that the angel spoke both literally and figuratively. For, in a later vision, received before the Bernalillo chamber had been dismantled, Joseph saw that the child had risen to the heavens in the arms of a giant redwood.

Begin the practice by sitting on the ground or in a chair, preferably a wooden chair. Face East like the angel. Start the square breath, concentrating on the inspanding kiva in the abdomen. After you sense the inner void, start the vertical arrow/ prayer stick breath and concentration. Remember the arrow/ stick/trunk is your spine, along which energy flows through the three worlds and the Center, Up, and Down.

You can inhale up four counts, concentrating on stretching the inner space up through the head. You can focus on abdomen, chest, head, and above. Add red/orange, yellow/green, blue/ violet, and white/crystal if you wish. Or you can rise up through the spectrum on seven counts/colors as we did with the arrow practice. Initially, hold your breath more than one count above the head so that you accentuate the transcendent Upper world. Exhale down naturally, using the same rhythm as the inhalation, but only pause one count after the exhalation. Use the water/ mouth exhalation.

Visualizing an ascending and descending elevator will help

this practice, an elevator that takes you through the roof, into the sky. Or visualize energy/sap rising through and out a hollow trunk or bamboo shoot. Once you sense the top of your head as open, and you sense a powerful upward thrust (that stretches your torso and head), visualize a luminous ring/crown above the top of your head. This is the ring of elders existing in the subtle realms of the *nah*. Communicating a very subtle impulse from the Source.

The ancients of the Judeo-Christian tradition (who inherited from the Zoroastrians) recognized at least nine orders of angels. They might have considered the elders to be cherubim or seraphim. You might want to hold your in-breath as you concentrate on the crown. If you need help visualizing, you can research the aureoles or halos that were painted above the heads of holy personages during the Renaissance. Seek out the paintings of Botticelli, Verrocchio, Crivelli, Mantegna, and Giotto. Sometimes, they painted halos as golden discs.

Remember from the three-worlds practice that we are the three worlds and that the upper and lower worlds extend infinitely. When we first experience the rising of the elevator through the top of the head (into the upper world), we experience peace, bliss, and liberation. Like a genii emerging from a lamp. We are temporarily freed from the illusion that we are only material, finite beings. When this occurs, we have a sense of eternity and infinity. Our very subtle body, our transcendent body or world, feeds off our attachment to the physical world.

More and more, we sense the relativity of the ordinary, personal mind, senses, and body. We become less identified with our self-image and importance. And, to some extent, we lose the fear of death because we realize physical existence is temporary, that Intelligence (consciousness without an object) is timeless. This is what Joseph means when he says that we don't exist. We don't exist as separate, isolated, encapsulated things. A well-developed halo corresponds to the permanent opening of the energy center in the top of the head: the first stage of wisdom.

This experience is sometimes called 'resurrection.' Consciousness/energy has, indeed, risen. We have died before death in the sense that we know we are not just the personal self. We may also have insight into our higher self, soul, or archetypal nature. This, our angelic body, needs to unfold while we have our physical bodies. It manifests (and projects) qualities of light and vibration through the physical/personal body. It is the perpetually reborn and unfolding child within.

As the rising energy/perspective becomes more fixed, it can develop into what mystics call the witness, transcendent eagle consciousness. Continually/consciously taking the elevator to the roof and from the roof to downward (the eagle sweeps to the surface), we link the three levels of mind. And experience a more profound wisdom.

When the ancient ones descended into Bernalillo as a disc of light, they subtlely embodied an impulse of revelation, the clear white light of Intelligence, sometimes called the divine mind. The descent of the transcendent light/energy is illumination, also called transfiguration. With illumination, transcendent energy descends, opening us up, penetrating into the ground of our being like a lightning bolt. Once it has opened and purified us by descending into and through the bottom of the spine, the angel and the child can descend into our hollow.

The descending, illuminating light, represented by the descending disc, creates the inner womb, the pure place into which the seed of the soul can be planted. This is the child. The child of the soul, who must mature and unfold, blessing the world as it does. The planting of the infant *(pa-ne-ne)* is *nah-mo-lo,* "descending into the inner recesses of Self so they can place themselves in heaven." We each become the Blessed Virgin: purified and impregnated by spirit. In alchemy this is the athanor, alembic, holy vessel in which transformation takes place.

In order to enact this according to Joseph's vision, you must exhale the luminous disc downward through the open elevator shaft. You must do it again and again. First inhale four counts upward to the roof, pause one count concentrating on the halo, then exhale the luminous circle down through the head, neck, chest, and abdomen, into the bottom of the spine. This will empty, prepare and purify us for our own child. Our child of soul, our next inspiration and revelation. Remember when you inhale, Sky, the upper world, is drawing energy upward and Earth is exhaling/pushing. And when you exhale, Sky is really exhaling and Earth is really inhaling/pulling.

On one of your exhalations, take the next step, exhale an orb of light downward into your lower abdomen. Into your metaphorical uterus, the luminous room below the navel. You are doing this from the consciousness of the elders, wisdom. This is the descending breath of Intelligence *(wa)*, what mystics call illumination. The elders are planting the seed; they are the seed. This is your experience. Joseph was called upon to give birth to the child of the peace chamber (himself), to nurture this child, this need, this revelation, world over. Spirit will impregnate you with Its Own need, which is your need, which is you.

As you breathe these breaths of resurrection and illumination, your being will swell with inner light and divine purpose. You will inspand and expand. You will look elliptical, pregnant. The child will push out to the four directions. The fertilization takes place deep in our being, in the lower world. It engages Earth, the body, the senses, our instinct. It activates our essence or animal. It requires every aspect of existence along this ray of energy/light/ sound that we are.

With every series of vertical breaths we prepare, we purify, we illuminate, we impregnate. After the gestation, the preparation, we eventually birth and nurture. The birthing and nurturing are the unfolding, the spreading/growing of the seed being. This corresponds to exhalation into the four directions that accompanies its maturity. The spreading of Joseph's child corresponds to his teaching and traveling, his sowing of the peace chambers. Together, the one hundred or so peace chambers around the world form a web of light and vibration.

Those who practice this interiorly magnify this web. Whether they build or enter a physical peace chamber, they build peace for themselves, this world, these worlds. The holy womb of the empty chamber is the focus for infusion from all worlds. For the energy of the child, its presence, was essentially that. The infant is/was the transcendent peace (*Sat* in Sanskrit) brought to Earth, brought into Earth. Its implantation echoes the incarnation of the high priest of priests, the heavenly messenger Melchiesidek, teacher of Abraham, who is said to have founded the city of Jerusalem, the city of peace. ('Salem' means peace.) The peace chamber practice incorporates the kiva/medicine wheel concentrations. Joseph was shown that the original peace chamber was half below ground, half above.

In his painting of this event, rain, the light of intelligence, *wa,* rains upward from the hole, the angel, and the infant. The holy, blessed rain is rising into the heavens. *Nah-mo-lo-ney,* the divine impulse has "descended into lower recesses of Self so they can place themselves in heaven." The lower recesses 'went' beyond placing themselves in heaven. They became heaven. And then they offered a reciprocal blessing. This is a paradox: the Above's becoming the Below. This magical reversing of natural and supernatural law is rarely experienced and understood in world mysticism. Tibetan Buddhism, Vajrayana, is one of the few paths that teaches the mystery of reversal of directions and the final disappearance of all orientation in pure Beingness, primordial, luminous, non-dual Suchness.

Joseph's work to bring inner/outer peace into the body/Earth, to make peace immanent, was further symbolized/signaled by his being initiated (by the same elders) in the underworld, and their subsequent emptying him of negativity. This emptying occurred in 1984, after Joseph finished the first physical chamber in Bernalillo. It marked the rooting of the peace child, the child that he was. And the pacification of his physical form. Remember, the elders were the walls. In this vision they blessed him when he hung head-down into a hole in his backyard, a hole he was digging for a well. Mirroring the action of his painting. Clearly, after the chamber was built and practiced in, the elders descended even deeper into Grandmother Earth.

If you want to taste this initiation by the elders in the underworld, visualize a descent deep into Earth as you exhale. Remember, your aura, not just your body, is the peace chamber. When you exhale down, your auric/energy field descends as a shaft of *chi.*

When you inhale, draw down a shaft of energy/light to your bottom, and then exhale it down from there. You will begin to experience the presence of the descending light, *wa*, below. This is a taste of the reconciliation of opposites. Through Joseph's building of the vision, the male Above force penetrated the Below. The Below of/in him.

Joseph was hanging upside down. So the transcendent energy above his head literally penetrated the immanent presence of the Below. Short of hanging upside down in a hole as Joseph did, and other mystics have done, stand on your head or hang downward from a limb or a bar. If you do so, send your breath down through your head as you exhale, and inhale up from Earth. This is the typical act of a *koshare*, a holy clown, a backwards/forwards. You, too, may have a taste of the Up becoming Down and vice versa.

Joseph's revelation/impulse was an infant. He had been having these visions for years. Then he was shown explicitly what to do and where to do it. He was even shown the precise shape of the chambers: ovals/ellipses, pregnant spheres rather than circular kivas. We, in our own small way, will be directed through steps. Once the being of our purpose births, it, with our own nurturing and the cooperation of creation, will unfold and respond to the need of manifestation. We will provide a specific spiritual food from the very subtle and subtle levels for creation, the manifest, temporal realm. The elders, our own wisdom, will convey revelation from the Source to the surface.

Though we become a true, responsible adult (knight/brave) in time, we still remain an archetypal child eternally, for only the pure, innocent child in us can receive. And the growing adult gradually becomes the wise, androgynous elder. Even though the archetype of the knight/brave exists eternally. As we evolve, we do not lose archetypes—though they unfold in time. This is a spiritual mystery. The archetypes exist eternally on the subtle level of the collective unconscious. We are unfolding, revealing, becoming them, in time and space.

The peace child came down. This is an early morning practice. But it can also be done in afternoon.

XXIV. Ascent of the Chamber

In 1991, seven years after erecting the Bernalillo chamber, Joseph envisioned the ascent of the chamber and child. The chamber, which was the incarnation of the circle of elders, came to rest a mile above earth, then sixteen miles nestled among the branches of a redwood. The angel and child, now seven, stood by. Together the circle, disc, and child—elders, angel, and child—composed a crystal sphere that streamed light as the Earth rotated. Somehow Joseph's chamber work, though grounded by the roots of the redwood shifted to the subtle level. Keep in mind that, according to Tiwa revelation, even while our primary work is here in the physical world, we exist simultaneously on all of the ten (infinite) worlds.

Though the energy/impulse ascended, it is still anchored to Earth, the lower world, through the deep roots of the redwood. Because it was planted, grew roots and branches (as the redwood), its presence, in fact, extends upward, permeating the atmosphere. Joseph says that it is fed by solar winds, fixed above Albuquerque, trailing a mantel of light. This is a mystery, a mystery worth contemplating. Perhaps the prototypical peace chamber encases/embraces Earth as an aura of protection. Try the following practice.

Sit in a wooden chair or on the floor/Earth. As you inhale, begin the kiva concentration. Start the square breath, breathing in and out the nose. Inspand the entire chest. When you exhale, let your focus settle behind the sternum, in the center of the chest. This is the Center, the first and last direction, the holy void, which is filled with pure potentiality. Gradually, as you inspand, sense that your entire torso is Earth, the sphere of the manifest Vast Self. Your middle is the rotating orb of oceans, land, and physical life—blue, brown, and green. Remember how earth looks from the space shuttle.

Now, envision that your head is the luminous, crystalline peace chamber, hovering a mile or so in the atmosphere. Now envision the Earth/midsection as rotating clockwise, toward your left shoulder. Once you can experience this, start rotating your head in that direction, at the same pace. Your head/chamber, tethered to Earth by the subtle redwood, rotates in concert with the planet. Exhale as your head rotates left, down, and up to the right. Inhale as the head rises from the right shoulder to straight up.

As your head/chamber rotates, it will radiate energy, primarily from your forehead, the center of awareness. It is a very fine energy light, more subtle than the auric light generated from the spinning Earth/midsection. You are strengthening two dimensions of subtle light/energy/magnetism or *chi*. The finer light of the head protects and the light of the middle body, which emanates most powerfully from behind the sternum. Perhaps the peace chamber, risen into the Above, is serving just this purpose, protecting and pacifying the spinning being of Grandmother Earth. Perhaps by practicing this, you will contribute to this protection and pacification. You will certainly protect, pacify, empower, and bless your microcosm—your own center (which is The Center), heart, and presence.

This is an early morning, morning, and daytime practice. If you do it at night, you may not sleep.

XXV. Becoming the Peace-Chamber Child

A variation of the previous practice focuses on the experience of the child rather than the mother/father, birther/nurturer, *key-ah*. As you did in the merging with Grandmother Earth, lie on your back upon the ground. If you have a hole, a sweat lodge, or a peace chamber, you can lie in it with your arms spread and your head facing East. (Remember, the descended prototype was half under earth.) Close your eyes and imagine being let down into an oval womb within Earth. Relax totally, surrendering to gravity. As you inhale softly, rise up to the consciousness of the subtle light that is planting you in the womb. As you exhale through the lips, let go. You are secure and protected in Grandmother. This practice evokes the opposite of effort: surrender.

This gives you the opportunity to relive your birth. Birth was traumatic for all of us. Being jostled by contractions, then squeezed through a narrow tunnel and into harsh light, feeling gravity more powerfully. Fear, as Joseph describes, arises from the sense of 'me,' from being caught (due to limited consciousness) in a physical body and concept. Some of us don't feel at home in our bodies, on this planet. We don't feel secure and welcome. Experience the security and love of Earth. You are in Her lap. Experience the protection and guidance of the luminous oval (wisdom/elders) that surrounds you. Let fear and anxiety descend into Earth as you exhale.

As you, the new-born, grow, you will naturally orient yourself more to Earth, to yourself as a swirling crystallization of light and Intelligence. So instead of connecting upward as you inhale, just experience the swelling up of Earth, allowing Her aura/energy to encompass yours. Again, you are merging with Her breath and rhythm. When you exhale, you are merging more deeply. You are sinking luminous roots. Your treeness is unfolding. The oval/chamber becomes your auric mantle, protecting you always, everywhere, in peace.

Now, as you recall, Joseph saw the initial chamber/child

ascend after seven years. If you want to replicate this, exhale straight up through your center. Earth is pushing up through your roots, through your back, up the upper world. But, more powerfully, Grandfather Sky is calling you back, inhaling, resurrecting you. So, you, the child, ascend as if on an elevator (angel). You, will, however, maintain your connection with Earth through the redwood elevator that penetrates Earth as you exhale.

This last concentration strengthens your subtle nature, your angelic counterpart, as Zoroastrians say. As the Tiwa say, we live simultaneously in ten (an infinite number of) realities. If you are becoming too materialistic, too identified with physicality and mind, this final concentration will relieve you. The only danger in ascending is if you are not at home on Earth and do not love life. Envisioning yourself above can imbalance you. The previous practice of rotating the head around the mid-section will balance and empower you.

This practice is for particularly for early morning. But you can do it in day.

Once deep in this inner chamber of immanent peace, you can dwell in the silent emptiness of the void, *key-ah-teh*. And you can birth the sounds of the directions, the names of the directions, and all the archetypal Tiwa sounds. Perhaps the most complete mantra you can sound in your chamber/kiva is *Wa-Ma-Chi*. Sit on the ground or in a wooden chair, facing east.

Wa-Ma-Chi is the Tiwa sound for the Great Mystery. Joseph generally translates *Wa-Ma-Chi* as Breath, Matter, and Movement, though his many elaborations convey extraordinary subtlety and nuance. *Wa-Ma-Chi* does not denote a dualistic, personified deity. In fact, it denotes nothing at all, no thing and everything, a chest-centered *ah* vibration akin to the Aramaic-Christian *Allaha*, the Hindu *Brahman*, the Zoroastrian *Ahura Mazda*, the Cherokee *Ywahoo*, the Lakota *Wakan Tanka*, and the Vajrayana *Ah*, the vibration of Great Perfection.

Put one of your palms over your sternum and guide the *ah* resonance down from your throat, behind the palm. This is your energy center of beauty, love, and harmony. As Joseph describes in his books, videos, and talks, vowel sounds are circular vibratory fields resonating in different chambers of the body according to their frequency and our vocal range. You recall, *ah* the first vowel, relates to the east, to rain, washing, and ritual purification. It is best imagined as liquid light, the archetypal blessings of the subtle realm. Resonating above the *ah* are the various *u* and *ee* sounds, which generally vibrate in the throat and upper mouth respectively, though we can extend their resonance through practice. The various *oh* sounds can resonate below the chest, into the solar plexus, even into the abdomen through practice.

In making the *w* sound, the lower jaw drops and the lower mouth cavity rounds and elongates, creating inner space. In *Being and Vibration*, Joseph says *w* conveys "twice carrying" (143). Connected to the *ah* sound, *wa*, stretches downward to the chest. For Joseph, *wa* is undifferentiated feminine energy or spirit descending, the movement of original breath toward manifestation, our primary world. In *Sound*, Joseph says, "*Wa* is the light that precedes creation"(88). At the end of its descent, *wa* encounters the infinite Self, and duality and reflection exist.

The result is *ma*, matter, land, *naa-meh-nay*. M vibrates on the upper palate, the roof of the mouth. Sounding it, one can sense vibration rising through the skull onto and through the top of the head. *M* manifests. Linked with *ah*, the heart vibration, it is materializing, the word becoming flesh. *Ma* vibrates against the ceiling of the mouth kiva. Together, *wa-ma* deepen and heighten the kiva, expanding it in all directions. *Ma* effectively seals *wa*, like cupping the palms and feeling the swelling energy interact between the complementary energy of the palms.

Chi, the final syllable, joins the power thrust of *ch* from the back of the throat outward to the center of the head where *ee* resonates. *Chi* is the energy, the explosion resulting from the merging of *wa* and *ma*. In this primary world, from the subatomic to the galactic levels, energy manifests as movement. *Chi* bolts out from between the lips and upper palate like a projectile or gust of wind. At the end of *Wa-Ma-Chi*, *chi* is action/energy/movement, a continuum. *Wa-Ma-Chi*, then, is the way, the Tao, in which nothingness becomes. When you practice this, allow your head to fall and rise slightly, paralleling the vibrations of the syllables. At a certain point, shift to saying it silently while inhaling and exhaling. Then, don't say it at all. Just experience it as you tell your personal mind that you will resonate *Wa-Ma-Chi* thousands of times. That you will temporarily abandon time.

The degree to which we do this, are this, guided by inspiration *(ni)*, is the degree to which *Wa-Ma-Chi* is present within and as us. Inspiration, inhaling *wa*, can lead to embodiment, *ma* (if we surrender), which can lead to appropriate expression, *chi*, what Buddhists call Right Action. So, appreciating Joseph's teaching that actuality is a slice of light, lightning piercing through the Very Subtle—Subtle—Gross levels/worlds, we might say *Wa-Ma-Chi* is creates-uncreates-creates, or becomes-unbecomes-becomes.

Essentially, your instrument will bring the very subtle

239

energies of silence and vibration/light into the gross, physical dimensions. Helping to erase duality. The world needs people to experience transcendent peace, to detach from subtle and physical existence, thereby realizing the physical is just a flash of crystallized light. To forsake the futility of action. But, more importantly, the world needs people to make peace immanent, to embody it. To be peaceful in the crowd. To act creatively, beautifully, altruistically according to inspiration. Oblivious to approval or disapproval.

This is a daytime practice. Try inhaling it at night.

XXVII. *Sounding Wa-chi-chi-hu*

As noted in the "Living Naturally" chapter at the first of this section, *wa-chi-chi-hu* is "the light that precedes creation's becoming aware of itself as the energy that crystallizes as creation." Once we add the simplified meanings of "becoming" and our "search for meaning," we can appreciate *wa-chi-chi-hu*'s being us, the two-leggeds. We are the only means by which It, the totality, can become aware of Itself. So entering deeply into this vibration, resonating it again and again in the peace chamber/kiva, will attune us to our essence and destiny.

You can try this practice in several ways, vertically and horizontally. Face Eastward. First, nod downward slightly, saying *wa*. Raise slightly saying *wa*. And speak horizontally with *chi-chi*. Sense how the *chi*'s are a doubly powerful output of energy/light/beauty/action. Then raise your head slightly saying *hu*. Do this until you permeate form with the subtle world of vibration. Then, silently sense your being as you say *wa-chi-chi-hu* silently, first on the inhalation, then on the exhalation. The final step is just to experience the vibration.

Another style is to repeat the four syllables while rotating the head, both sunwise (left to right) and moonwise (right to left). *Wa* to East, through your chest; *chi* to South, through your right shoulder; *chi* to West, through your back; and *hu* to North, through your left shoulder. Your body is the prayer wheel. Just as you did with the vowels for the cardinal directions. When you need to inhale, do so through your top and bottom, in the center/Center. Rotate many times in one direction. Then many in the other. Eventually, say the words silently, continuing the concentration. You can try exhaling sunwise and inhaling moonwise.

You can also do this practice by sitting still, focusing on the central axis, and sending the vibrations to the four directions with your concentration. Now, the prayer wheel is moving inside you, on the subtle level. Strengthen your focus and visualization. As with the previous physical rotation, you can shift to silent practice, and you can work sunwise then moonwise. And you can alternate directions, exhaling sunwise, inhaling moonwise. Always end a practice in silence, still savoring. As indicated earlier, you can practice it walking.

This is a daytime practice.

XXVIII. Gracing Food

Eating is inhaling and ingesting. Pausing is assimilating. And
exhaling is eliminating downward and sharing in six directions.
Inhaling, pausing, exhaling. Eating is also extracting quality
from quantity. All our relations *(qah-weh)* are alive. All eat
each other. However, humans, two-leggeds, have the unique
opportunity/responsiblity to eat consciously, thereby extracting
more quality from the quantity that enriches our physical bodies.
In addition, the Tiwa teach that we also extract essences that feed
our other nine (or infinite number of) bodies and the worlds in
which they exist. First we feed this primary body/world; then we
feed the others.

Primal peoples, who raise, harvest, gather, and kill what they
ingest, have a sacred, intimate relationship with food. They pray
and worship at every stage. Praising, asking, and promising
the Creator and Sustainer, the heavenly bodies, the archangels
of the Elements, the seven Directions, light and vibration, the
archetypal beings of the animals and plants. Others die in
order that we may live. They know this. They do the killing and
harvesting. They feel the pulsing, breathing, bleeding body. Feel
the pain. They know that the flesh, energy, and archetype of the
being will be extracted and ingested. Will become them.

Most of us have been removed from this sacrament. We
further remove ourselves by conceptualizing beings as 'food.'
Reducing their inherent quality to egocentric utility. Natural
peoples perceive the food's quantity (perceived through senses)
on the physical level, and quality (perceived through *nah*) on
the mental, emotional, and subtle levels. For the most part, we,
conditioned by technology and advertising, are oblivious to this
sacred metaphorical act. We eat processed beings for pleasure.
We do not honor that which has died that we may live. We do not
realize that 'our' food has the same inherent worth, the same
integrity of life, as we. Animals at the top of the food chain have
nothing more than more responsibility.

When we inhale, we are charged with our fundamental food,

air. We pause and extract oxygen in lungs. We are charged, exhaling carbon dioxide. Without air, we die quickly, in a few minutes at best. Next, we eat water. We can live for three or four days without water. But we can live for a month or so without flesh or vegetable food, depending on our resources. Clearly, air and water are the most essential foods. And it is most important that they are pure. Primal people know that they are beings, archangels to Zoroastrians, Wisdom Sisters-Dakinis to Tibetans. They sustain us and exist within us. These archangels permeate us, physically and subtlely. (For the Tiwa, water is light.)

Every flesh and vegetable being we eat provides a combination of these elements/archangels. Most people don't realize that we also fuel ourselves, our subtle nature, with impressions, consciously received perceptions. In the Eastern mysticism, this is known as etherizing the breath, drawing prana/*chi* from air. Consciously drawing impressions at the physical, emotional, mental, and intuitive levels charges us, empowers us, and connects us with life on the ten (infinite) levels. Remember, this is what Joseph and the Tiwa call *ah-tschlu*, "doing with full attention." Mystics enhance feeding on the subtle and very subtle levels by fasting from food and water, temporarily forgetting physical food. Thereby filling the physical with metaphysical food.

If you carefully read *House of Shattering Light*, you will find many references to eating, on all levels. We include a few here. We start with the teaching he received from his first sage, Grandmother Rael:

> Eating was a ceremony. We would use little dippers made from gourds. She would do some singing about the bowl, about the food. The significance of eating was a major Picuris teaching. We were taught that everything was eating—that life was eating all that lives, and all that lives was eating life—that the soul was drinking [*sooh*] light. Life was providing the food for us and we were life's food. (80)

We are food for life, Vast Self. We know that our bodies become physical food for Earth, Vast Self, when we die. But Beautiful Painted Arrow teaches that our becoming *(wa-chi-*

chi-hu) also feeds Earth/Vast Self. On page 103 he speaks of our feeding plants and animals as a result of our physical, emotional, mental, and spiritual efforts. Technology and laziness has decreased our physical effort. This, in turn, creates irritability and conflict. "And without the effort, the planet sickens." To compensate for this lack of human quality, two-leggeds multiply (quantify). Joseph conjectures that the human population must increase to provide effort-food for the Vast Self and our non-human relatives.

A few more references to physical/metaphysical eating in *House.* On page 23 he writes of his soul's being fueled by his family's vitality, before he was born. On 39 he writes of intuition's drinking the light of perceptions (impressions). On 54, he talks of eating corn *(ii-hooh)* and venison *(peeh-waa-ii-eh-ney)* while in the kiva as a boy. Corn allows "what is known to die so that new potential can emerge." Venison allows us "to see how life is constantly placing itself in total awareness." The corn, by the way, contained a black fungus that "helped me expand my perception of what was happening in the kiva and also later in my life."

On 57 he describes that "echoes feed our soul." On 61 he describes sacred running and how, when the "runners lay on the ground, exhausted, the people of the village started 'feeding' or blessing our bodies by sprinkling us with cornmeal." On 75 he has an enchanting story of plant's teaching him to "eat them for their medicinal properties because they enjoyed traveling the human digestive tract. . . . I would eat the leaf of a plant. . . . The plant part that I had eaten would send back a report to the plant that had given the leaf and translate the messages of the eaten plant leaf back to me." Finally, the sweat lodge, which he describes in *Sound* but not *House,* is the black hole, the cosmic womb into which we enter to drink silence, the black light *(key-ah-tey).*

Joseph offers this prayer (recorded by Marchand) to say/remember before eating:

> *Kaa-la-who (God is eating us)*
> *Oh Great Spirit*

We thank you for this circle of life.
In the beginning we came
And formed the very first circle,
And we come again in this way.
We thank you for this food;
We thank you for this day;
We thank you for the friendship.
We thank you for all of the traditions
That made it possible for us to be here.
And we thank the elders of ancient times
And all the others who made it possible
For us to be here
That they come forth and be here today
And feast with us.
So that after we have feasted together
We will go forth until such times that
We come back together again in this way.

Before the practices, and after each practice, you will have
seen the suggestion that certain practices tend to be solar (best
performed in day) or lunar (best performed in night). This, as
explained, is because energy tends to move down and out in day
and in and up at night. Sun time, particularly morning, is the
time for action, for breakthrough, opening doors in the outer
world, primary world. It is exhalation. Day is the unconscious
manifesting through the conscious. Morning practices should
pull energy, our center of gravity downward, into the body,
the gross body. Empowerment. Charging and grounding our
personal selves with energy from the subtle and very subtle
levels. *Wa-Ma-Chi* is acting through us, so we are actualizing
the will of the Creator. In order to do this, be this, we would have
had to have been a cup. A cup *(tee-uh)* that receives inspiration.
And in order to have been a cup, we would have had to have
been innocent. Early morning, before and during sunrise, is the
most important time to meditate and pray. All mystical/religious
teachings know this.

Afternoon is the time for consolidation and completion. For
tying up loose ends. For gathering. Before sun sets and we begin
to turn within. You can always perform practices to enhance
awareness in afternoon. You can also perform empowering (fire
and earth) practices if you need them. Very often energy starts to
turn inward and we need it outward. Practices for awareness and
power will help. Unless you are nocturnal or must work at night,
you should be home when *to-le-ne* sets, seeking its own home
beneath the horizon. You should also eat early in the evening
while you still have some energy in your physical body, before
it rises too much. Eating early will allow you to have digestive
energy, *chi* (fire) to break down food. Eating too late will pull
energy down from its natural ascendance. Despite this, you will
not digest food well. This will inhibit sleep. Sunset is the third
important time to pray/meditate/remember.

Evening is the time for assimilation, contemplation and

inspiration. For receiving, for allowing, letting go. It is inhalation. The unconscious. It is the time for inner work and prayer. In day we do. In evening we ask. In day we are a fist or arrow point, so to speak. In evening we are an upward palm or cup. Energy turns within and rises. We become still. Night becomes still. Energy gradually moves from the gross to the subtle and very subtle realms/worlds. This would be the time that we visit other heavens or dimensions, as we often do in dreams. Our mental, brain-wave activity shifts from alpha, to beta, to theta, to delta. Delta is deep sleep without dreams. Before sleep is the second most important time to pray/meditate/ remember. As evening progresses, we experience *weh-leh-who,* "going up into the heavenly planes."

At night, we reflect upon our day, the daily breath. We express our deepest wish to the Creator. Some mystics have referred to prayer as conscious wish, meaning we sincerely ask for what we/It needs, rather than what we (little me) wants. Tiwa have a special relationship to night. They commune with stars, with constellations, with distant ancestors, with black holes. They gaze *(ti-lah)* at black stars, generating light that is too clear to see. Night is awe, wonder, unlearning, erasing the slate. Night is *no-we-ah. No-we-ah* is prayer to the infinite nothingness: "May the dark of the night bring me to what I am searching for." You can say this prayer peering into the night sky. Seek out the unpolluted darkness if you can. With *no-wee-ah* we can bring into being our perfect nature, that for which we are ignorantly, naively, longing. Particularly practice *no-wee-ah* leading up to and from the new moon when the sky is darkest. When the moon is near full you can speak directly to her, praising the moonlight "that impregnates us with knowledge that births in morning." You can, of course, speak directly to *No-wee-ah,* regardless of the station of the moon. You can start by whispering it as you exhale. Then you can repeat it as you softly and subtlely *inhale* and exhale. In the end, you *(pa-ne-ne)* should repeat it only on the inhalation. Finish with pure receptivity and surrender.

In addition, night is also time to call the ancestors *(weh-ya-who)* and cry for a vision *(weh-seh).* We can repeat both of these as we inhale up through the body and ultimately just up above the head, like a fountain rising into the beyond. Again, always end evening practice with stillness and transcendence. With *oh-high-oh,* "innocence in a state of possibility." Typically we will receive energy and inspiration as we sleep or enter into a transcendent state. And we will understand when it strikes the ordinary mind when energy descends to the gross/personal level. The naturalness of this cycle will change if we are dancing, making vigil, or taking a retreat because we are intentionally shattering the natural rhythm and time in order to be spiritually broken and remade.

Lastly, as you lie on the ground looking up or lie in your bed facing the infinite sky, we can say *pa-peh-yeh.* This is the way the Picuris say the "Our Father" prayer that Jesus taught. They were already doing it in their own way, so when the missionaries came, they adapted it. Lying with their backs on the breast of Mother Earth, they say, "*Pa-peh-yeh*: Our father who art in heaven, hallowed be thy name." Or, as Joseph says, just "Our father who are in heaven." You can repeat *pa-peh-yeh* as you exhale and inhale, falling asleep while breathing finely. Lying on our backs looking upward to sky, we are the face, the *pa-ne-ne* prominent in all of Joseph's paintings. The metaphor of face is "Every single moment wants to praise its creator." Face is the "power that allows us to receive." At night we re-enter the womb of nothingness (sweat lodge) in order to be reborn.

Early morning, the hours before sunrise, is the transition from night to day. One can perform all the practices of night, as long as one ends by drawing energy down into the body, down through the three worlds, ending by rooting us in Earth. This is when we gather the blessings of evening. We are the cup being filled with inspiration/light/energy of the higher planes, *ti/chi.* Just before sunup is the perfect time to do the breaths of the elements, ascending and descending the mountain. If you are in sync, salute the sun as it arises. And practice the outward solar practices described in the saluting sun chapter.

XXX. *Crying for a Vision: We-seh*

The keys to crying for a vision, *weh-seh,* are seclusion from
society and immobility. Seclusion causes us to fast from our
social self, our personality, our yearning for attention, approval,
and self-importance. The aspect of the mind that performs for
others. Eventually, through witnessing and the natural rising
of energy, it can quiet. The energy devoted to performing can
sublimate inward and upward. If we are fortunate to fast from
others in nature, nature can commune with our "crystallizing
power of carrying the Vast Self," *tu-nay,* and essence, *pee-ah-who.*
As noted earlier, only essence can grow/become, *wa-chi-chi-hu*
("Life that is talking and walking with higher source").

Immobility, as opposed to dance, drives energy inward and
upward. Energy is simply not expended or wasted in outer action.
Crying for a vision, we sit, *laa-aa-ii-eh. Laa-aa-ii-eh* is "bringing
clarity into awareness." Beautiful Painted Arrow says, "Train
yourself to sit. Sitting you can experience cosmic enlightenment.
You cannot experience it standing. Why? Because sitting in
silence and cosmic enlightenment are one and the same."
Inhalation gradually takes over. By not moving more than we
must, we also root ourselves *(pee-ah)* in silence to Earth and Sky.
The energy expended in the cardinal directions withdraws to
Center and the central axis. By witnessing immobility, we charge
Center with *ti/chi.* We are the heart, *tu-tah,* the kiva, which is the
house of shattering light.

We also fast from physical food (and water) so that we more
fully rely on spiritual food of the three directions. If one is not
used to solitude, start with a night and day alone and work up
to three or four days. Beautiful Painted Arrow says that once
medicine people of Picuris could fast for thirty days. Ancient
mystics of the Himalayas, on perpetual vision quest, survived
on ground minerals and plants. If you quest for longer than a
day, you should have a companion nearby or better yet a guide,
someone who has quested many times before, someone familiar
with the inner workings of energy, breath, and consciousness.

The guide should check the person crying for a vision twice a day, in morning and evening.

If you intend to fast, prepare a week or two before by refraining from caffeine, salt, and sugar (and television). Gradually restrict your intake to juice. Do not fast from water in the extreme heat. The first time you fast from water, fast for a day, or the last day of a three-day quest. Sometimes, questers purify themselves in the sweat lodge before 'going up.' You can cry for a vision in a hole, on a hill or mountain, in a tent, hut, lean-to, or rockless sweat lodge. All primordial cultures sent individuals off alone to encounter their fears, prove their reliance, commune with nature and the universe, and ask for guidance. This is crying for a vision. "A vision always comes from that place of the unexpected. It comes when it comes and stays only until it has completed its message; then just like it came, it leaves."

If we still have the illusion that we control our lives, that security exists, that we are self-sufficient, we shouldn't seek a vision. We must, in fact, feel desperate, fragile, ignorant, childlike. Knowing that we do not know. Overwhelmed. By fasting, we empty ourselves at all levels. Remember, we are the paradoxical empty center/Center. We need help. We need direction. Sometimes the guide will sweat while the quester cries. Vision means guidance in any of the myriad forms it appears. Everything is a sign. Often the guide is asked to interpret what the quester perceives.

Remember, you must sit "and bring clarity to awareness." Sitting on the ground is best. You can dig out a little hole that will support your back. Prop yourself in a wooden chair if necessary. Resist lying down. When you do, merge with Vast Self, facing both downward and upward. If you sit straight, but not stiff, the circulation of *chi* up and down the spinal cord will strengthen. It will straighten your posture. Energy from the left and right sides of the body will seep to your middle. Talk to your body; endure discomfort. "Endure discomfort by going beyond it and letting it go." In referring to the stages of vision quest/crying for a vision, we will use Joseph Campbell's stages for the hero's quest: Departure, Initiation, Return.

Departure

The first day (or two) is primarily DEPARTURE, transition from personality/ordinary consciousness/smaller self to essence/ evolved essence, *pee-ah-who*. Remember we are always beginners. We only have the illusion of achievement in the material world. Our child, *pa-na-ne*, looks up in gratitude, recovering bliss, appreciating the blessing of existence, asking for guidance. In this transition to *nah*, witness every phenomenon. Let your social self and the outer world, with its anxieties and stresses, fall away. Slough them off like old skin. Molt the old. Exhale all excess down and out. After concentrating on exhalation and elimination, begin the water breath: Rise up while inhaling through the nose, and exhale downward though the lips. Let go. Allow yourself to be purified by liquid, luminous *wa*. Send everything foreign and unnatural away. Grandmother Earth will accept and transform the unnatural. Remember the little mind will figure out nothing. Flush out thoughts with the exhalation. Surrender to Vast Self. Departure culminates with emptiness. In the morning do sun practices. In evening, before sleeping, lie on your back and embrace the infinite nothingness of night sky.

In this stage of transition, you can perform two more practices (in addition to witnessing and accumulating *ti/chi*): breathing the five elements/climbing the inner mountain of ourselves and consciously repeating *chaah*. Start doing *chaah* mechanically, one time aloud as you exhale, one time silently as you inhale. Then repeat *chaah* four times while exhaling and inhaling. Then be receptive to where *chaah* 'wants to go.' *Chaah* might become the song of essence, *pee-ah-who*. If it does, follow it. It means the universe is starting to tune you. Sing the song that sings you.

Initiation

The INITIATION stage of your quest has two parts. You start the INITIATION stage of your quest by Sending a Voice, talking to the universe. This phase begins when you sense a connection to Above and Below, that you are the axis connecting Above and

Below. When you sense the presence of ti/chi, you send a voice.
You can send your voice to the powers of the seven Directions.
You don't need to talk aloud. If and when the internal dialogue
of the gross mind quiets (has been 'sucked into Subtle and Very
Subtle mind), your breath will have merged with the breath of
Vast Self. Send your voice like the smoke of the pipe and incense.
Smoke is *kuuh*, "opening to receptivity." Your voice/wish/prayer
is unique, unscripted. Every essence has its own prayer. Let your
nah speak. Though the gifts of our *nah* differ, our emotional
pleas are similar: "Help me," "Show me," "Make me real." At
night you can breathe *no-wia*, "calling forth that which longs
to come into existence from the darkness." The problem is
separation. The gross, ego/mind. We must become nothing, the
new moon, so that It becomes everything. One. The Nothing/
Everything is the hollow Center, *tu-tah*.

After talking to the universe, you listen. Listening/Receiving
is the second part of INITIATION. It begins when you are in a
state of *the-ooh-oh*, "innocence, in the state of high awareness
and teachability." Listening involves tuning into the subtle
inner light and sound, the energy of the Subtle and Very Subtle
realms. Everyone receives guidance in her/his own way. The
greatest obstacle to hearing and initiation in general is thought.
However, when we are finely tuned, inspiration *(ni)* and
guidance naturally flow into our cup, *ti-uh*. (Reference Joseph's
books, *Sound* and *The Way of Inspiration*.) We receive as a deer,
the four-legged whose horns, *my-eh-neh*, are antennae receiving
the fine vibration of the Upper World, whose firmly planted
hooves penetrate the Lower World. Perhaps you will be the deer
upon the mountaintop. Or you might be the high-flying eagle,
falcon, or hawk, whose feathers catch the subtle and very subtle
vibration and light. Or the crescent moon.

When you have finished crying for a vision (in this immovable
state), you initiate your RETURN, the transition back into
life. You pray to maintain the presence *(who)*, to implement
the vision, to sing and dance your song. To maintain solitude,
sincerity, and authenticity in the crowd. Once again, you enter
wa-chi-chi-hu. Beautiful Painted Arrow has an ancient Tiwa

recipe for transition, transmitted to him by Antonio Simbola. Since that time, he has practiced this archetypal series of actions every day. Bringing the inner life back into the outer world, maintaining the certainty of one's axis amid the confusion of the crowd, is life's greatest challenge. For this reason, RETURN has its own chapter.

XXXI. *Return: Transition Back to Everyday Life*

Transition takes us from sleep to awakening in life. It infuses
reality into illusion. Authenticity into falseness. Essence into
excess. Naturalness into artificiality. When we wake on the
final morning of our vision quest, we birth ourselves into new
life, just as we do every morning. Physical sleep represents the
sleeping of consciousness, when awareness has identified with
its content (personal thought, emotion, sensation). Relegating
us to an existence of reaction and separation from Spirit. The
precious energy of *ti* has been uncollected. Physical sleep is
also the time of recharging, the time when the primary body/
world sleeps and we visit the other worlds in which we exist. We
have become pure inhalation. *Nah* withdraws into its Source,
the womb of Nothingness. It harvests the infinite energies of
the universe. In rising from sleep, you rise like *to-le-ne*, with
concentrated *ti*. You have been freed from the past. You can *ah-
tschlu*, act with absolute attention. Contemplate the sounds and
the archetypal positions and actions of the body in each of these
stages.

Kou-ee is when you awake, lying with your back toward
Grandmother Earth, looking toward Grandfather Sky *(paah-peh-
thah)*. With *kou-ee* you are present in this body, in this primary
world. As you breathe, you focus the energy of all the other
worlds in which you simultaneously exist into this body/world.
You are the Very Subtle, Subtle, and Gross world.

Next, you sit up, *thlai*. Sitting, you straighten the spine. This
is a major accomplishment for the child. You are stationary. You
become the central axis of the Three Directions, just as in the
vision quest. Sense the energies spread from the Center, return,
and flow up and down into each other. No outward movement.
Feel yourself become the tree, then the mountain and sky. The
sky watering the mountain with light. With lightning. *Wa-ma-
wa-ma* . . . infinitely. Remember, "sitting is enlightenment."

Rising, getting up, is *wee-weh*. We rise further into heaven, become the stem rising from Underworld to Middle World.

Standing is *Kweh*. *Kweh* is the straightening, the 'verticaling.' It is the jackknife snapping fully open. Standing, the child begins her becoming as a two-legged. She tastes becoming a tree, a tree as yet without roots. She thrusts further into the Upper world. In order to balance, she must grow roots, send *chi* down through the spine, deep into Earth. She must send the energy that has risen in rising, downward, even as she thrusts higher. When you stand, *kweh*, you are standing for some thing, some value. Every time you stand; ask yourself what you stand for every time you stand. Humans stand for *Wa-Ma-Chi*-ing. They must act upon their inspiration, energy received in sleep and realized as we sit.

Once you see, you face and see, *moo-who*. *Moo-who* is perceiving with the eyes of Spirit. The divine is looking through our eyes. We are the divine glance. We breathe through the eyes, sending out light/*chi*, drawing in light/*chi*. Your glance, *Wa-Ma-Chi's* glance is both search lights peering through darkness and radar. The Vast Self can only experience this world through us. Seeing represents all of the senses, the senses being interfused with awareness. *Moo-who* transforms what it perceives. *Moo-who* means we perceive ourselves and the world around us before we act.

Walking is *ta-chi-who*. The tree would move purposely. Shifting its weight from side to side, left to right, receptive to active. It shifts to left or right, then thrusts out the opposite leg, then slides diagonally, shifting again. We try to move straight, to act upon what we stand for. We walk toward a worthy destination, away from a previous achieved destination. In doing so, the body is actually zigzagging. Antonio Simbola once told Joseph to walk as if he were drunk, accentuating the lateral shifting, so he could slip in and out the alternating slices of light, pulses of energy/breath from the Source. Doing so, he could pass in and out of existence and perceive the alternate realities in between the flashes. He would also guard against being caught in the momentum of a previous, now irrelevant, inspiration.

In order to have *ta-chi-who*, the two-legged must shift her center of gravity to the navel, the physical center of the body. To be balanced, she must achieve equanimity between Above and Below, from side to side, and from front to back. Every movement necessitates a return of the breath to the physical center. *Ta-chi-who* represents all right action through which we grow, *wa-chi-chi-who.*

This sacred movement—aiming, advancing toward that for which we stand, shifting, centering ourselves (remembering), advancing—embodies the lateral explosion/evolution of *Wa-ma* into *chi.* As Joseph explains it, two-legged walking (by which *Wa-Ma-Chi* realizes itself) is a metaphor for our life's work, *t'ah-lah.* The inner work of RETURN is rightly implementing intuition. Joseph states it another way in saying that we have "a sacred duty to enact our epiphanies." We enhance our capacity to enact epiphanies by staying centered. By maintaining the inner connection of *ti* and *chi*, the energies of the forehead and abdomen *(ti-uh).* By sensing the rising of Earth energy up through the soles of the feet and out through the top of the head, and the descent of Sky energy down through the top of the head and out through the soles of the feet. By sensing the sun inside your kiva *(tu-tah).* By resisting the pull of mass unconsciousness and artificiality. By conserving the precious energy of *ti/chi* by not falling into, or at least not getting stuck in, the web of reactive/egocentric states.

Inner work, maintaining the thread of inner awareness in all situations, is *i-lo.* By working interiorly while we are engaged exteriorly (acting), inner and outer work become one. In this way, we make outer work sacred *(t'ah-lah)*, and thereby actualize the archetypes, fulfill our purpose in life, and contribute to overall goodness: *wee-weh.* Departure culminated with your becoming the new moon. Return culminates with your becoming the newborn sun, *to-le-ne.* You may intuit other powerful, luminous, magnetic, and grounded animals and symbols. Such as the dragon, horse, elephant or buffalo. You are the moving throne, the moving mountain, the sovereign king/queen. Share naturally, with no expectation, just like the sun. Inhale and exhale fully, always returning to Center. Sing and dance your song. The song of the moment.

XXXII. DYING NATURALLY

Dying and living are a continuum. They are not opposites. What we call dying is just the shedding of one of our ten/infinite bodies, our primary body. To understand the Tiwa experience of death, you must appreciate a bit of Tiwa cosmology. According to Tiwa esoteric teaching, ten worlds or levels exist. Joseph stresses that ten represents infinity because Tiwa count in sets of ten. In this text, we, like Joseph and some Tibetan teachings, have simplified the map of the universe by condensing the ten/infinite worlds into three: Very Subtle, Subtle, and Gross.

So the universe contains infinite worlds/levels. So do we. This material reality that we experience through the senses is our primary world. But we, the microcosm, are all these worlds and levels. In fact, Tiwa teach that we exist simultaneously on all of these worlds/levels. But we are usually only aware of the gross/material world. Unless we consider that the function of mind and emotion are separate realities/worlds, as some traditions do. Some mystics, like Joseph, are conscious of several realities, of the Gross, Subtle, and Very Subtle simultaneously. This is complete awakening. Allowing the infinite riches of the worlds to breathe through one body. Then, one is, indeed the Vast Self. And the Vast Self is one. One.

Most Westerners are comfortable speaking of heaven, even if they don't believe in heaven per se. In fact, European mystics and theologians have posited many heavens and assigned to them various orders of angels. Collectively, heaven is the Subtle realm, the world of *nah*. Jesus the Prophet said heaven is within. Of course. Heaven is the presence of love, joy, generosity, compassion, as well as the peace of practicing presence. Heaven is goodness. The everlasting right now. It is a so-called parallel reality/world.

The Tiwa recognize neither heaven nor hell. The thought of place, itself, limits soulness, *nah-ness* on its infinite journey. Joseph communes with his ancestors regularly. After one sun dance, he saw generation upon generation of ancestors, beyond human, stretching back to animals and vegetation, all relations. Every time he meets human ancestors, they appear middle-aged and blissful. Picuris souls enter into and emerge from the side of a mountain to the southwest of Picuris.

Tiwa, like Tibetans and Navaho, for instance, understand that most souls hover around their former gross bodies for three or four days, depending on the way in which they die and their degree of attachment to physical reality. Though I have never heard of Joseph speak about lost Tiwa souls, I have heard him speak of guiding other souls, confused souls that linger in perceptual reality. You can read one of these stories in *House of Shattering Light* where he describes guiding such souls onward to the subtle realm.

When we are stuck in conceptual thinking, our energy or center of gravity is fixed in the mind function or world. In the limited aspect of the East instead of the Center. One can see this in body's posture. The mind level is not heaven/the subtle realm. But, when we experience love, we transcend thought and enter heaven. And when we are aware of thought or emotions, we encompass those with a 'higher' world/energy. The subtle realm also includes the aforementioned dimension of archetypes or metaphor. Joseph teaches that the worlds/dimensions are stacked like pancakes or cards. Some mystics see the worlds concentrically. Whatever their metaphor, mystics experience life as multi-dimensional, with time being a property of the crystallized physical realm.

Whatever the map, death is the shifting of one's primary world from the Gross/physical Earth realm to another more subtle, essential world of being. This is all. We experience death every time we sleep, or meditate, or witness the aspects of ourselves. Every time we watch/ practice presence, we detach, weaken our identification, our illusion that we are just our body/ minds. This is why Joseph constantly repeats that we don't exist, that only Vast Self exists. So that we can overcome the illusion of death before we die and therefore live eternally. So we can experience eternity, now, now. Not just later. And not just after the suffering that some souls experience because of trauma, fear, or attachment to body/mind, the Gross level.

Mystics often practice death, relaxing deeply into Earth, as we did, and enhancing the witness, which ushers the body into a sleeplike state and awakens luminosity. Indeed, some people experience lucid dreaming, being fully aware while sleeping. But the aim of this practice of spiritual death is not to merge with Earth as we did but to drop the body, so to speak. To let the parts subject to gravity be taken by gravity and allow the everlasting Subtle body and Very Subtle bodies to 'rise,' become more prominent. In practicing this, one lets the breath become very subtle. One does not control it. One simply lovingly abandons bodiness to Earth, its origin. If one were to do this every evening, one would "die daily." But truly dying daily requires more detachment, disengagement. We must also watch and detach from mind, emotions, and even essence/*nah*. Joseph's teachings concord with Buddhism, which teaches that there is no soul because even the idea of a higher, finer, special, eternal Self prevents freedom and liberation. More importantly, all forms, even subtle forms, are temporary orientations.

Remember we don't exist. You will read this again and again in Joseph's books, hear it again and again in his talks. Only Vast Self, in Its Nothingness. In this particular practice of spiritual death, you are not remembering that you, *Wa*, are also all these functions. You detach from them as you abide as clear, white light that is No-thing. Absolutely no content. You are experiencing the exclusiveness of the Great Spirit not Its inclusiveness.

Some traditions enhance this experience by visualizations, by suggesting that you see the body in ultimate peace and rest, beatific. Like the sloughed skin of a snake, the molted shell of a lobster, the discarded garb of a butterfly. Miraculousness. Beautiful Painted Arrow suggests a practice with some of these elements, a practice that permits death each day, each breath. You are cleansed of wounds, in all four directions, mentally, emotionally, physically, and spiritually.

After you have lain upon Earth and detached from your various contents, see yourself from three or four feet above the body. Notice that that being/body has effectively died. Myriad slices of light have come and gone. The dissolving and re-amalgamation of infinite nebulae. You, *wa*, are not that being which expressed itself through limitation, ignorance and egocentricity. See the new being/body as infused with light, the purifying and illuminating light of *wa*. It is the primary body of the luminous, innocent, receptive, light-drinking *pa-ne-ne*. While acknowledging its limitation and error, and committing oneself to greater presence, you envision the new being. This practice is the precise experience of many who have had near-death, out of body experiences.

The practices of climbing the mountain/breathing the elements, and the painted arrow are also practices of spiritual death, with some variation. When practicing spiritual death, you are not the mountain rising into sky, Upper world. You experience pure consciousness passing from the experience of one element to another, from Earth to Ether, consciousness itself. For instance, the Dalai Lama practices the progressive dissolution of the elements every day. In fact, the dissolution of the four elements (from Earth, to Water, to Fire, to Air, to Space/Consciousness) corresponds to the first four stages of death. The last four stages of death involve the dissolution of consciousness into clear white light. Practicing spiritual death, you temporarily lessen continuity. You ascend and detach. You are more like the kite that has its string cut and is lifted into silence.

If you use the arrow meditation for this purpose, turn the arrow around with its nock downward and its arrow pointing toward the infinite beyond. Rise again and again from the infrared to the ultra-violet edge of the spectrum as you inhale. Pull the center of gravity upward, first inhaling through the mouth, pulling upward from the Lower world of your body. Increasingly empty the lower abdomen as you inhale and push energy from the Middle world of the chest through the top of your head into Upper world as you exhale through nose. In the beginning, stress the inhalation. You're not just emptying your lower half, you're erasing it.

Next, keep accentuating the inhalation, but draw the energy

up into the upper chest and neck, and exhale through the top of the head. You can imagine a volcano spewing cold, clear white light. Or a fountain rocketing cold water into the beyond. But the source of the clear lava/water disappears. Over time, erase the chest and neck. Then erase the head. Until only pure upwardness exists. At this point, you surrender to the lifting power of the Very Subtle realm and inhale above. Periodically hold your breath in the beyond. Your exhalation will become very, very fine, almost cease. The same will happen to the inhalation. In this transcendent state of spiritual death, breath virtually ends. You approximate sleep without dreams, coma, the delta level of brainwave activity (and the Vajrayana practice of *phowa*). Remember that while this state is the aim of some mystic traditions, it is only preparatory for the healthy Creation-based mysticism taught by Joseph. We practice resurrection and nothingness in order to be filled with the presence of the Vast Self, which we are potentially. We experience nothingness in order to love more fully and completely. Out of love to be only the love of *Wa-Ma-Chi. Wa-Ma-Chi*-ing.

Beautiful Painted Arrow teaches another practice, sacred to the Tiwa. One of serene detachment and surrender. Practice the ascending painted arrow to the point where you are peaceful and highly aware, *ti*. "*P-you* is the word sound of death." Repeat it silently as you enact the previous meditation, on inbreath and outbreath. Continue the practice of silently repeating *p-you* until you are only concentrating on the inhalation and the exhalation becomes very fine. "P is heart. Y is a human with its two hands (arms) reaching for the heavens." You can raise your arms to heaven, orchestrating the rise of energy into the transcendent. "O is innocence full of creativity *(pa-ne-ne.)* U is carrying, meaning that only Creator has absolute charge of the soul after death. No other entity has entry to the soul at this point of the journey. The lesson here is: Don't mess with what belongs to God. What the Creator creates belongs to Creator, the Tiwas say. The white dove that comes for the soul *(kai-pia-neh)* is the garden tender of Creator's heavens."

What an extraordinary example of Joseph and his people's

poetry and profundity. When your inhalation rises high above
the head, lifted by the beyond, you can visualize the ascent
of the dove, drawn by your yearning inhalation. The dove,
representative of purity and peace for Tiwa, resides in Sky. It is
the Great Mystery's Breath embracing us with its exhalation and
carrying us with its inhalation. The dove, like soul, will rise,
not tarry upon Earth. This exquisite practice and prayer teaches
surrender. We ultimately have no control. Or just relative control
within the ten worlds. We exist perpetually subject to Divine
Will, the Creator's intention. As in the Tibetan (Vajrayana) *phowa*
practice, if you do this for yourself, let the ascendant light/sound
descend into the heart—unless you are dying or practicing for
someone who has died.

This practice will, paradoxically, prepare one for the end,
with every inhalation. Every inhalation that carries 'us,'
consciousness, from this primary world through all the other
worlds back in silent Nothingness. Whatever it is that we
temporarily are will be carried off like a blade of grass or piece of
string to that garden/nest of heaven. We can practice this at night
as part of our surrender to omniscient Nothingness. And we can
practice this as we near our own transition or the transition of
others. If we are at someone's bedside or far away, we can breathe
P-you with them. And one can pray "What the Creator creates
belongs to the Creator. Surrender to the white dove who comes
for your soul." Since the soul often lingers around its former
body for four days, practice and pray with them often during that
period of time. (Joseph also suggests lighting a match or candle
for the dead, indicating that they should seek the light without
form. And putting a feather in their hand to guide them to the
angelic realm.)

Placing a feather or a 'fan' of feathers in the hands of the
dying or dead is common practice at Picuris, according to
Harrington (*Indian Tales from Picuris Pueblo*). Harrington relates
that people put a *plumero* (plume) in their hands, as well as a
line of black mica on their faces. Black is the color of the West.
Someone sings a song of death to the one leaving the primary
body. The song will guide him along the path to the southwest

toward where the sun sets. In many native traditions, black wingeds (ravens, crows, vultures) guide departing souls into afterlife, like angels of death. Sunset is a window, an aperture to the infinite. Also, one can pray to the power of the West, *Who-kweh*, that those who have already left their physical bodies might continue on to the light, shedding attachment and confusion. As Harrington describes, the Picuris put drops of water (light/awareness/eternal life), representing the mountain springs around Picuris, into the mouth of the departer. Significantly, the waters of eternal life emerge from within the Vast Self. She is then surrounded with candles. On the evening of the fourth day after death, the *nah* of the dead body departs this primary world, following the spring water into the mountain (78–79).

Joseph's prayer also means that what happens to the soul after transition is the will of the Creator, the compassionate Powers. The soul may reside in any one of the ten worlds. Joseph says that we have work in every world though our primary work is here while in the physical body. Our work here is enhanced by bringing the beauty of the other worlds here. Too few of us have the experience of nurturing flowers and plants, but many of us have the experience of nurturing children, friendships, partnerships, beneficial projects, true art. Bringing beauty through love.

When we leave this world/form, we pass on to cultivate another world, one in which our ancestors may exist. (Joseph teaches that we can commune with our ancestors with the mantra/prayer *weh-yah-who*.) Joseph, in fact, teaches that those who leave this world and other worlds first prepare the next world for their loved ones. But many worlds, infinite worlds exist. Even the *nah* world, heaven, has, as we have described, many rooms or dimensions. Perhaps some souls have not finished their work here and reincarnate. Perhaps some souls, kernels of energy, become what Buddhists refer to as bodhisattvas, illuminated, liberated beings who vow to return here to alleviate suffering. The beauty we bring forth largely depends upon our longing for Light, inspiration, and dedication (effort). What happens when consciousness leaves its husk depends on our cultivation of that consciousness and the will of the Creator.

If using these practices for yourself, if you are not dying or near death, perform them at night, late night, or very early morning. Or practice them any time if you are on retreat from daily routine. Still, they will be most effective at night and early morning. Remember, if you are not dying or practicing for someone who is, allow consciousness/light/vibration to descend and settle in the heart.

XXXIII. *Efforting*

The practices in this manual, based upon Joseph's unfolding mystical experiences and visions, allow us to enter into Joseph's attunement/perspective, to experience/appreciate his mission, and to better allow the same 'process' to occur to us.

While spirituality essentially awakens/grows/unfolds/matures by mysterious grace, it also depends upon our conscious cooperation, through effort. Effort is our capacity to do what we don't want to do. Effort and surrender (innocent allowing) are absolutely central to Joseph and his forbears, as they are to several other ancient spiritual paths. (Effort opens the door, *show-peh*.) But for the Tiwa, effort is present in their name for the supreme, *Wa-Ma-Chi*. What begins with surrender to *wa*, culminates in *chi*, right action. When we, the microcosm, the agent for the moving of *wa* (wisdom/Intelligence) in the world, stop moving from inspiration, the totality breaks down. Right effort widens our aperture, our *ma* (the window/pore that we are) so that more spiritual energy/inspiration can flow through us. Some mystics liken us, our *ma* (material form) to a flute, through which the universe breathes, producing unique melodies. Our effort keeps the flute playable. Joseph says that the energy/blessing we receive from effort accumulates above us like a balloon. For a time in which we truly need it.

Effort also empties us and draws more Very Subtle energy down. It also opens us, making us more receptive to the Vast Self as creation. It shakes us up, realigns us, permits new combinations, like the *koshares*, sacred clowns *(ah-wa-yeh-ne)*. Permits us to overcome personal resistance, laziness, and torpor, sloth as Christianity calls it. Guides us through threshold after threshold, from second, to third, to fourth 'wind.' To stop efforting, to cease growing and becoming *(wa-chi-chi-hu)* is to hasten death. Even as awakened elders necessarily make less physical effort as they age, they still move vigorously on the mental, emotional, and intuitive levels.

In summing up effort, Joseph says effort has the following effects:

1. gives power and the energy of placement.
2. puts us in touch with the father *(tah-meh-ney)*.
3. magnifies innocence, teachability, capacity to learn.
4. gives peak experiences, ecstasy, epiphanies.
5. strengthens faith.
6. clarifies and simplifies.
7. creates power to crystallize, give shape, actualize.

We exist in a society geared toward so-called luxury and leisure, wherein those who work less and hire others to work for them are superior. Holy acts have been turned into burdensome, esteem-lessening chores. Those who are working *(t'ah-lah)*, particularly with their hands *(ma-neh-neh)*, are most inferior. So we must be vigilant against the deadening pressure of materialism and mechanization. Vigilant against life-destroying psychosomatic disease.

Even as Joseph rarely dances now and undergoes fewer austerities, he paints and builds. Furthermore, he assists the movement of energies throughout his microcosm, from the Center, to the other six directions, and back to void of the ever-expanding Center. While the growing boy of the peace chambers exists in the subtle realms, the child/plant of his painting blossoms. Producing exquisite flower after exquisite flower.

Once you have made effort (efforted) with these concentrations (as well in the more strenuous physical/Western domain), challenge and feed imagination by exercising intuition, mind, and emotion by contemplating Joseph's living art. Peace.

GLOSSARY

(Remember, in Tiwa, as in verse, meaning occurs in relationship/context. Meaning is essentially connotative and figurative in Tiwa: the interplay of vibration. Everyday actions and things are meaningful because they actualize archeyptes. Remember also that Tiwa is an oral language. These phonetic renderings are close, not exact. Over the years, attempting to better communicate these vibrations, Joseph has refined these renderings—in lectures, books, ceremonies, and film. For instance, a word/vibration may appear as 'e,' 'eh,' or 'ey.' The sound, however, is precisely the same. Don't allow the ordinary/ little mind to exaggerate these variations. Enter the subtle world of pure vibration which is pure meaningfulness—beyond computer mind.)

Aah breath and heart

Ah-who breath of highest inspiration that is washing us

Ah-tschlu doing with full attention

Ah-wa-yeh-ne Koshare, sacred clowns who embody opposites

Chaah song of now, the moment; the descending of the beauty of the heavens so we can have spiritual clarity; our going back to our original purity

Chai-ka feed soul, plant a soul

Cheh-eh-ney awareness capacity of eyes

Chi subtle energy/light; cold truth that knows, that awakens body for creation

Chu-ha-men-ten at the sand/crystal place of emergence; pristine consciousness

Co-wen goodness, all is well/beautiful

Ee-eh-mo two-leggeds as awareness/placement/movement

Eh-pee-ah play, G-d is making here

Haah breath, breathing, being breathed; identity

Haah-ley circumference

Hai skin

Hli-o energy descending

I-lo inner work

Ka buffalo; to dream

Kah-weh all our relations

Kai-pee-ah-neh arrow/light ray of the soul (*also* Kai-pia-neh)

Kap-ah-neh elder, Man/Woman being who has reconciled opposites

Key-ah Mother/father/birther/nurturer

Key-ah-teh silence, stillness, nothingness

Kee-wah feather

Key-ah-tah-meh-nay storytellers

Key-ah-teh peace chambers, peace, silence, void, emptiness, black light (*also* Keh-ah-teh)

Kola-oh-omo beauty that defines itself to the deepest recesses of the infinite self, that carries with it power of teachability and has eyes that see

Kos(h)are holy clowns, tricksters, reconcilers of opposites

Kuuh smoke, opening of receptivity

Laa-aa-ii-eh sitting, bringing clarity to awareness

Leh-lee-ah bringing up ancient wisdom

Lo-Le-La descending, spreading, ascending

Ma-neh-neh hands

Mo-sa-neh mountain lion

Moo-who manifesting in a state of grace

My-eh-neh horns, antlers

Nah the higher self, Self, or soul

Naah-aah-uu-kwil Grandmother Earth, Below

Nah-mo-lo drumness (the essence of drum)

Nah-mo-lo-ney Nah descending into the lower recesses of self, so they (recesses) can place themselves in heaven; drumming (*also* Nah-mo-low-neh)

Nah-pooh wiping clear the screen so that wisdom can be projected, "I am hearing myself"

Na-weh vibration of earth element

Ni inspiration

No-we-ah night, prayer to the infinite nothingess, calling that which longs to come into existence from the darkness

O-hee-o innocence in a state of teachability

Oh-kaa-meh-neh farmer, essence of childlike innocence of highest goodness that sits

Oh-oh-ney inseeing, seeing within, little child

Oh-tol-lo the brain; subtle link between brain and sun

Paah vibration of water element

Paa-tuh-hey Direction of South

Pah-ai-yah Grandmother Spider, spider's web, matrix

Paho prayer stick

Pa-ne-ne children of planes of light, the face of innocence

Pa-peh-tah Grandfather sky, Direction of Above

Pa-peh-yeh our Father who art in heaven

Pai-eh-ney Direction of North

Pee primary body, place of convergence, arrow; used to drive out habitual thought

Pee-ah vibration of fire element, tip of arrow (*also* pi-ya)

Pee-ah-who essence, clothing yourself in your song, how the universes are uniquely present in/as you

Pee-tah where center of life is (*also* pii-tah)

Pii-ini-aah-ii Direction of Center

Poh-ceh blowing breath with eyes that see

Poo-meh black hole, inner space

Qu-weh-yah-who presence of unconditional love

Soh swallowing, the soul's drinking light

Sho-peh opening the door, stepping into the unknown (*also* Show-peh)

Sibapu original emergence hole, kiva entrance, womb

Taah plow, seed; purifying Father that gives clarity of mind

Taa-chi-who walking, analogy for vibration

Taah-keh big bang

T'ah-lah work (holy work)

Taah-uh-lo sage, clearing pathway to inner/divine self

Taah-me-ney Father, creator

Tau-lee-uu-tah point of light that acknowledges abundance

Tai-eh-neh we are doers in states of placement so that the holy self *(nah)* will place itself among the heavenly planes; people are vibration and their work is to create

Ti-lah gazing

Teh stopping, nowness, holding the door open

The-ooh-oh innocence in the state of high awareness and teachability

Thlii wood, G-d's wisdom

Ti awareness

Ti-uh cup, the capacity to receive/contain; abdomen; awareness and time come together

To-le-ne Sun, solar consciousness

Tol-liaah-who running, abundance of clarity that is aware

Tsc(h)la-Tsc(h)lo butterfly, up and down movement of wings

Tslah-ah-nay tree, greatness

Tsclo-ii rain falling on parched land

Tso-leh-neh Direction of East

Tu-nay body, crystallizing the power of carrying the Vast Self

Tu-Tah love, center, kiva

Tu-tah-teh-nay the Tiwa, where the center of life is, where kiva is the center

Tu-yuh-ah-ney inward

Wa transpersonal light, life, creative intelligence descending, pure feminine energy, potential

Waaw vibration of space or ether element (*also* Ah-wa-yeh-neh)

Wa-Ma-Chi Being of breath/matter/movement; spirit/mind/body; the Vast Self revealing Itself in manifestation

Wa-chi-chi-who growth, becoming, unfolding of *nah*

Wa-chi-who consciousness of Vast Self

Weh-ley rising energy/consciousness

Weh-leh-who going up, climbing, G-d is carrying us

Weh-mu incoming of meaning

Weh-seh crying for a vision, divine longing

Weh-ya-who ancestors, the ancient ones

Who grace, presence of mystery that carries us into unknown

Who-kweh Direction of West

Wu-leh-neh (*or* Wu-leh-ney) outward

Woo-hah vibration of air element

<h1>Works Cited</h1>

Blake, William. *The Complete Poetry & Prose*. New York: Anchor Books, 1988.

Campbell, Joseph. *The Hero With a Thousand Faces*. Princeton: Princeton UP, 1968.

—, *The Power of Myth*. New York: Anchor Books, 1991.

Cook, Jeffrey. *Anasazi Places*. Austin: UP of Texas, 1992.

Corbin, Henry. Trans. by Nancy Pearson. *Spiritual Body and Celestial Earth*. Princeton: Princeton UP, 1989.

Decker, Peter. *The Utes Must Go*. Golden: Fulcrum Publishing, 2004.

Deloria, Vine, Jr. *The World We Used to Live In*. Golden: Fulcrum Publishing, 2006.

Dickinson, Emily. *Collected Poems*. Philadelphia: Courage Books, 1991.

Dutton, Bertha. *Americans of the Southwest*. Albuquerque: UP of New Mexico, 1993.

Halevi, Z'ev ben Shimon. *Kabbalah*. Golborne: Thames and Hudson: 1979

Halifax, Joan. *Shamanic Voices*. New York: Penguin Arkana, 1991.

Harrington, John. *Indian Tales from Picuris Pueblo*. Santa Fe: Ancient City Press, 1989.

Hildegard of Bingen. Trans. by Bruce Hozeski. *Hildegard of Bingen's Scivias*. Santa Fe: Bear & Co., 1986.

Jung, C. G., *Memories, Dreams, Reflections*. New York: Vintage, 1965.

McConnell Simmons, Virginia. *The Ute Indians*. Boulder: UP of Colorado, 2000.

Neihardt, John. *Black Elk Speaks*. New York: Pocket, 1972.

Ortiz, Alfonso. *The Tewa World*. Chicago: UP of Chicago, 1969.

Pettit, Jan. *Utes: The Mountain People*. Boulder: Johnson Books, 1990.

Rael, Joseph. *Beautiful Painted Arrow: A Medicine Story*. Virginia Beach: Path-ways, 1984.

—, *Beautiful Painted Arrow: Stories and Teachings from the Native American Tradition*. Shaftesbury: Element Books, 1992.

—, *Being and Vibration*. Tulsa: Tri S Foundation/Millichap Books,

1993.

—, *Ceremonies of the Living Spirit.* Tulsa: Tri S Foundation/Millichap Books, 1998.

—, *House of Shattering Light.* Tulsa: Tri S Foundation/Millichap Books, 2003.

—, *Sound: Native Teachings + Visionary Art.* Tulsa: Tri S Foundation/ Millichap Books, 2009.

Raine, Kathleen. *William Blake.* London: Thames and Hudson, 1970.

Sando, Joe. *The Pueblo Indians.* San Francisco: Indian Historian Press, 1976.

Taylor, Vaughan. *William Blake.* New York: St. Martin's Press, 1977.

Tulku Urgyen Rinpoche. *Blazing Splendor.* Boudhanath: Rangjung Yeshe Publications, 2005.

INDEX

A

aah 29, 180

ah-tschlu 154, 244, 255

Ahura Mazda 75, 238

ah-wa-yeh-ne 162, 266

ah-who 155

alchemy 45, 56, 144, 155, 157, 188, 230

Anasazi 33, 52, 74, 167–68, 214

Avalokitesvara 95

B

BIA Indian school 91

Black Elk 6–8, 18, 27, 35, 37, 112–14

Blake, William 9–10, 11, 61, 75, 98, 142, 193, 198

Blue Corn Woman 53, 80–81, 167, 173

Blue Stone People 119

bodhicitta 72, 95

Bohm, David 177

Botticelli 229

Buddhism/Tibetan Buddhism 17, 42, 48, 114, 133, 169, 232, 260

C

cacique 19, 53, 81, 117

Campbell, Joseph 9, 19, 24, 32, 45, 47, 57, 61–62, 69–70, 93–95, 109, 112, 126, 172, 176, 251

chaah 30, 145, 151–52

cheh-eh-ney 193

Chewaa 82–83, 94

chi 27, 66, 72, 86, 140–41, 143, 152–53, 157–58, 162, 178, 193–94, 196–97, 202–04, 217, 220, 232, 235, 239, 241, 244, 247, 249–53, 256–57, 266

chu-ha-men-ten 24–26, 172

co-wen 142

D

Dalai Lama 14, 261

Deloria, Vine Jr. 17–18

Dickinson, Emily 10

Dutton, Bertha 120

Dzogchen 13, 67

E

ee-eh-mo 142

eh-pee-ah 147

Elf Boy ix, 44–45, 61–62

F

feeding shrines 22–23

Fools Crow 6

G

Giotto 229

Grandmother Rael 62–65, 68, 80, 161–62, 244

H

haah-ley 159, 183

hai 143

Halevi (Z'ev ben Shimon) 31

Halifax, Joan 18

Harrington, John 25, 263–64

Head, Beatrice 50

Hermes, Thrice-Great-Hermes 23, 78, 89, 158

Hildegard of Bingen 11, 142

hli-o 158, 166

About the Author

Kurt Wilt, PhD is Professor of English at Saint Leo University, a specialist in comparative mysticism and Native American literature. He has studied with Joseph Rael for 30 years and attended Joseph's mystery school workshops in northern New Mexico.

Made in the USA
Monee, IL
07 July 2026